NATIONAL LAMPOON ®

FAVORITE CARTOONS OF THE 21ST CENTURY

Published by National Lampoon Press

National Lampoon, Inc. • 8228 Sunset Boulevard, Suite 1000 • Los Angeles • CA 90046 • USA • AMEX:NLN

NATIONAL LAMPOON, NATIONAL LAMPOON PRESS and colophon are trademarks of National Lampoon

National lampoon, favorite cartoons of the 21st century, / edited by Jay Naughton -- 1st ed.

p. cm.

ISBN 0-977871-819   978-0977871-810 - $14.95 U.S. - $19.95 Canada

Book Design and Production by
JK NAUGHTON

Cover Design by
MoDMaN

Front Cover Cartoon by
Dan Reynolds

FAVORITE CARTOONS OF THE 21ST CENTURY

NATIONAL LAMPOON® PRESS

From the Editor

Centuries from now, scholars will ask, "How could National Lampoon have predicted the world's favorite cartoons of the 21st Century so accurately only six years into the new century? Was it sophisticated humor analysis by the finest minds of the day? Customized computer algorithms designed to predict the everlasting appeal of fart gags? Or did they have some uncanny premonition of that the Apocalypse would begin January 3, 2007, and wipe out all humans with a sense of humor?"

Sadly, our methods must remain a secret.

So enjoy our "Favorite Cartoons of the 21st Century" while you can, and rest assured that they will remain so.

At least until Volume 2 comes out.

Jay

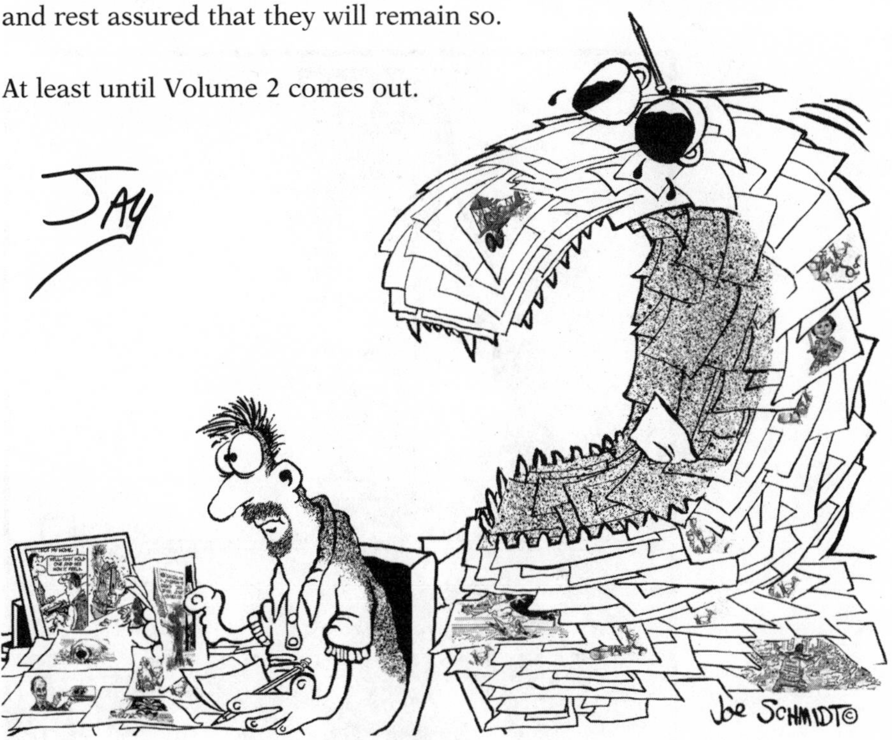
Joe SCHMIDT©

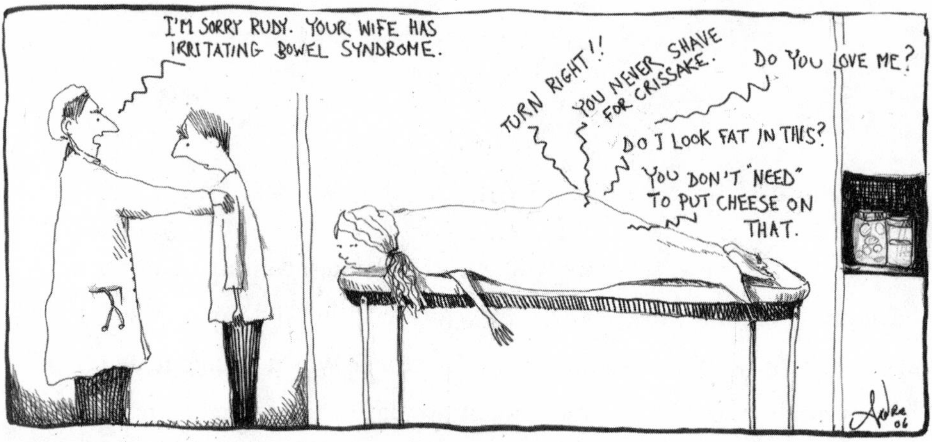
I'M SORRY RUDY. YOUR WIFE HAS IRRITATING BOWEL SYNDROME.
TURN RIGHT!!
YOU NEVER SHAVE FOR CRISSAKE.
DO YOU LOVE ME?
DO I LOOK FAT IN THIS?
YOU DON'T "NEED" TO PUT CHEESE ON THAT.
Andre 06

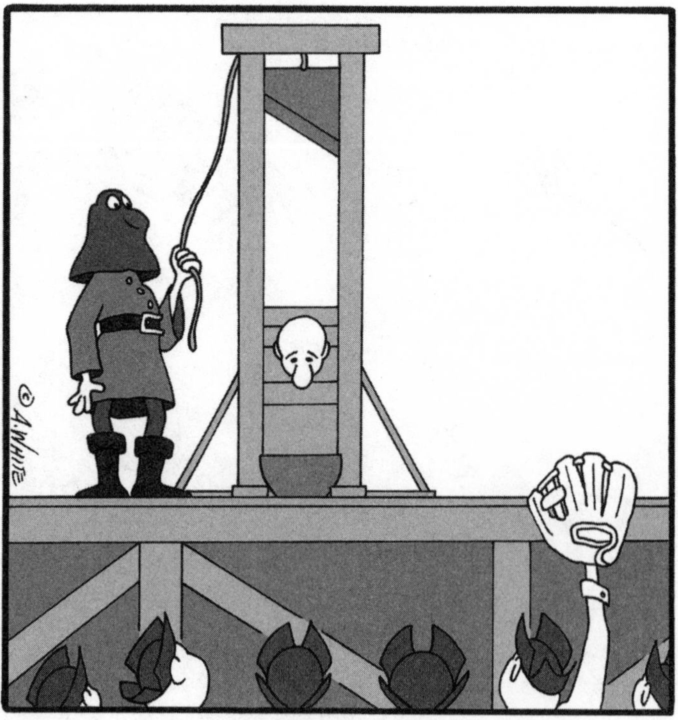
© A.WHITE

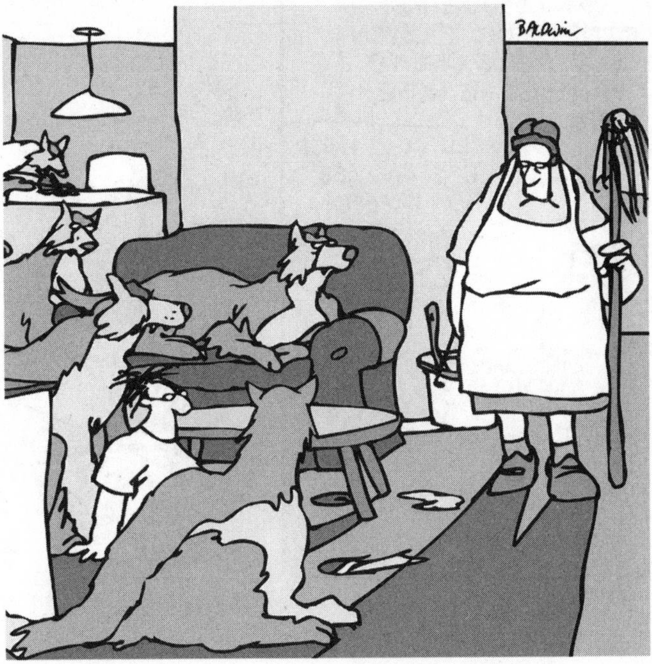
BALDWIN

He was raised by a pack of wolves, and the cleaning lady who came in twice a month.

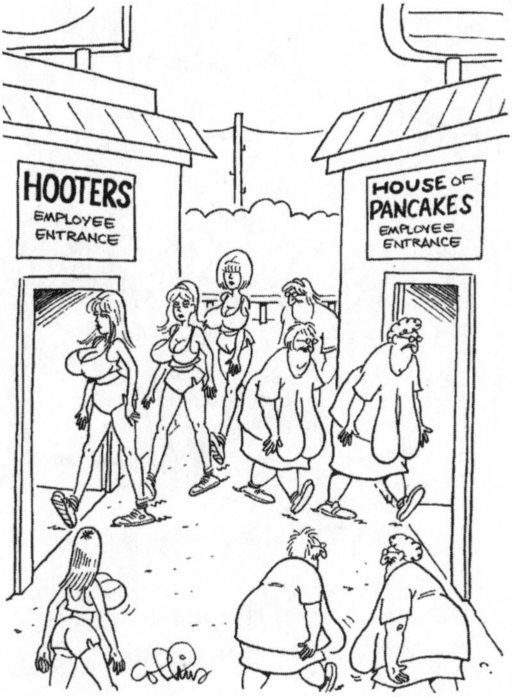
HOOTERS
EMPLOYEE
ENTRANCE
HOUSE OF
PANCAKES
EMPLOYEE
ENTRANCE

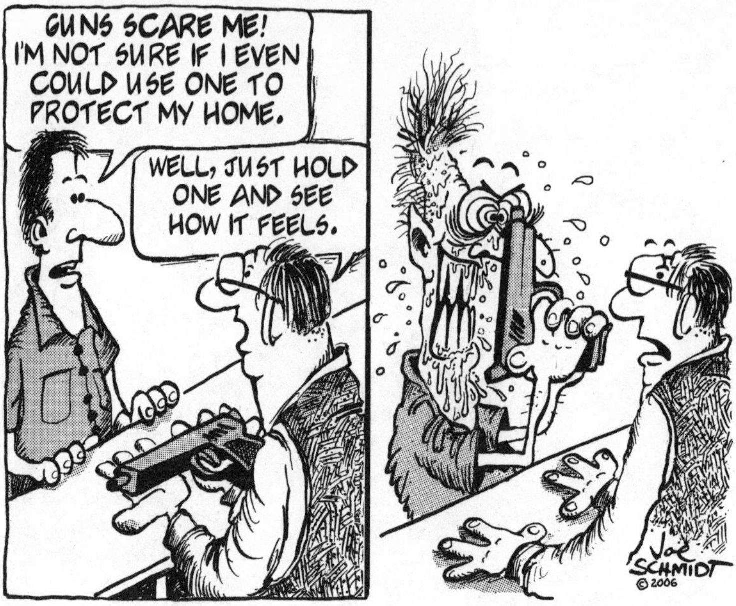
GUNS SCARE ME! I'M NOT SURE IF I EVEN COULD USE ONE TO PROTECT MY HOME.
WELL, JUST HOLD ONE AND SEE HOW IT FEELS.
JOE SCHMIDT
© 2006

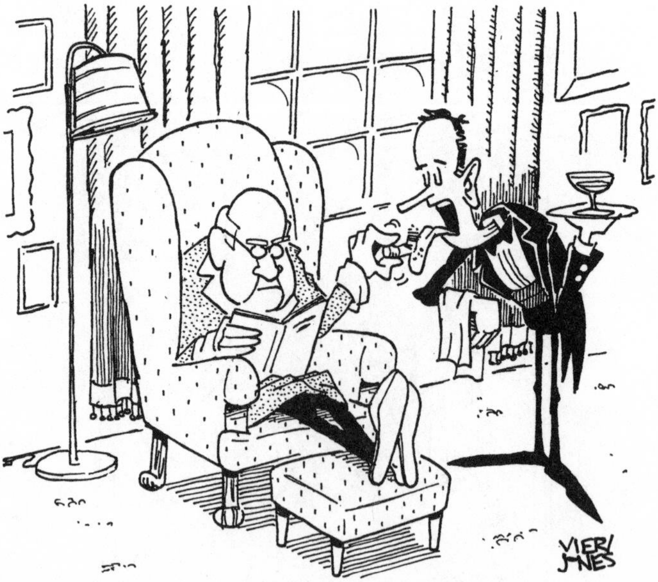
VIER/JONES

Once a month, the ashtrays are sent out to be cleaned.

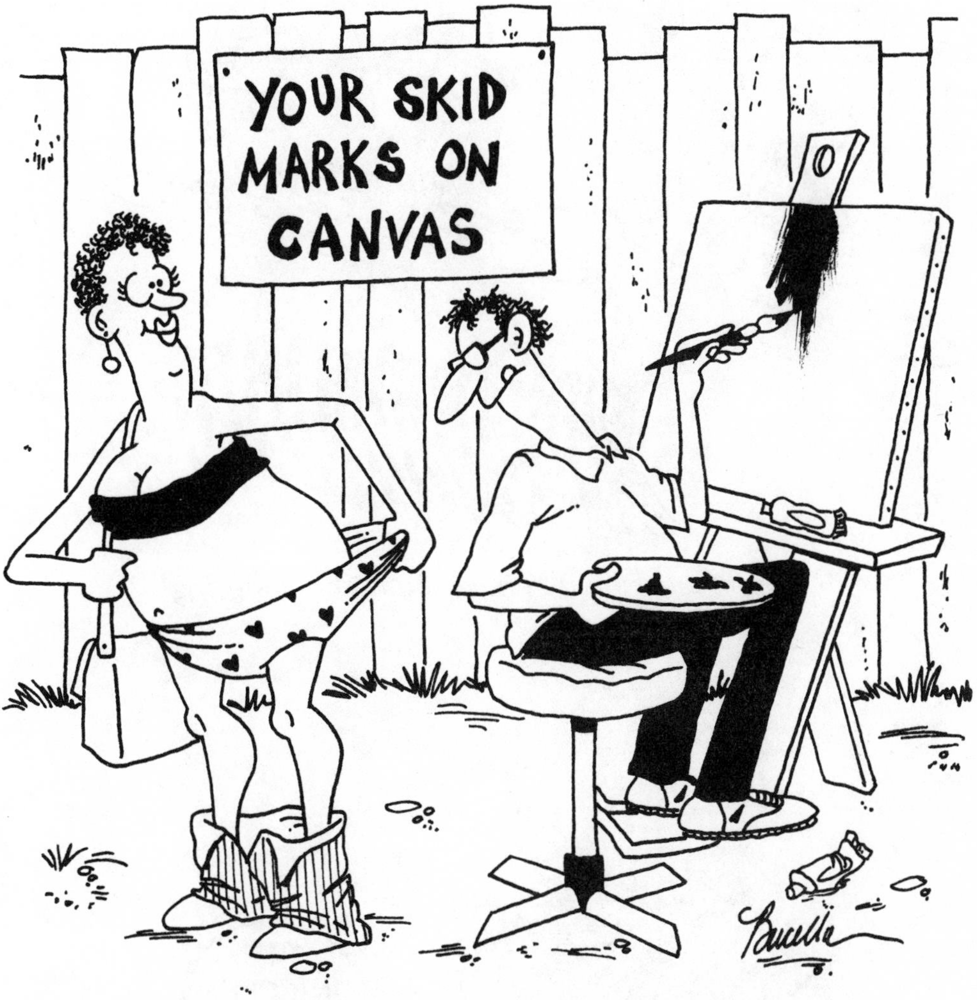
YOUR SKID
MARKS ON
CANVAS
Bucella

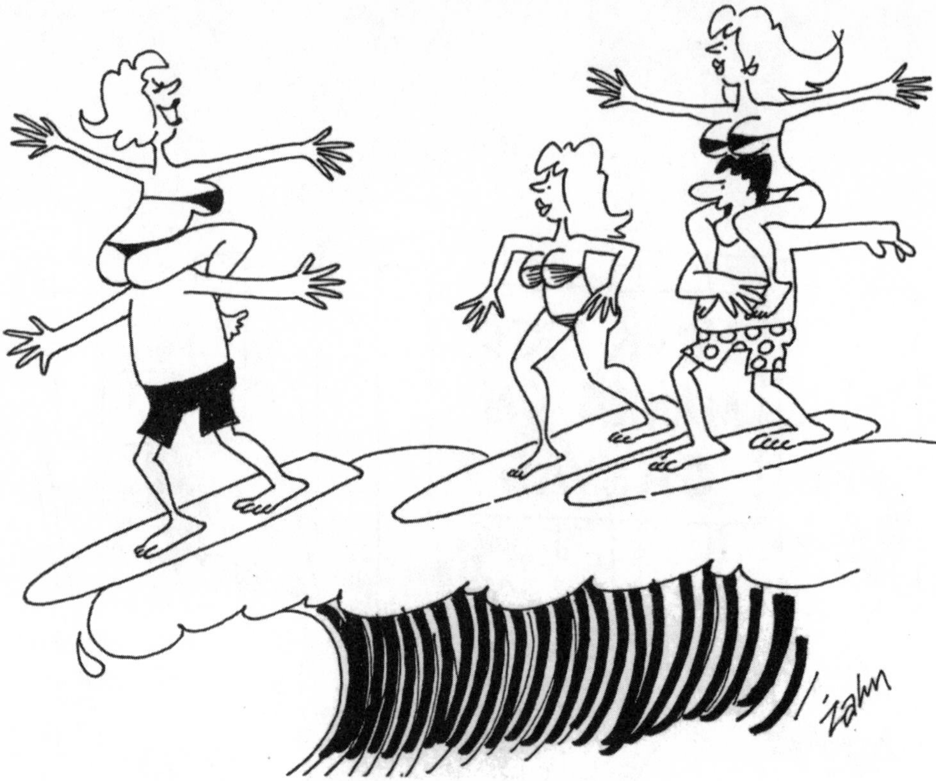
zahn

"They obviously don't know squat about surfing!"

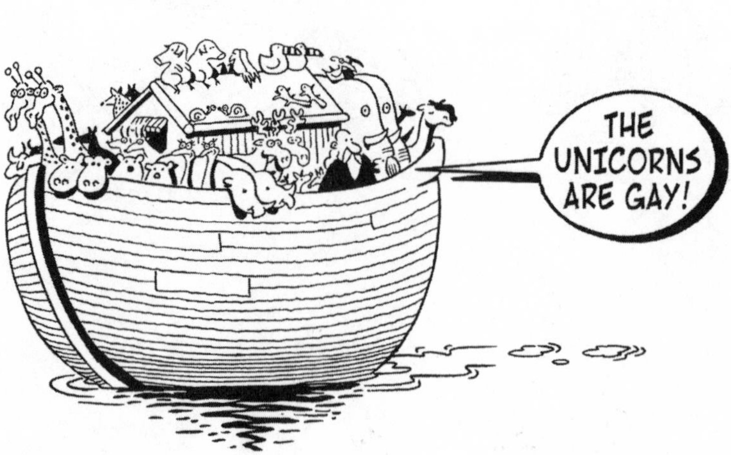
THE UNICORNS ARE GAY!

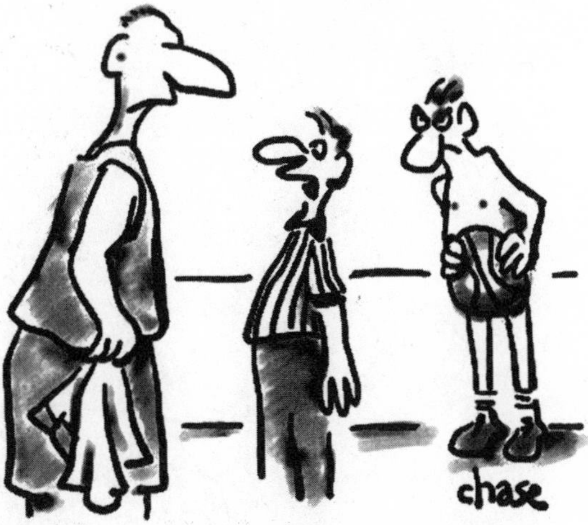
chase

"Yeah, I'd call that a personal foul...
now give him back his uniform!"

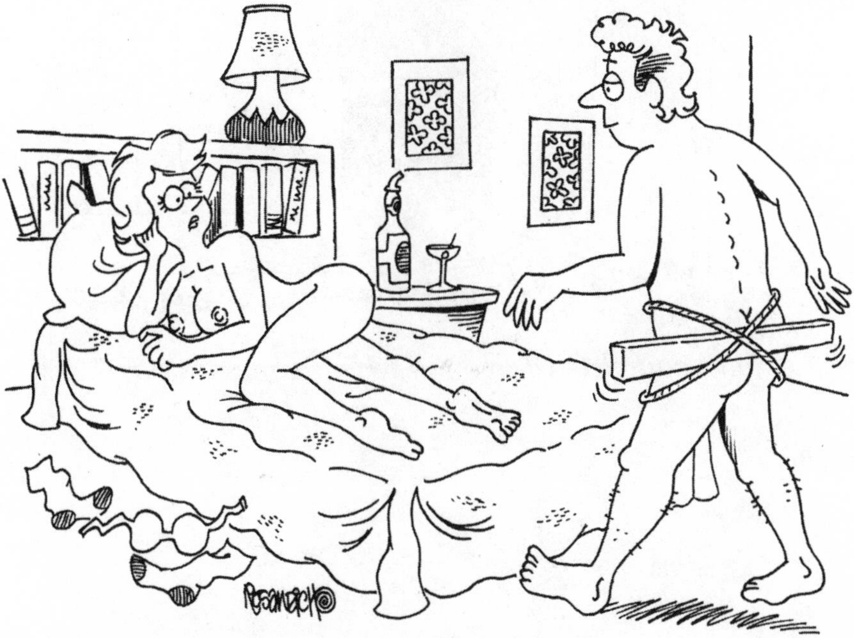

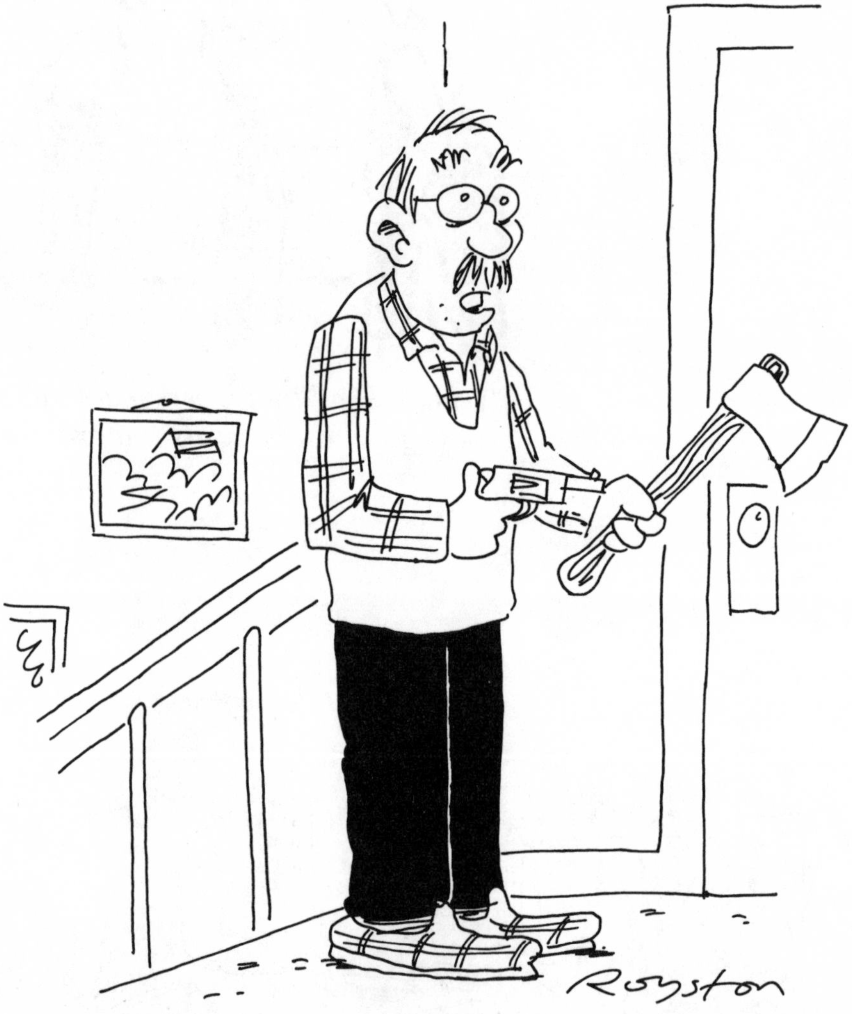
Royston

"I've completely forgotten why I came upstairs."

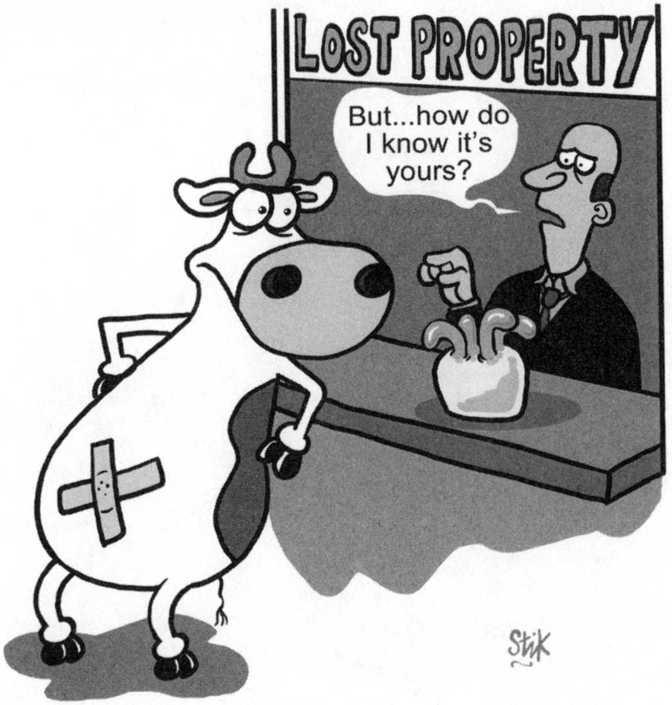
LOST PROPERTY
But...how do I know it's yours?
Stik

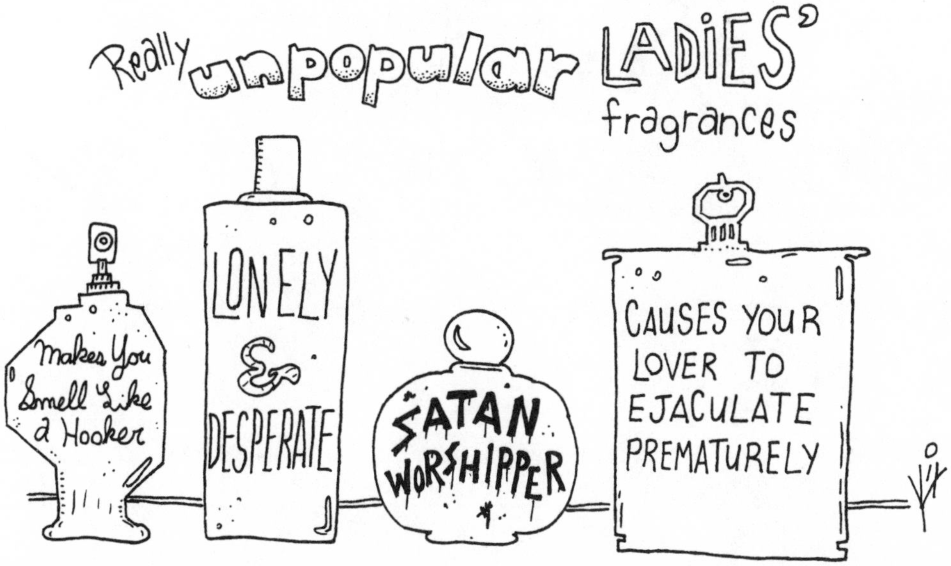
Really unpopular LADIES' fragrances
Makes You Smell Like a Hooker
LONELY & DESPERATE
SATAN WORSHIPPER
CAUSES YOUR LOVER TO EJACULATE PREMATURELY

WHEN GOD GETS BORED
HE PASSES THE TIME
SQUISHING THE HEADS
OF SINNERS

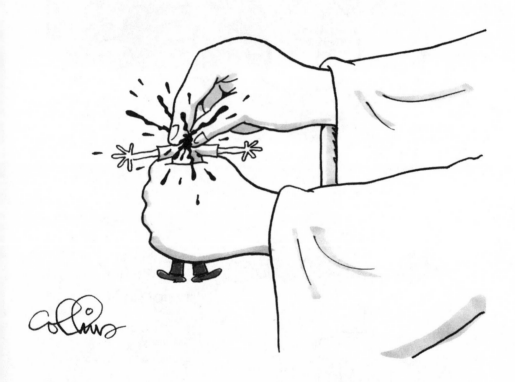

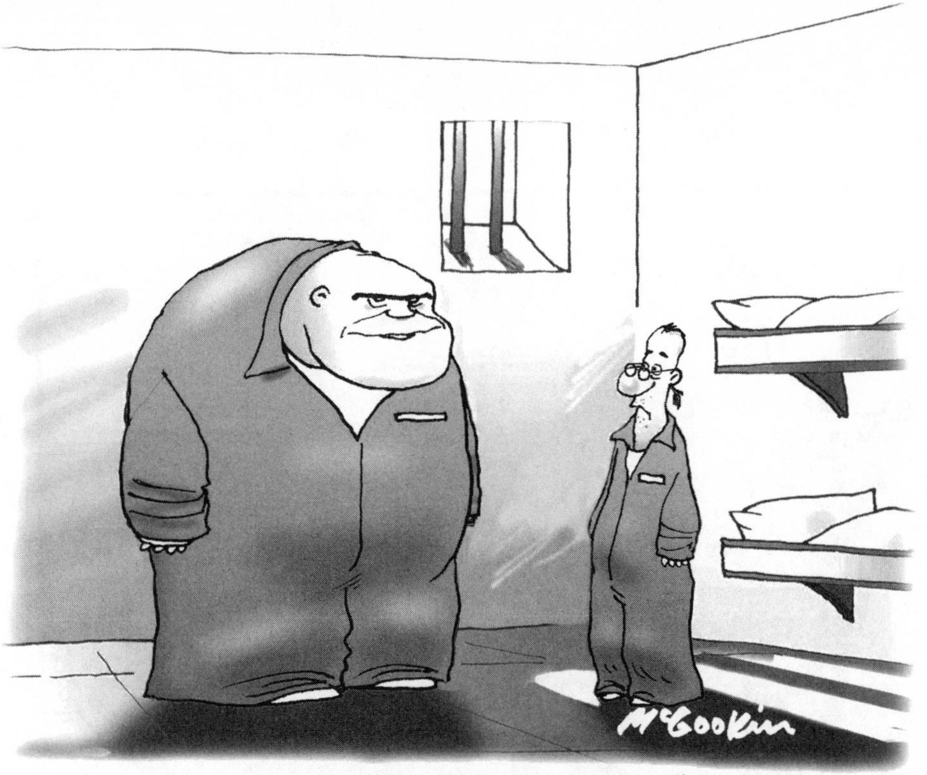
McGookin

"You're in for hacking? Me, too."

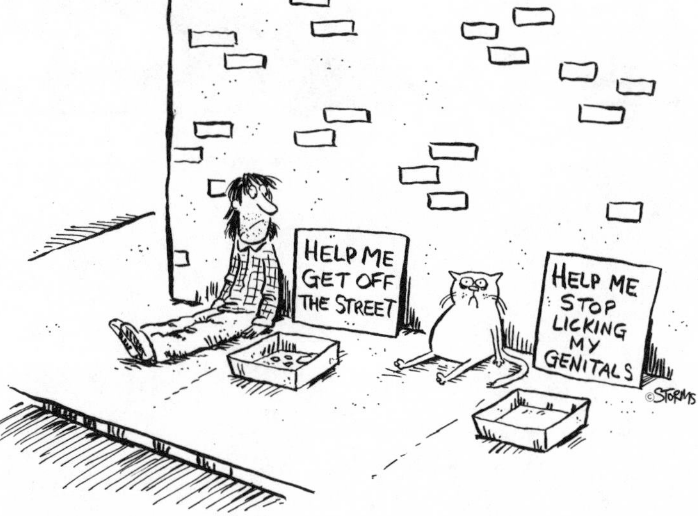
HELP ME GET OFF THE STREET
HELP ME STOP LICKING MY GENITALS
©STORMS

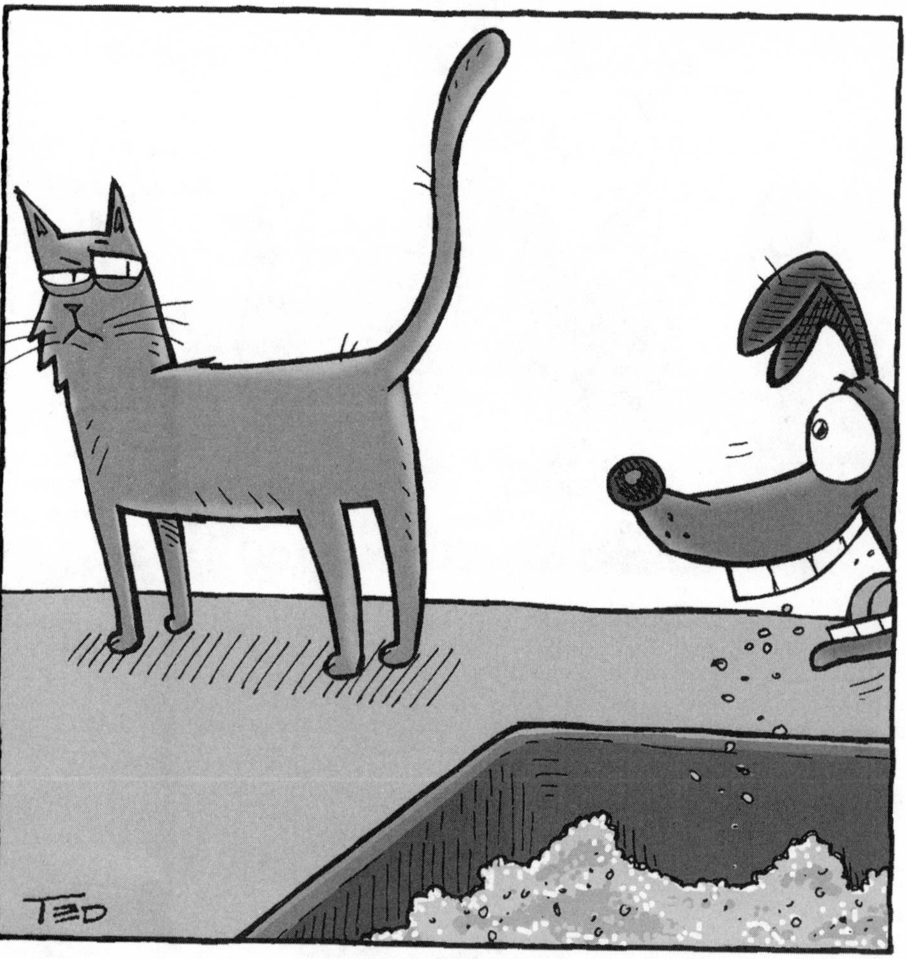
TED

"Five second rule!"

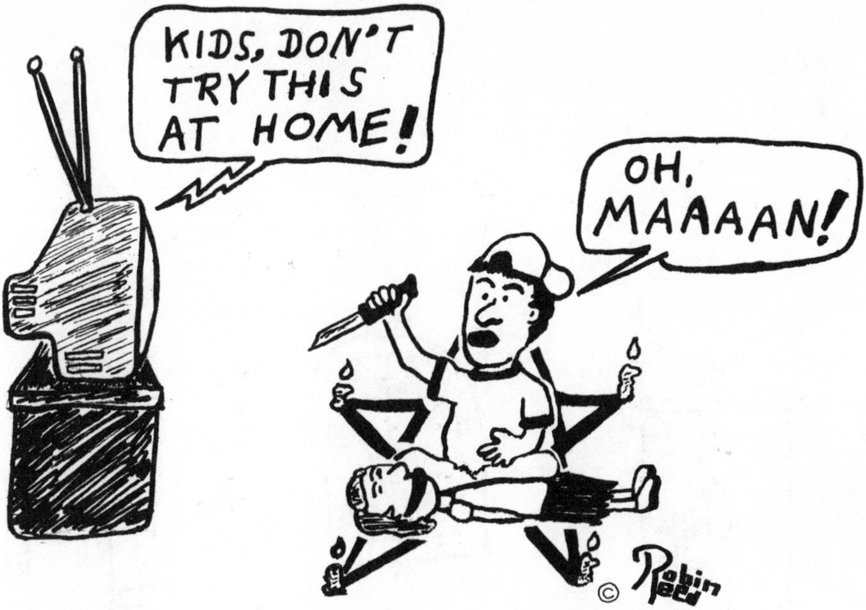
KIDS, DON'T TRY THIS AT HOME!
OH, MAAAAN!
© Robin Reed

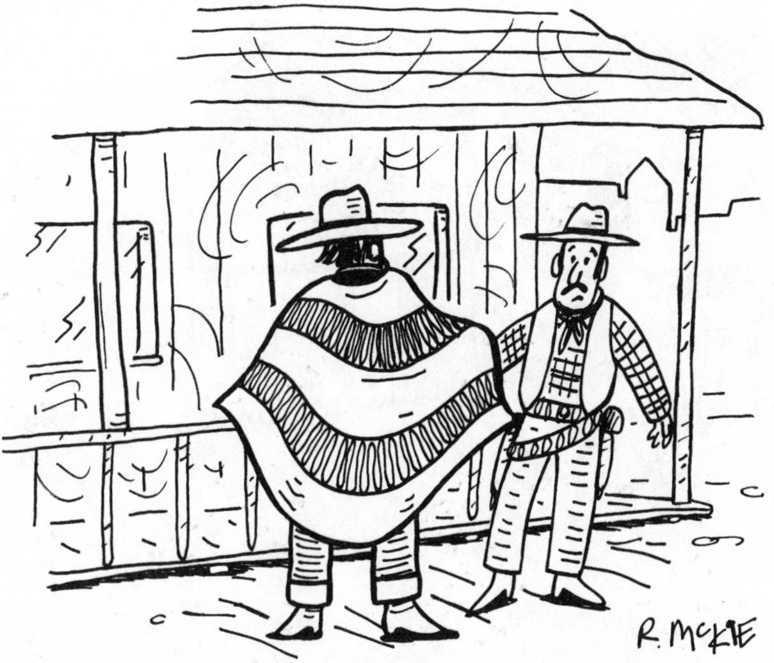
R. MCKIE

"I said, 'Is that a gun under your poncho, or are you ju...' Oh, it's a gun."

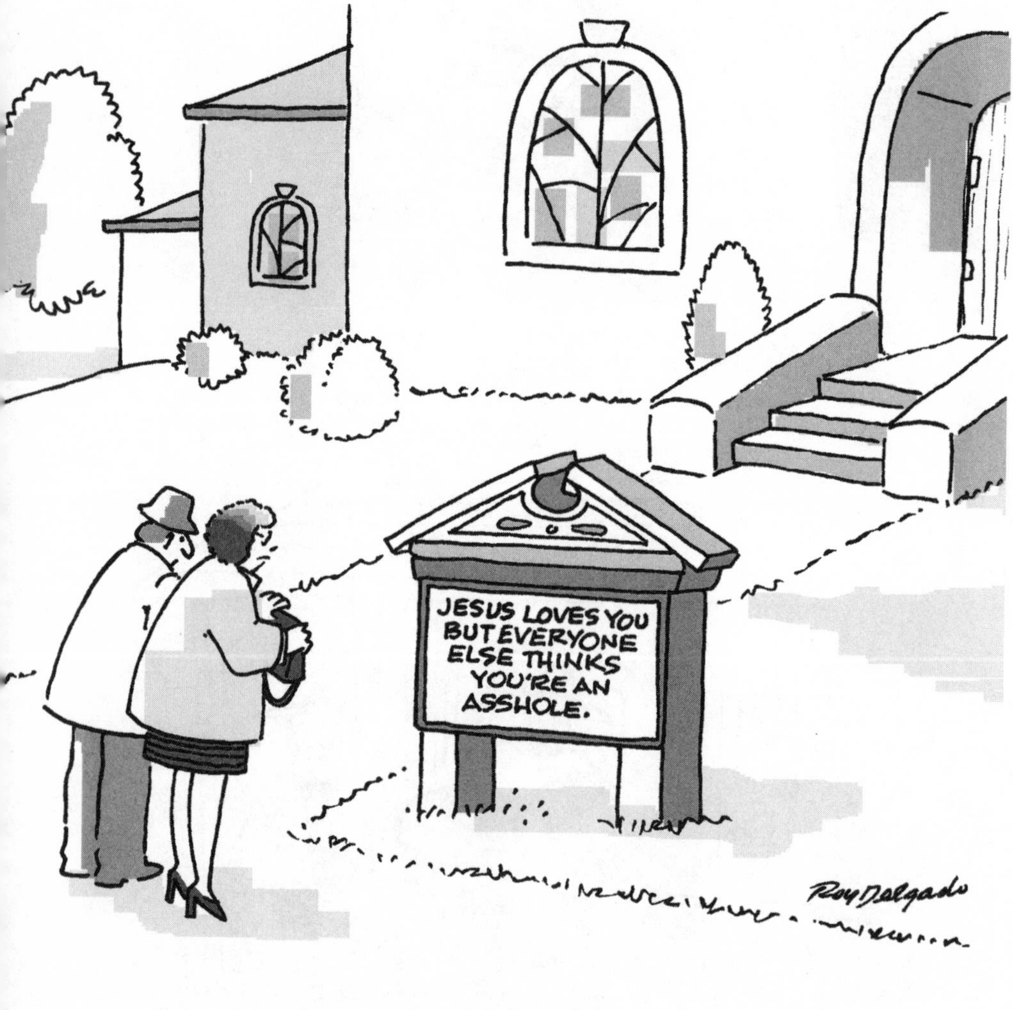
JESUS LOVES YOU
BUT EVERYONE
ELSE THINKS
YOU'RE AN
ASSHOLE.
Roy Delgado

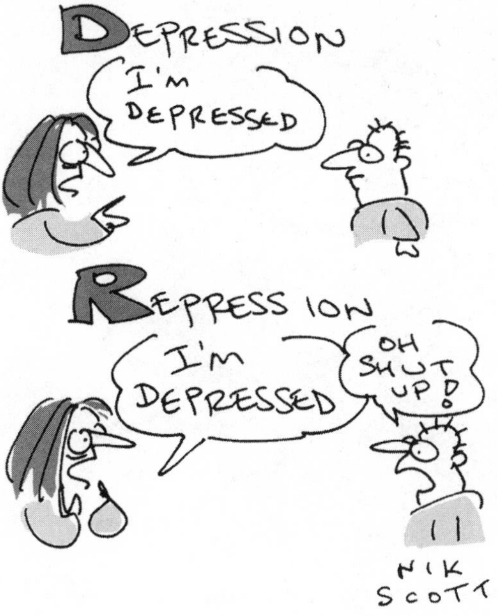
DEPRESSION
I'M DEPRESSED
REPRESSION
I'M DEPRESSED
OH SHUT UP!
NIK SCOTT

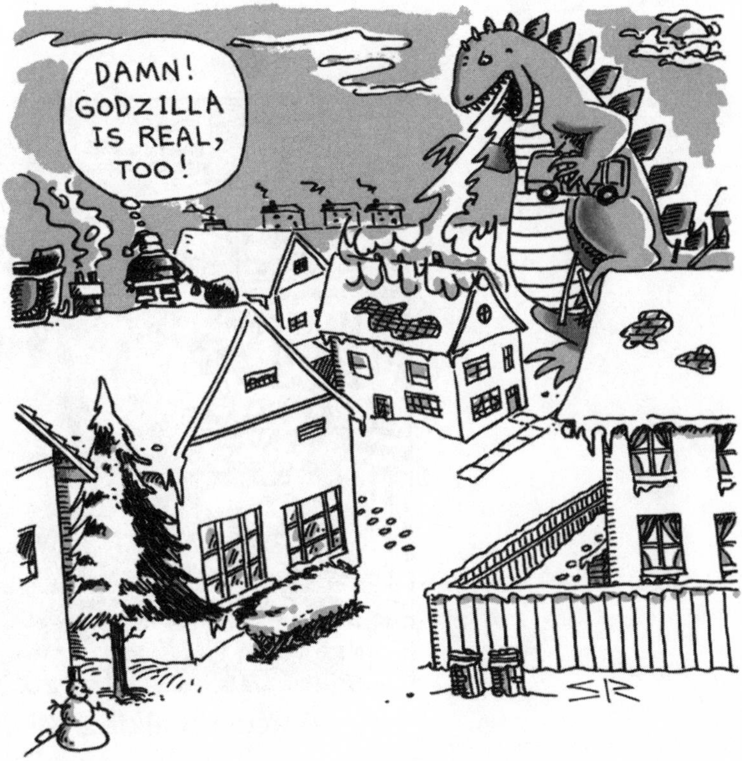
DAMN! GODZILLA IS REAL, TOO!
SR

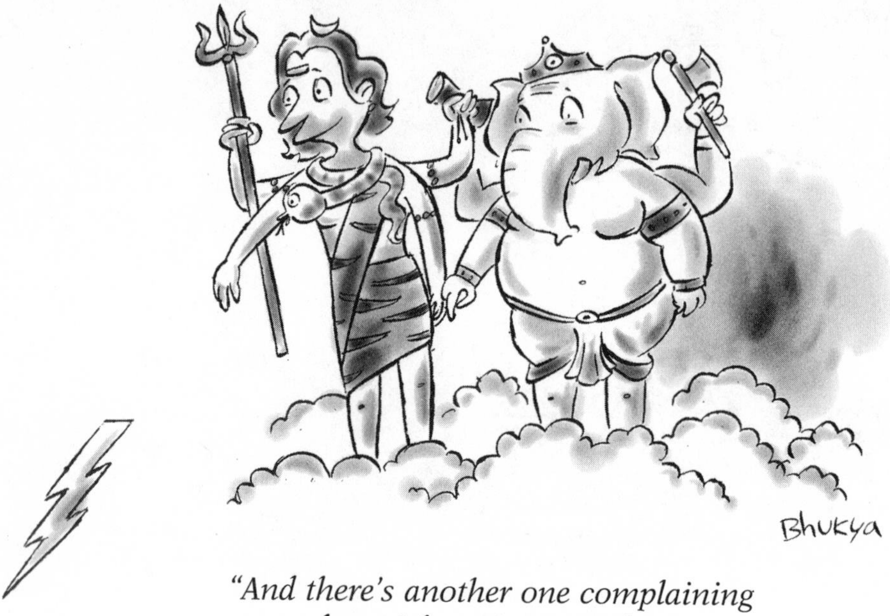
Bhukya

"And there's another one complaining about jobs going to India."

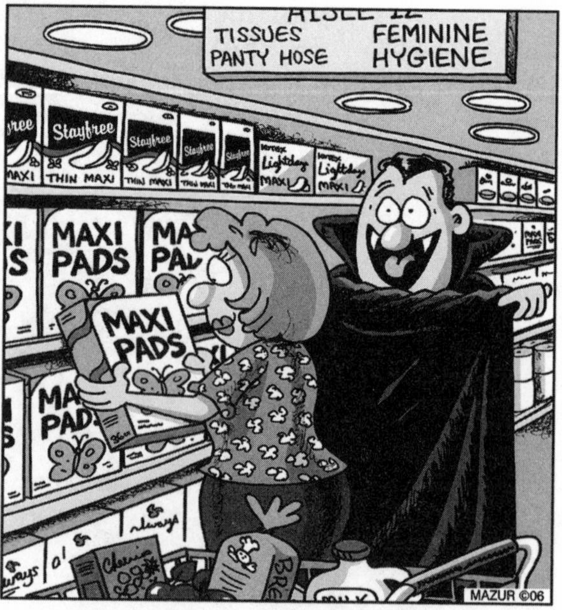
TISSUES
PANTY HOSE
FEMININE
HYGIENE
Stayfree
THIN MAXI
Lightdays
MAXI
PADS
MAXI PADS
MAZUR ©06

Dracula Stalking His Prey

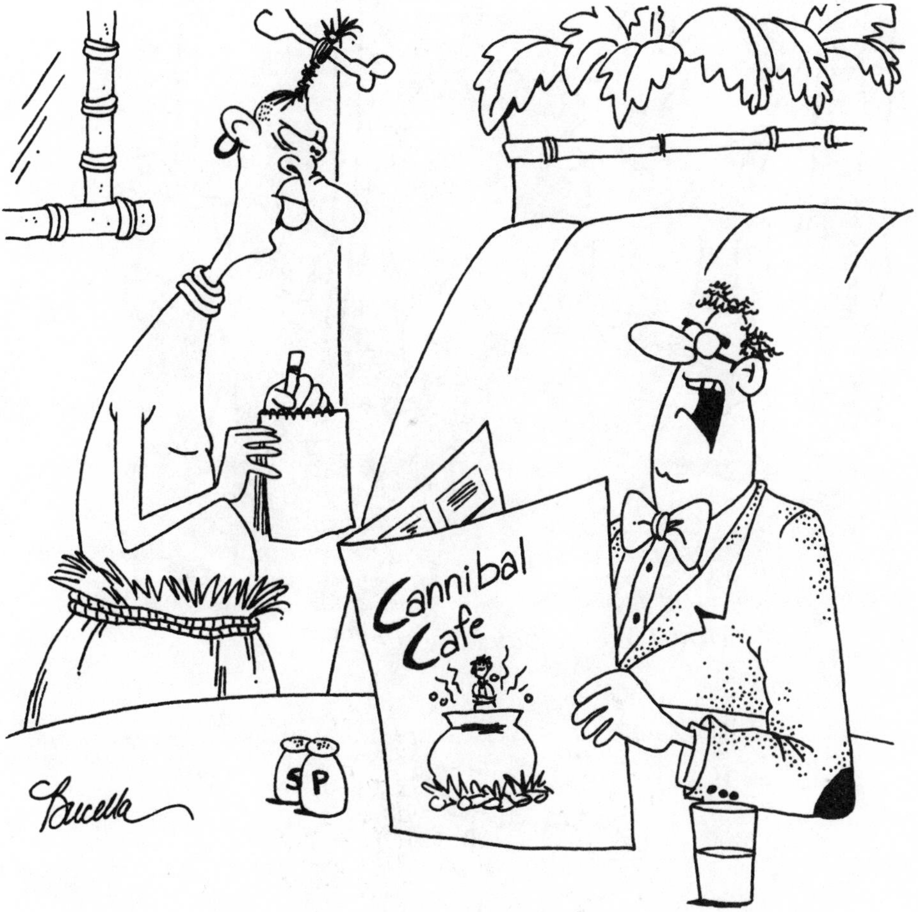
Cannibal Cafe
S
P
Baccella

"Does Denise come served in her own juice?"

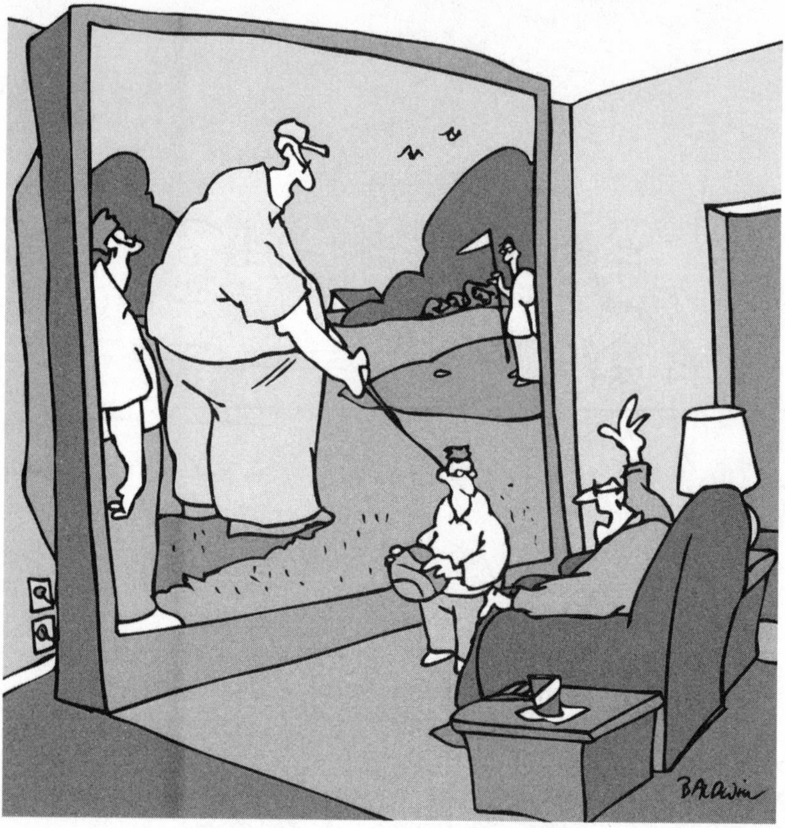

"Move! You're blocking the TV."

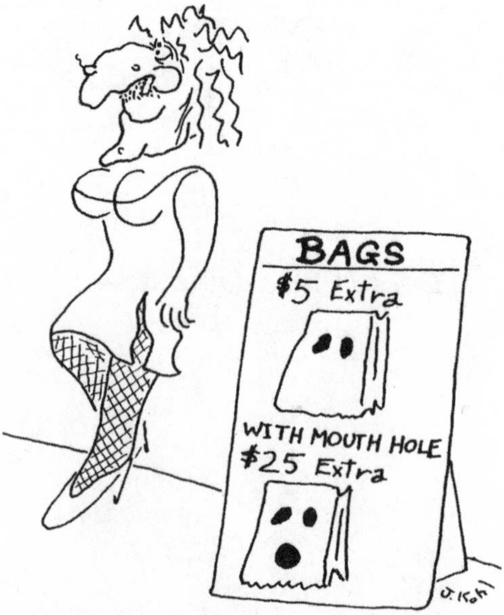
BAGS
$5 Extra
WITH MOUTH HOLE
$25 Extra

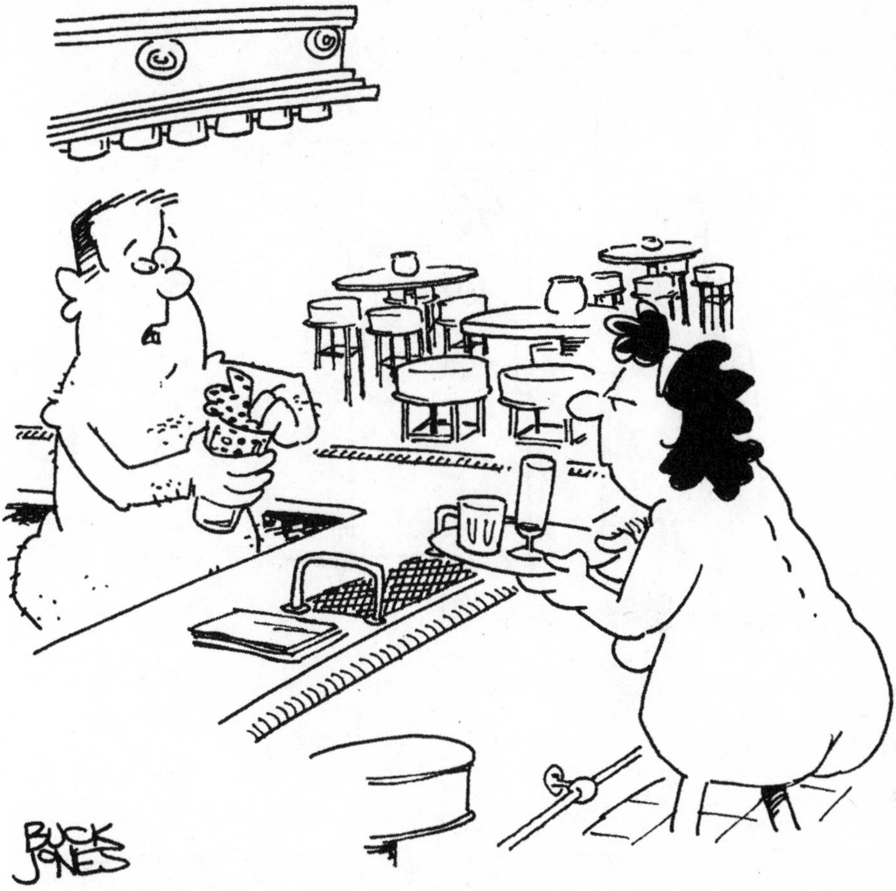
BUCK JONES

"I really thought Casual Friday would be more popular than this."

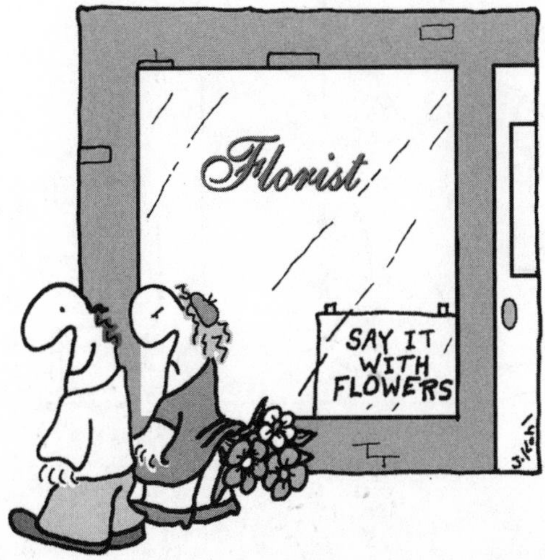
Florist
SAY IT WITH FLOWERS

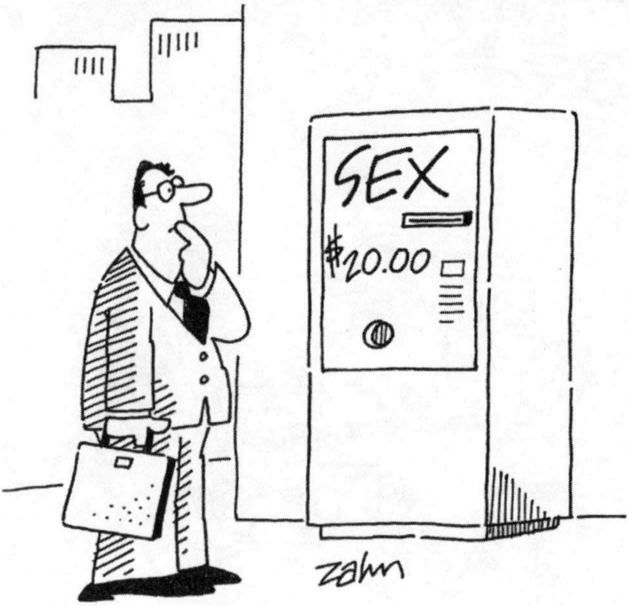
SEX
$20.00
zahn

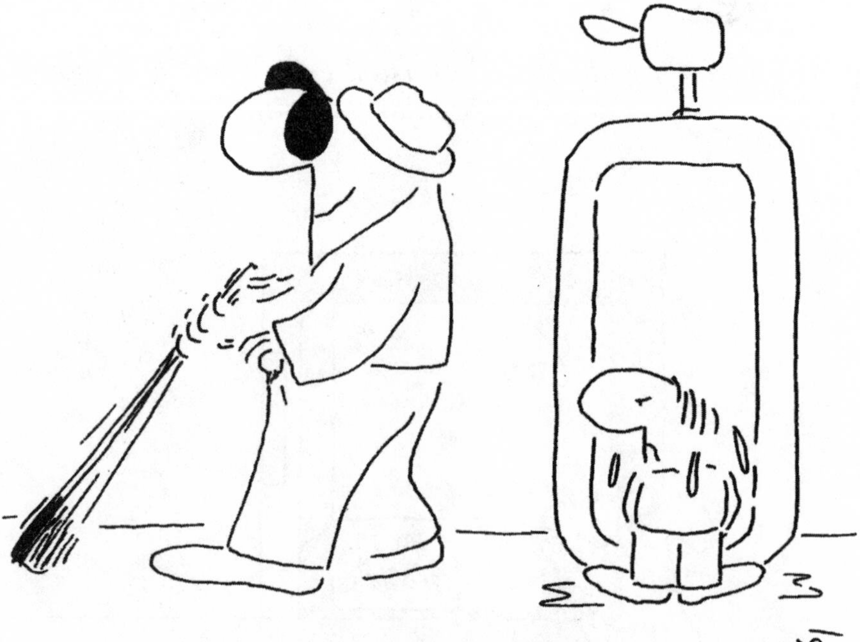
J. Koh

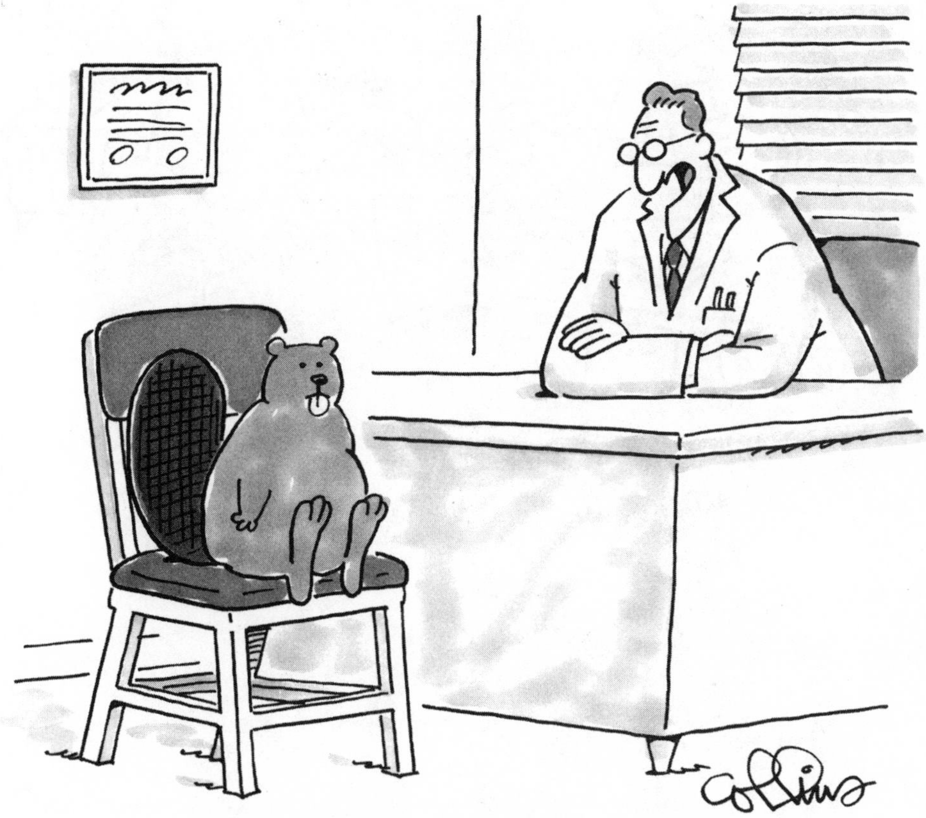
Collins

"Of course you're retaining water! You're a goddamn beaver!"

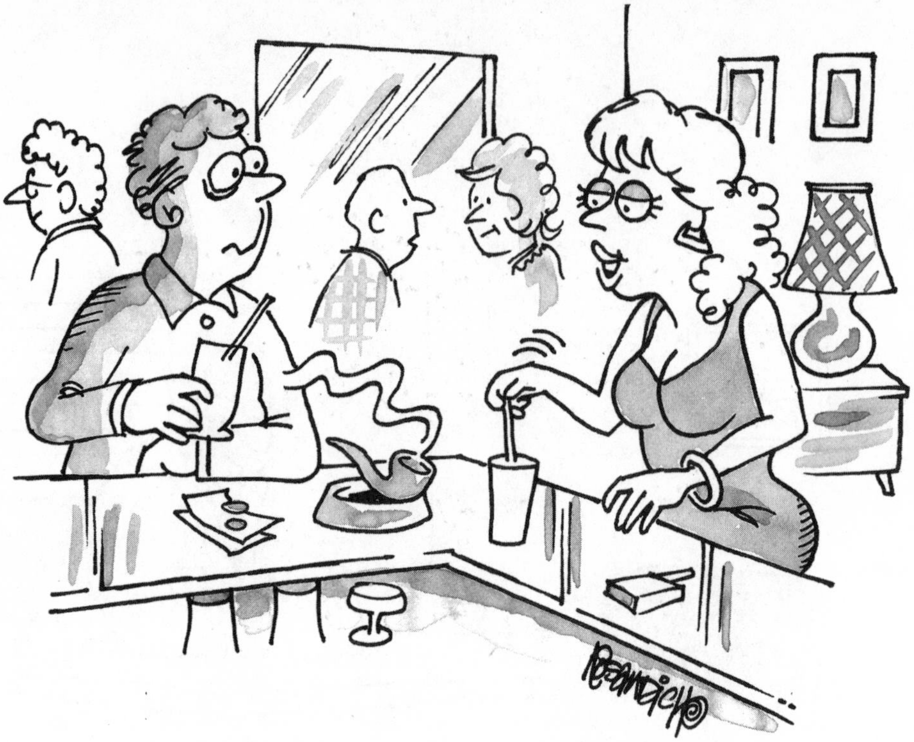

"No thanks, I'm into masturbation."

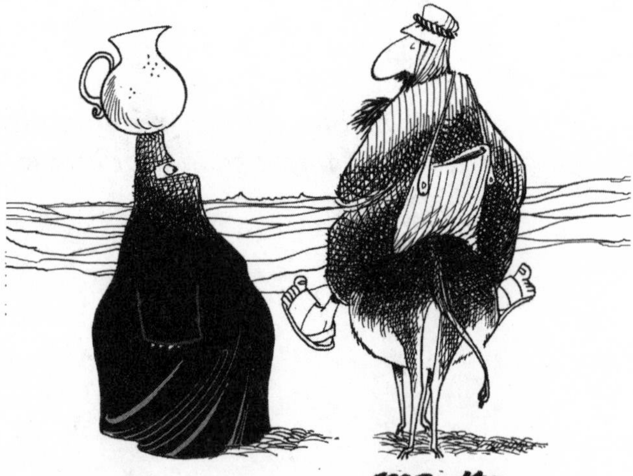

"Does my ass look big in this?"

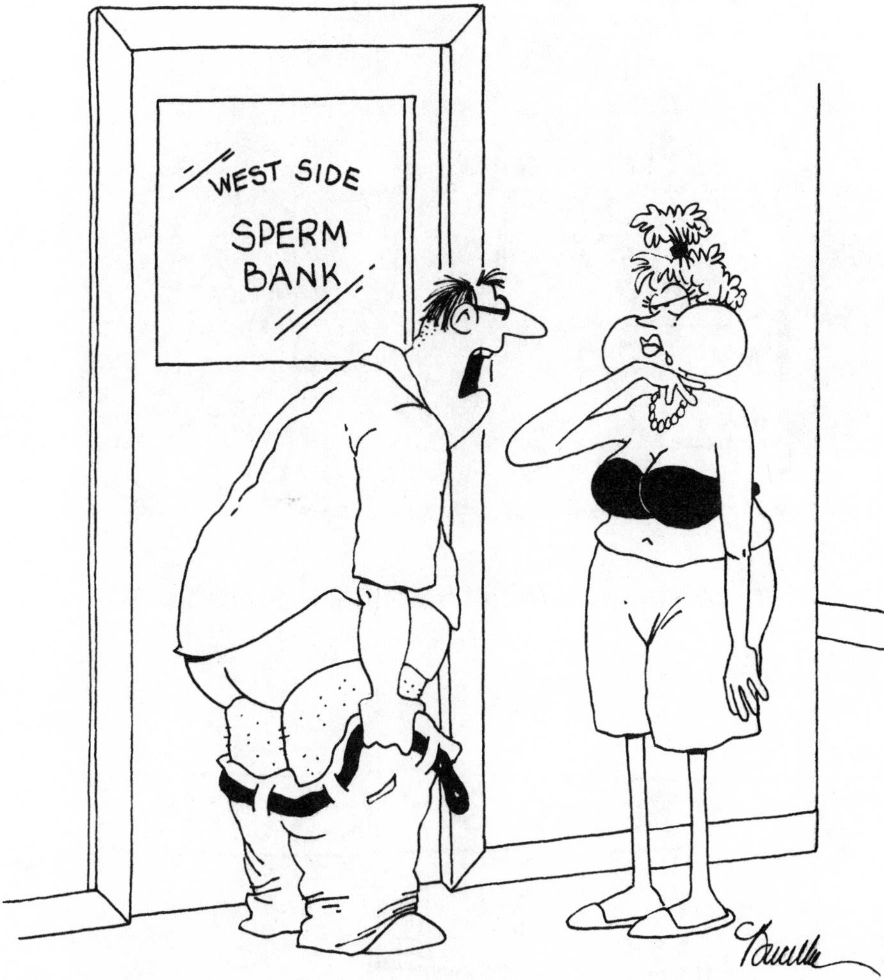
WEST SIDE
SPERM
BANK

*"This is the last place in town.
This time, let **me** do the talking!"*

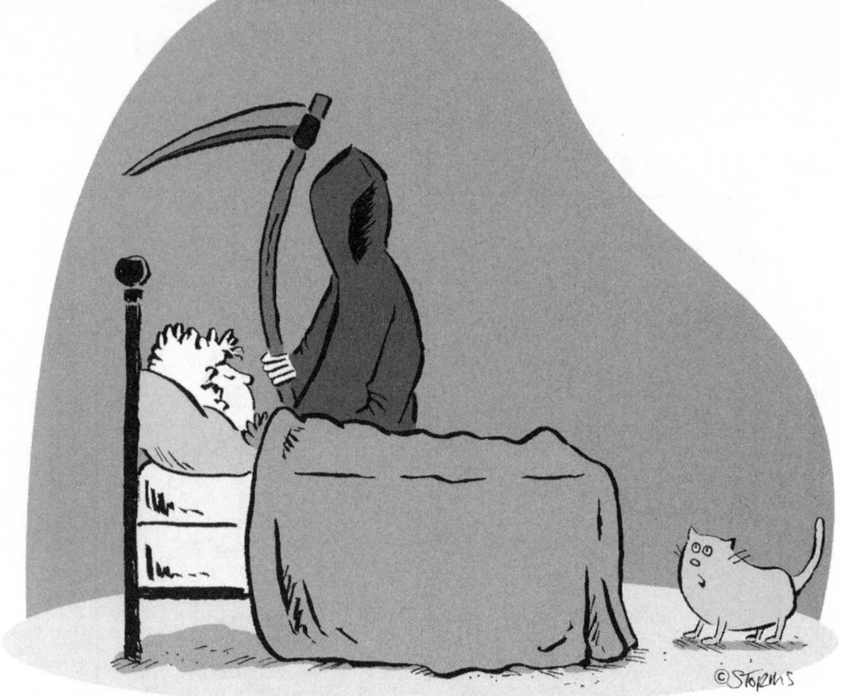
©STORMS

"Can't you wait until after she's fed me?"

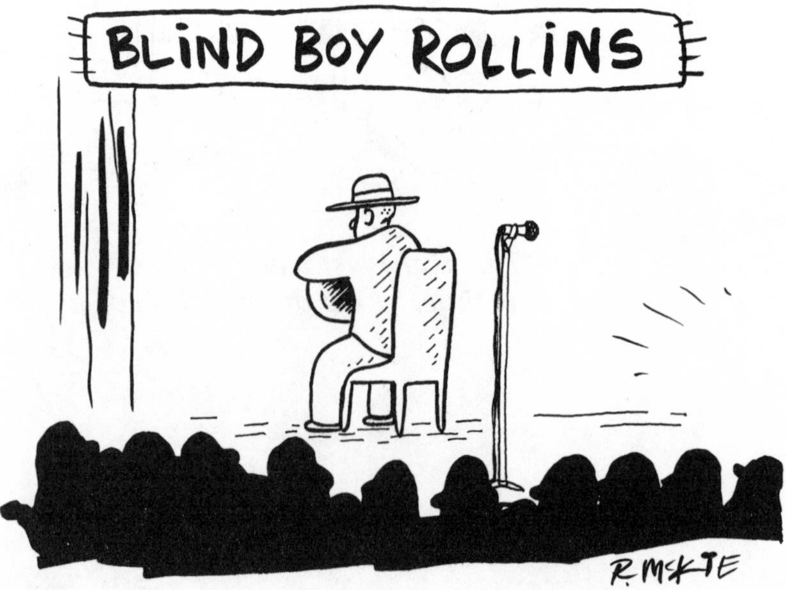
BLIND BOY ROLLINS

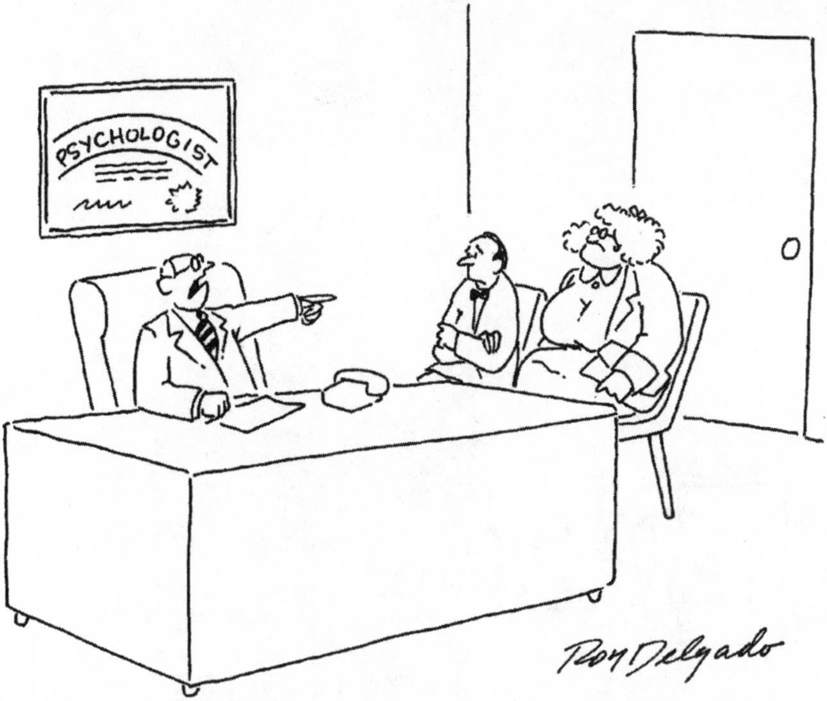
PSYCHOLOGIST
Ron Delgado

*"Okay, now it's **your** turn, you LITTLE JERK!"*

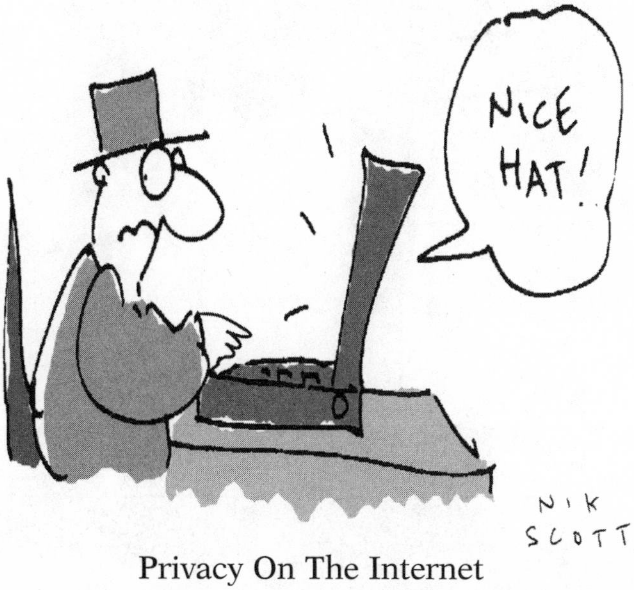
NICE HAT!
NIK SCOTT

Privacy On The Internet

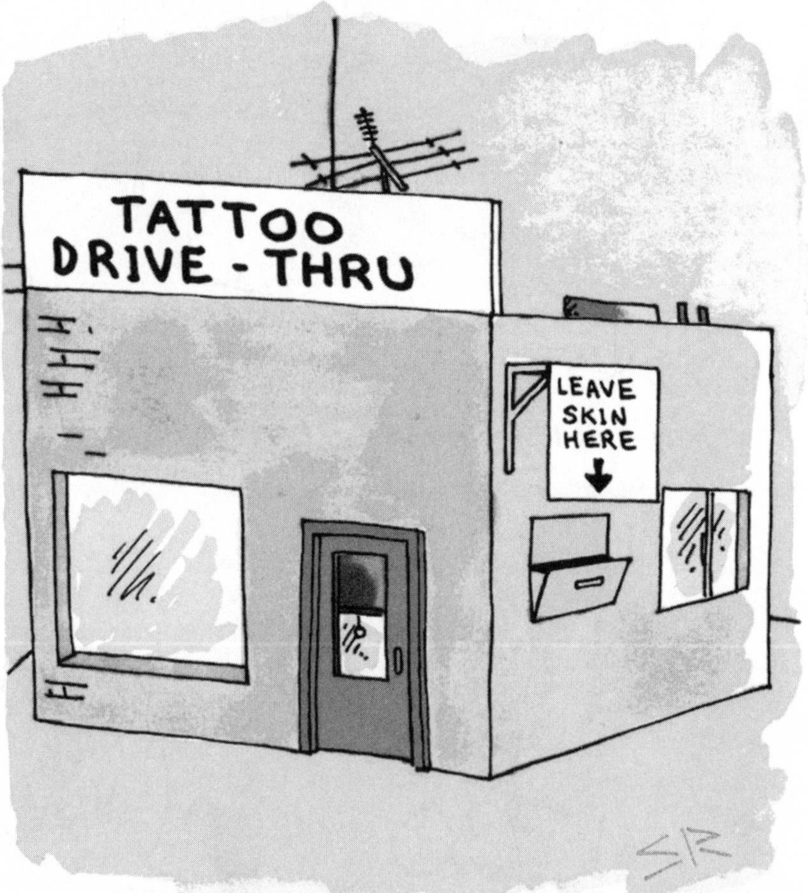
TATTOO
DRIVE - THRU
LEAVE
SKIN
HERE
SR

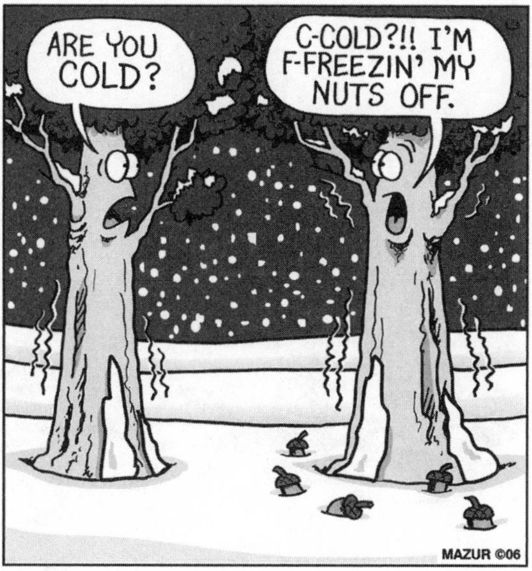
ARE YOU COLD?
C-COLD?!! I'M F-FREEZIN' MY NUTS OFF.
MAZUR ©06

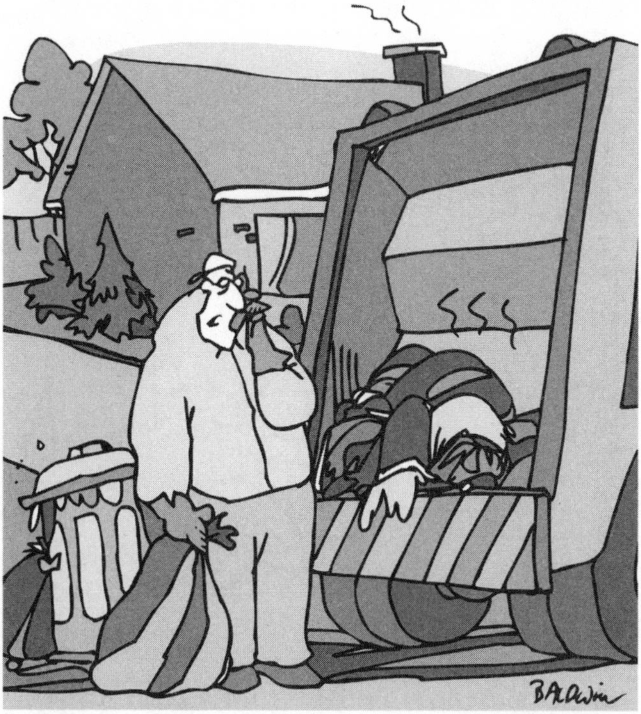

"Don't call me at work. My gloves stink."

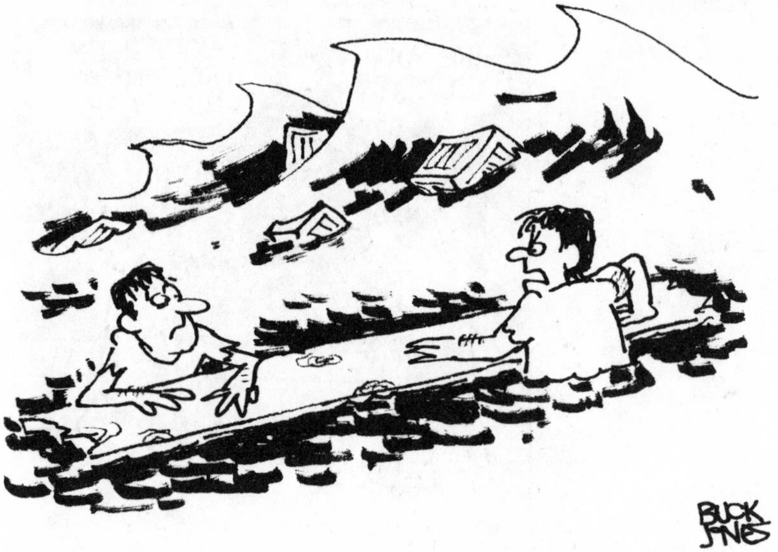
BUCK JONES

"Did you just pee?"

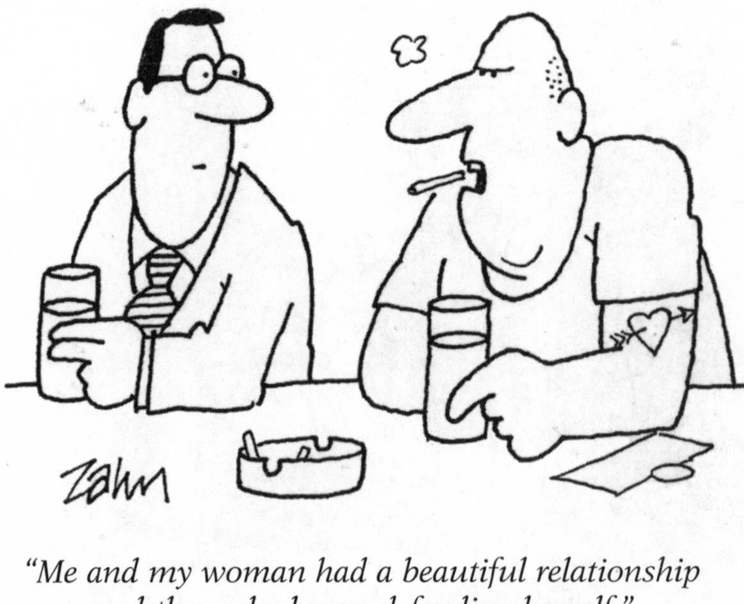
Zahn

“Me and my woman had a beautiful relationship and then, she began defending herself.”

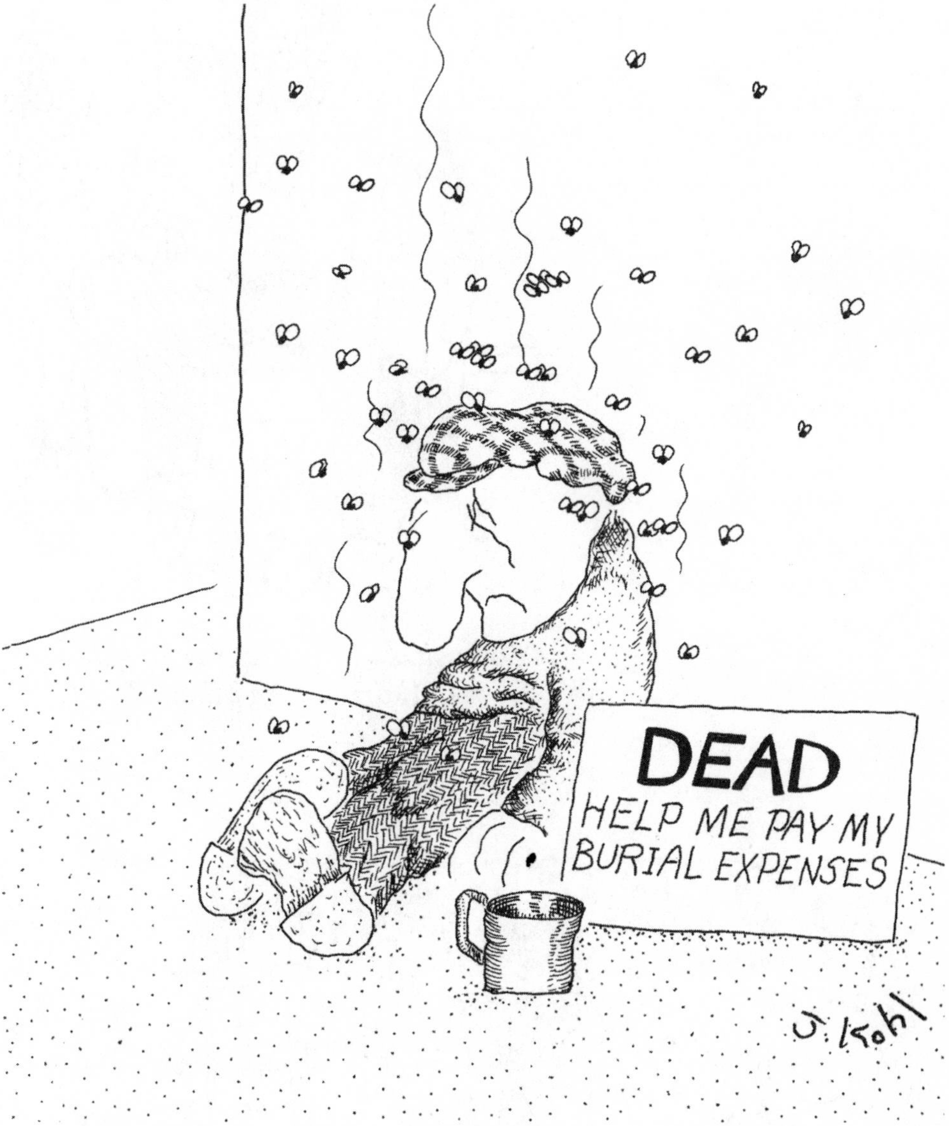
DEAD
HELP ME PAY MY
BURIAL EXPENSES
J. Kohl

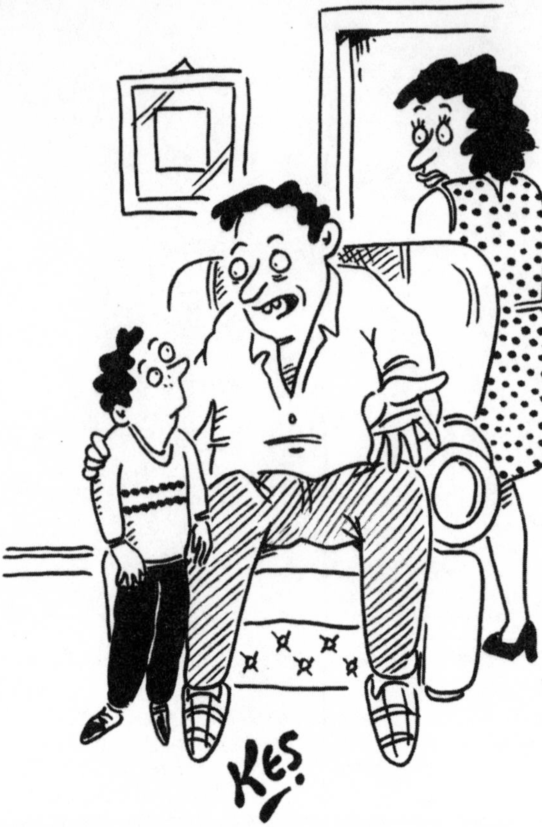
KES

"So basically, the bee tries to get the bird drunk. And then..."

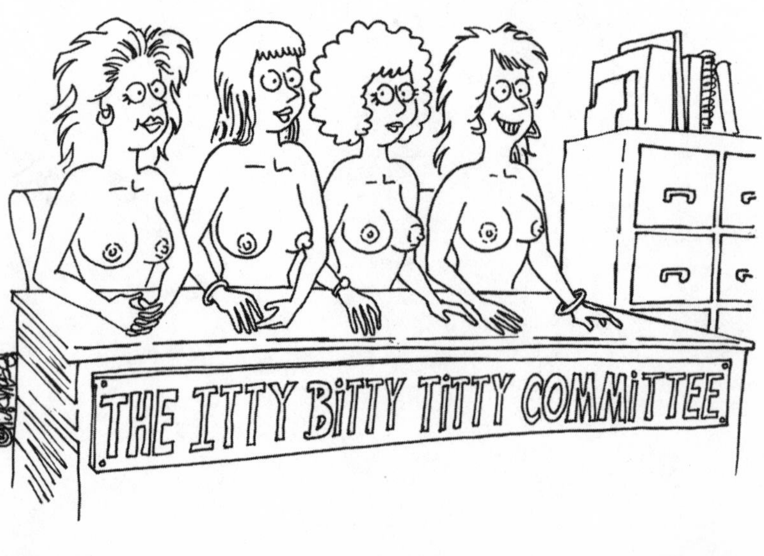
THE ITTY BITTY TITTY COMMITTEE

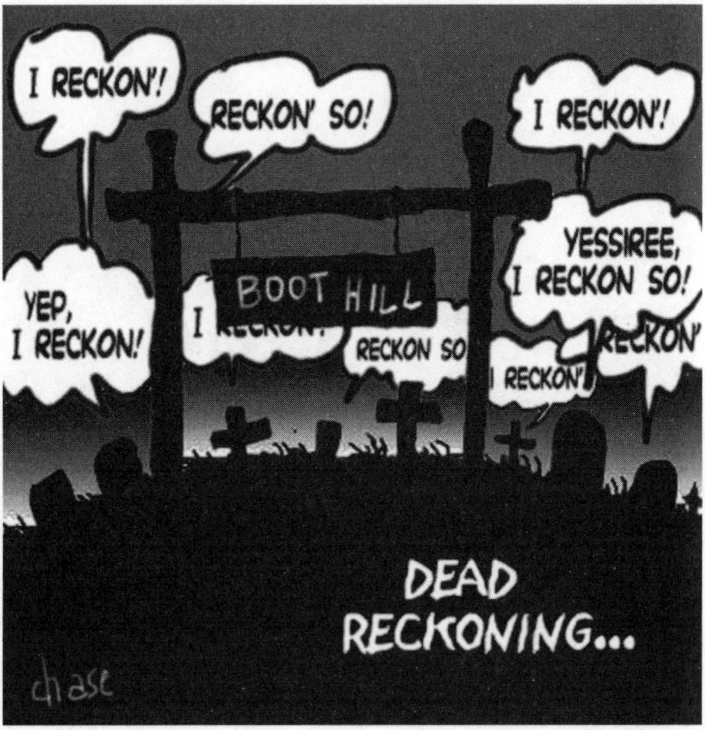
I RECKON'!
RECKON' SO!
I RECKON'!
YEP, I RECKON!
BOOT HILL
YESSIREE, I RECKON SO!
RECKON SO
I RECKON'
DEAD RECKONING...
chase

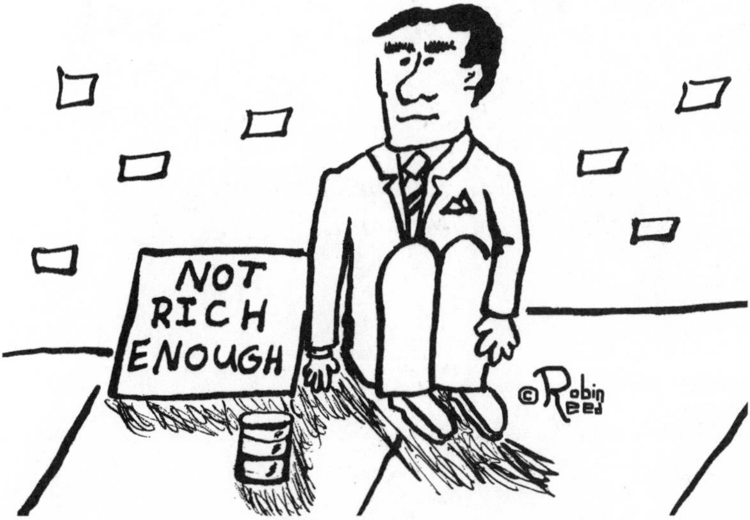
NOT RICH ENOUGH
©Robin Reed

"Have you noticed how zombies dress better
on this side of the island?"

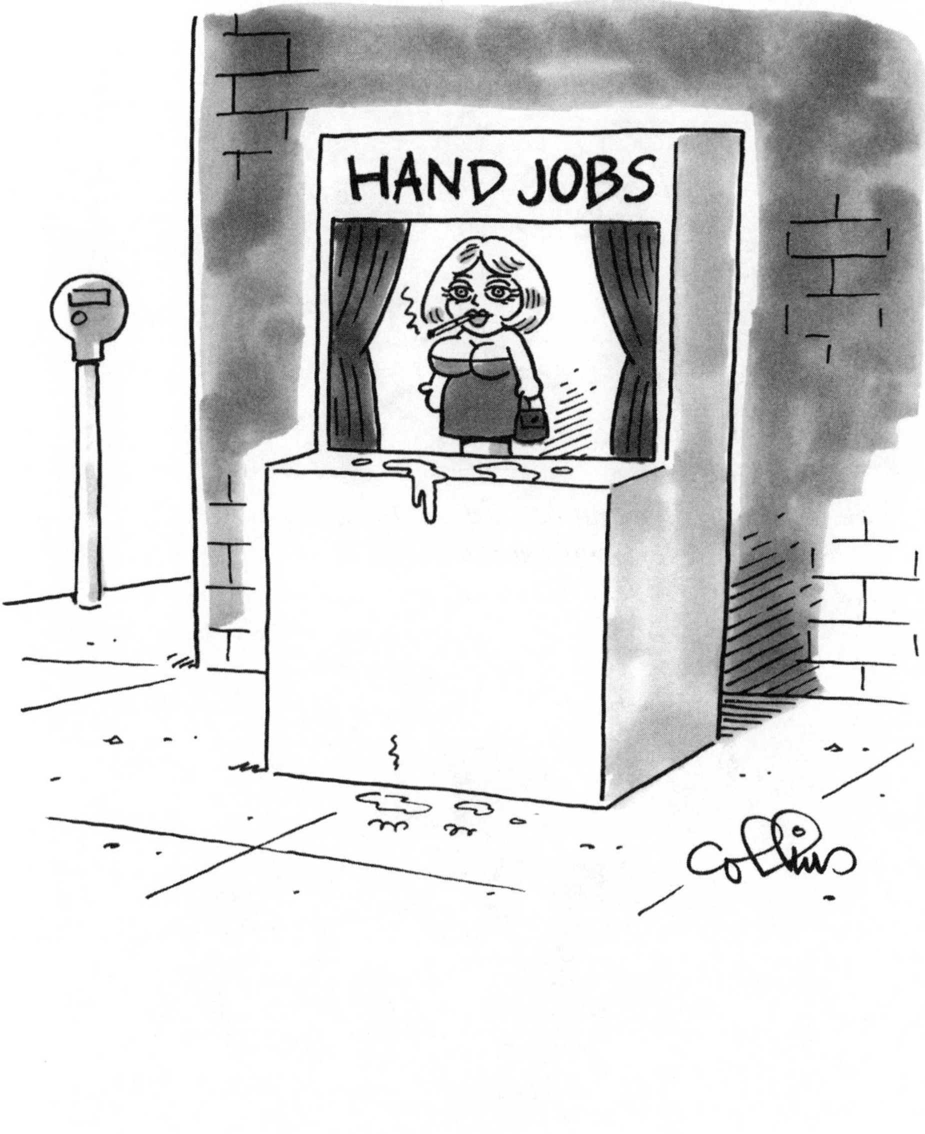
HAND JOBS

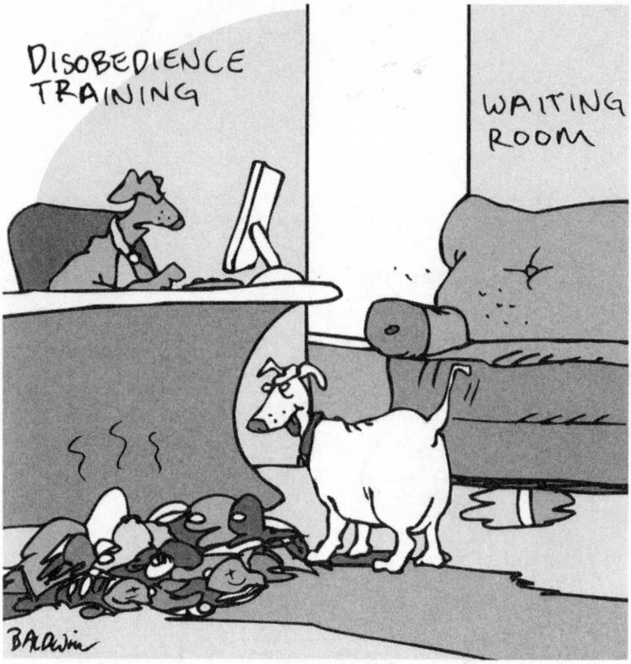
DISOBEDIENCE TRAINING
WAITING ROOM
BALDWIN

"Roll in the garbage and hop up on the sofa. Someone will be with you shortly."

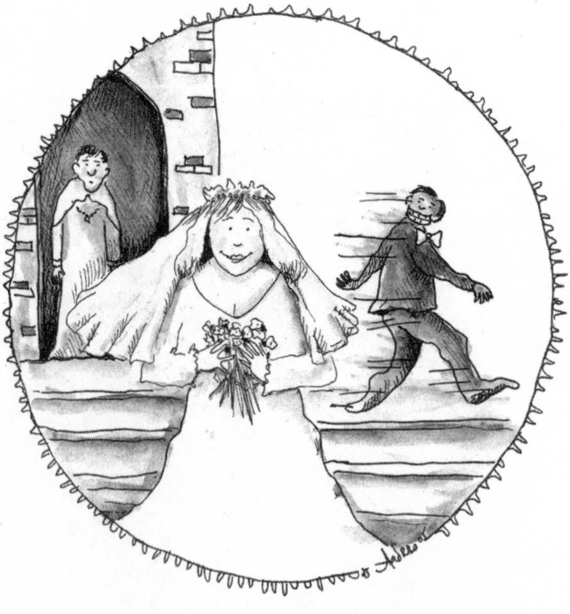

Bigfoot's Wedding Photo

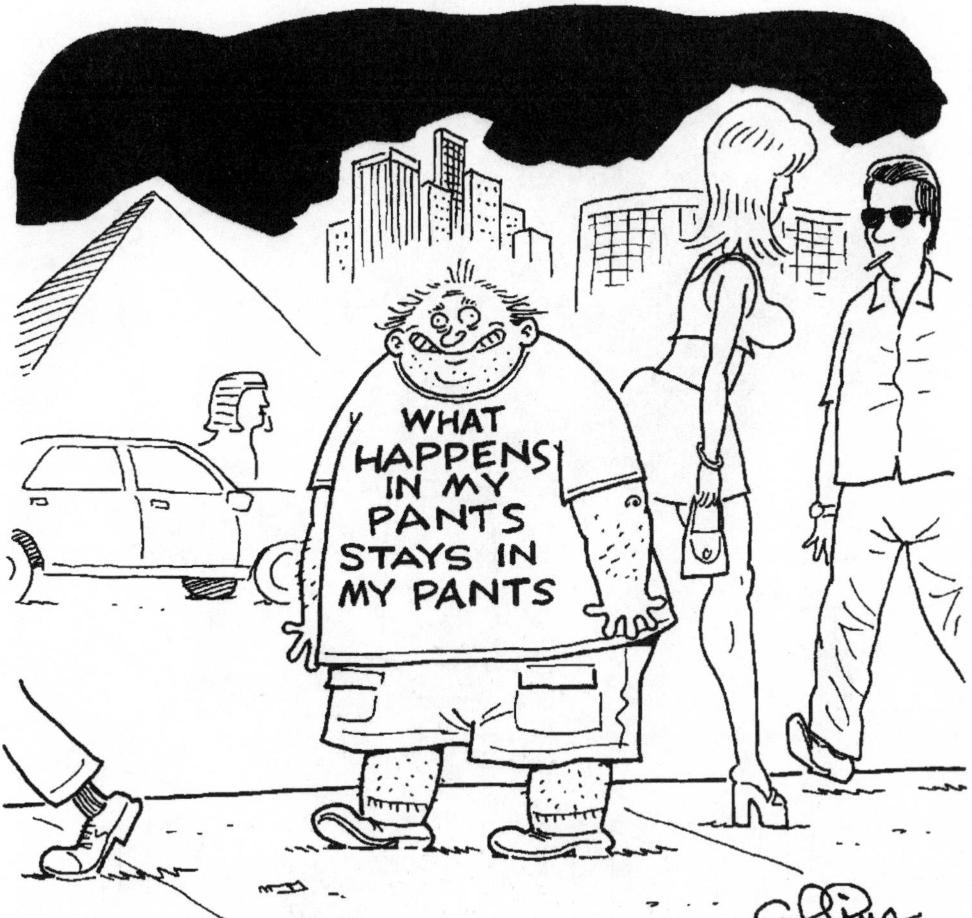
WHAT HAPPENS IN MY PANTS STAYS IN MY PANTS

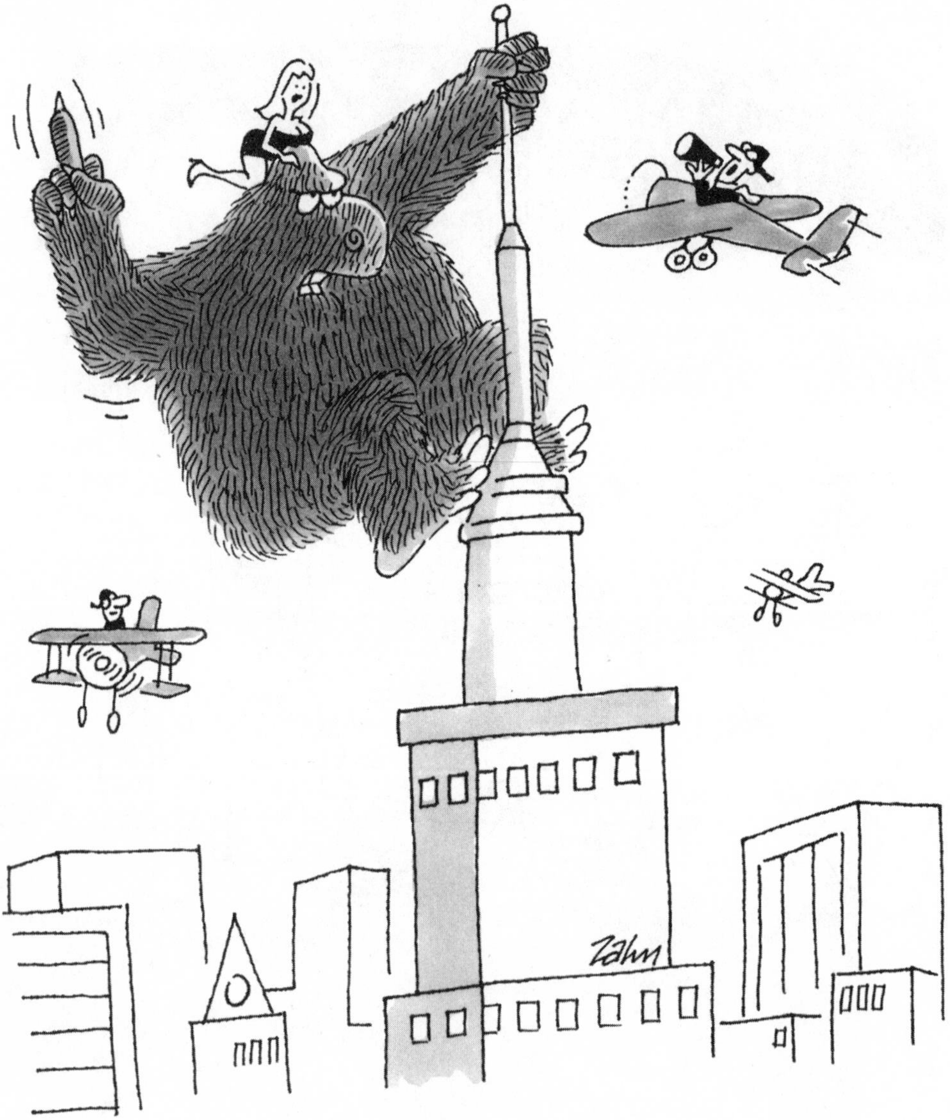
Zahn

"He's really mad now!"

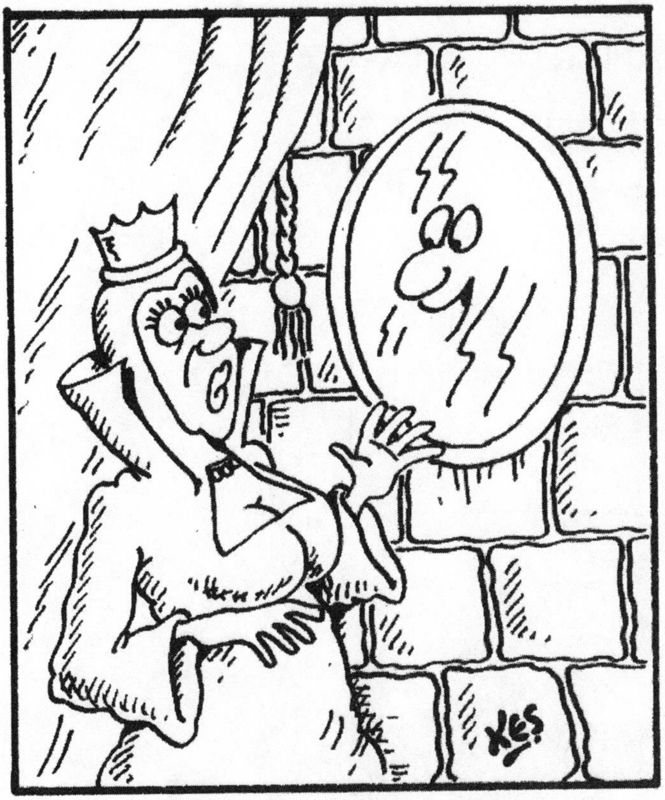
KES

*"Snow White is the fairest of them all.
But you've got the biggest tits."*

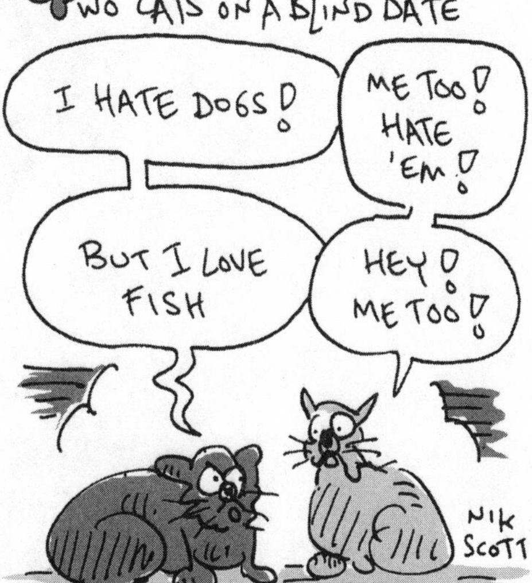
TWO CATS ON A BLIND DATE
I HATE DOGS!
ME TOO! HATE 'EM!
BUT I LOVE FISH
HEY! ME TOO!
NIK SCOTT

MULTIPLE AMPUTEE TWISTER

THIS SUCKS...
Enlightenment

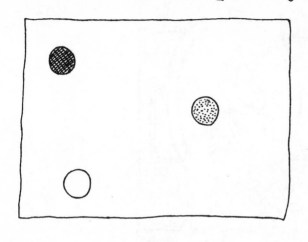

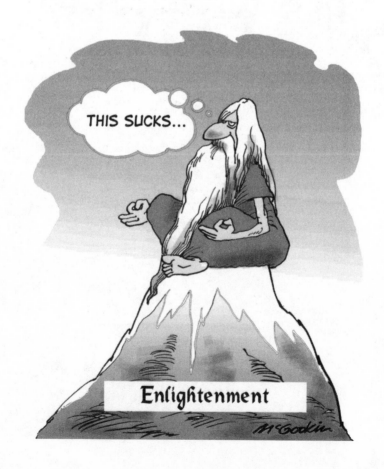

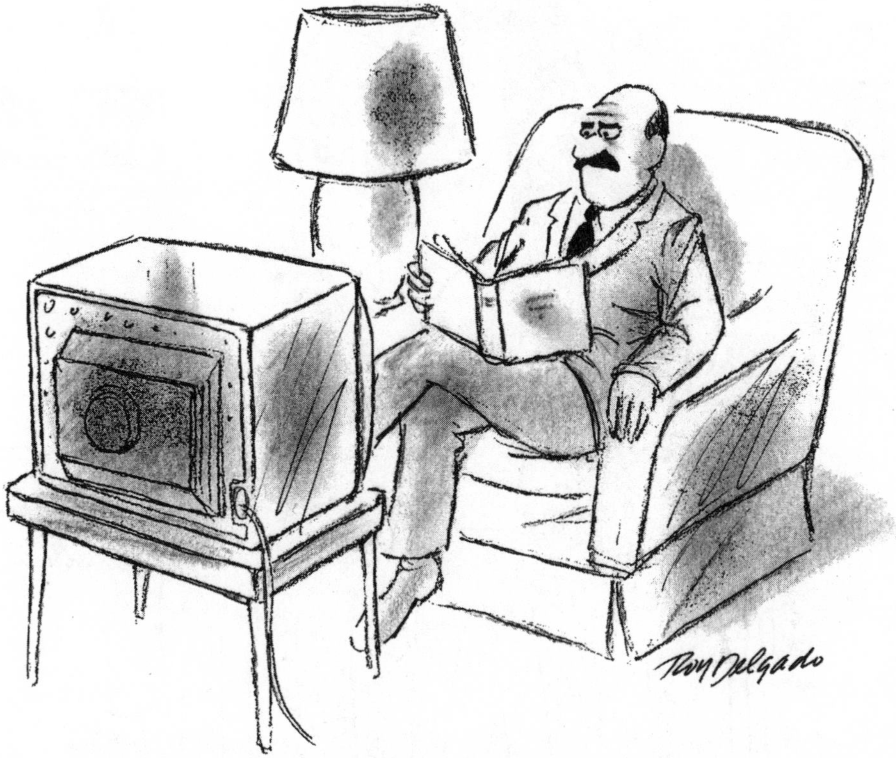
Ray Delgado

"The following PBS Special may not be suitable for Honkies..."

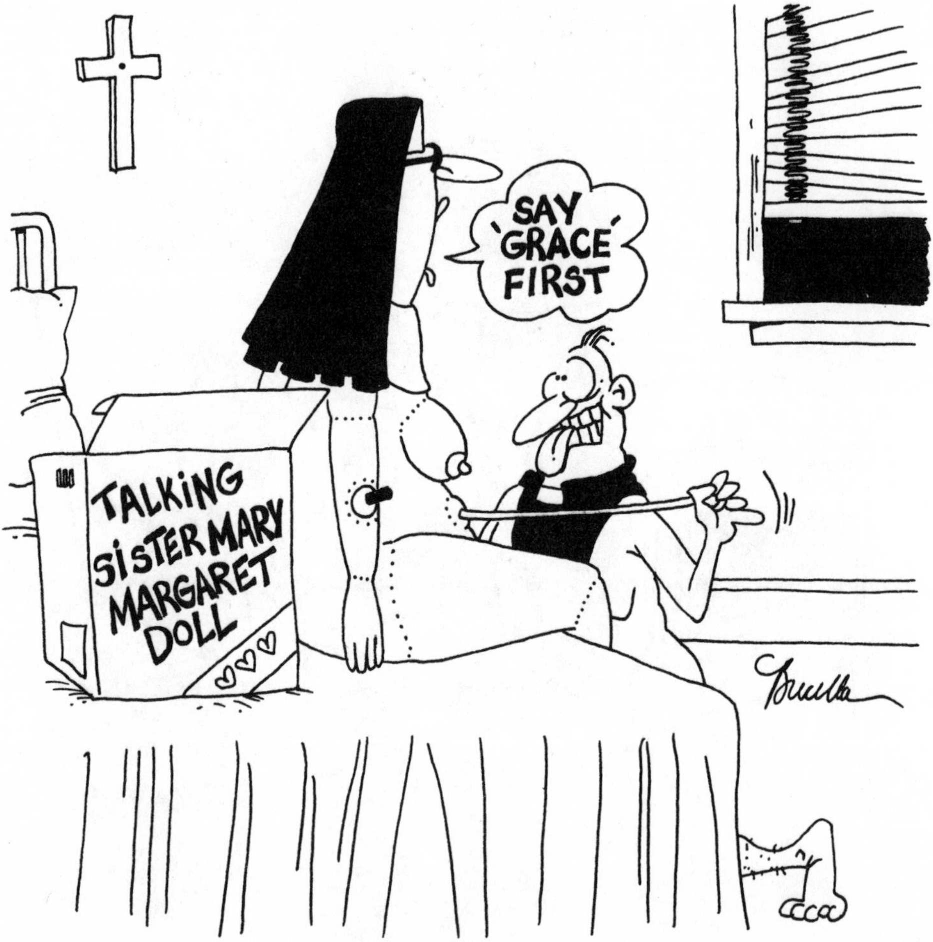

TALKING SISTER MARY MARGARET DOLL
SAY 'GRACE' FIRST

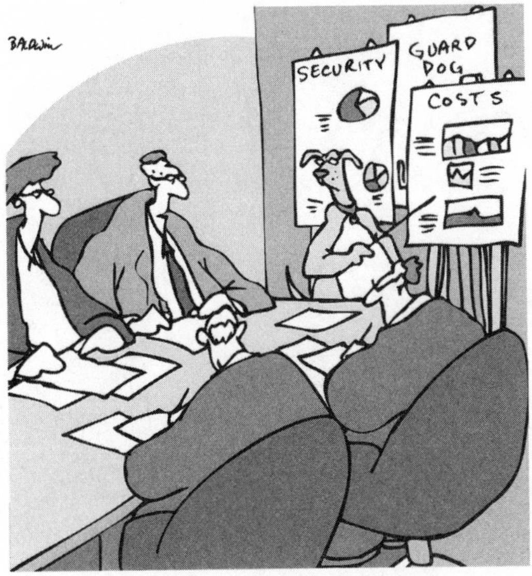
BALDWIN
SECURITY
GUARD DOG
COSTS

"Good proposal. We'll get back to you. We still have to hear from the cat."

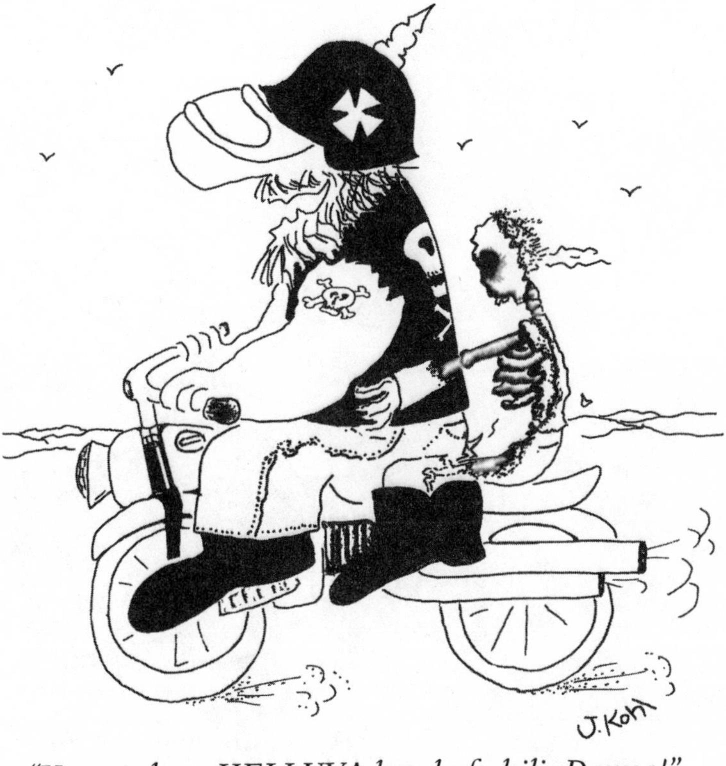
J. Koh

"You make a HELLUVA bowl of chili, Donna!"

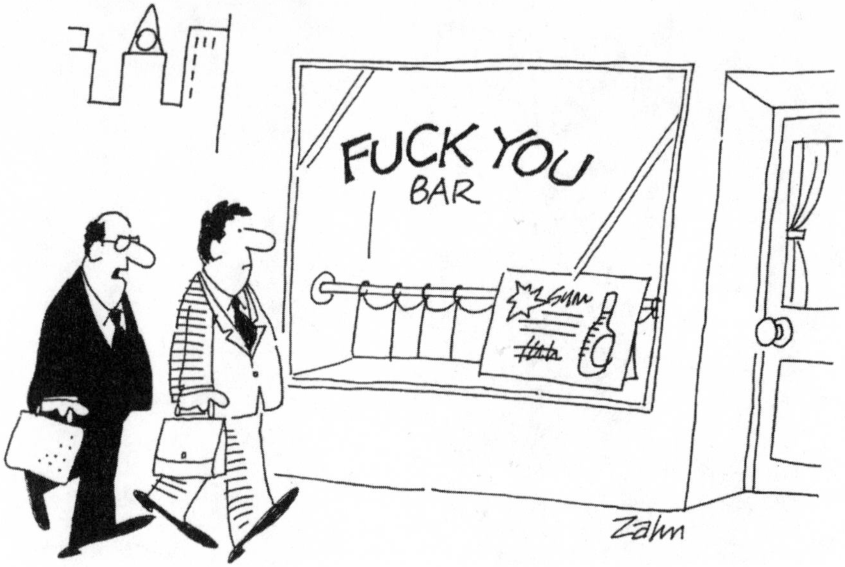
FUCK YOU
BAR
Zahn

"I hear they have a lot of fights in there."

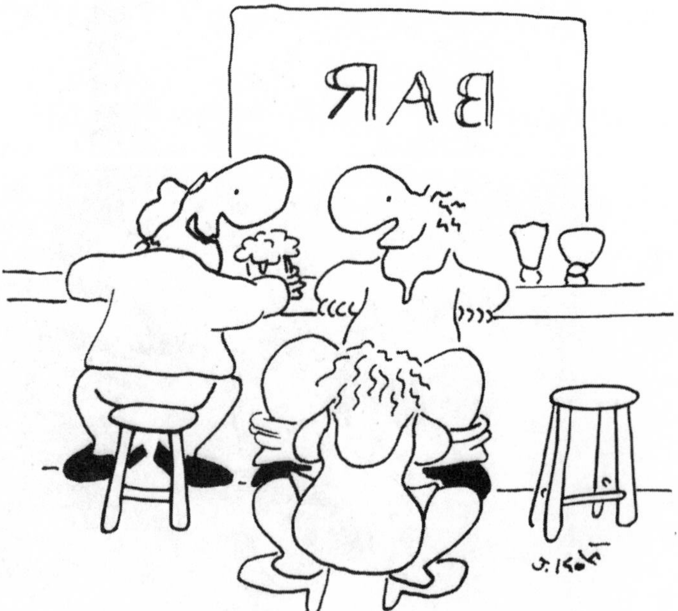
BAR

"You're doing great, Fred! See if you can get her phone number."

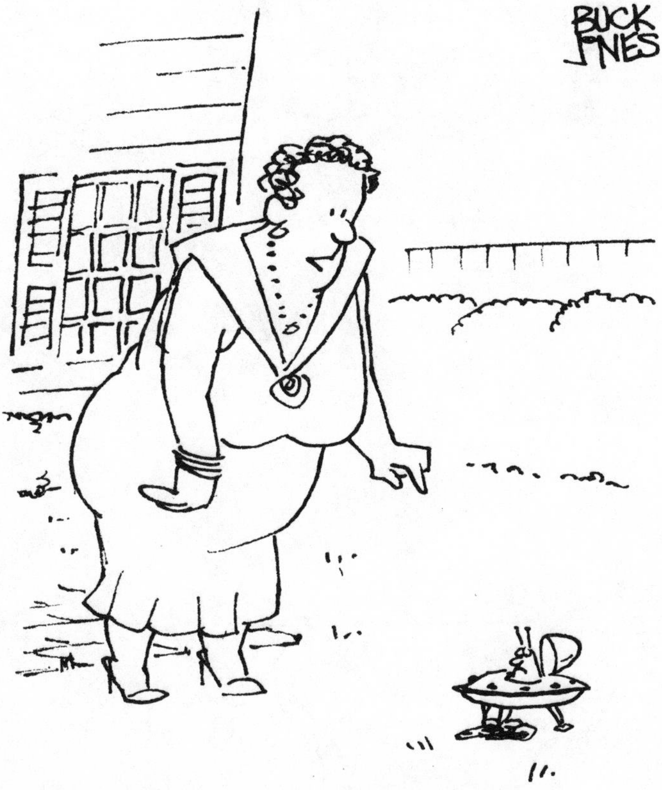
BUCK JONES

"Oh darling, you've landed in Fifi's poo."

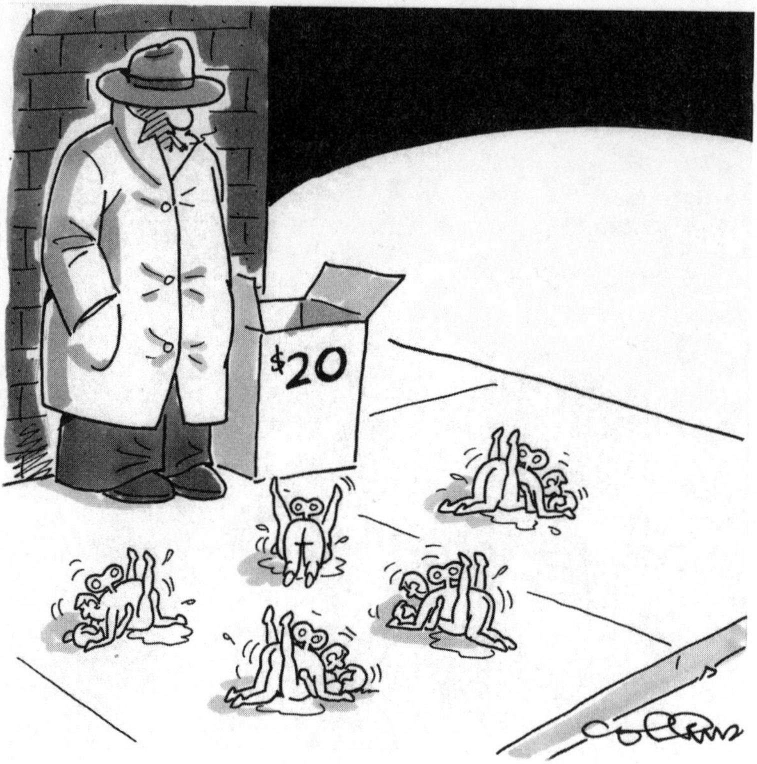
$20

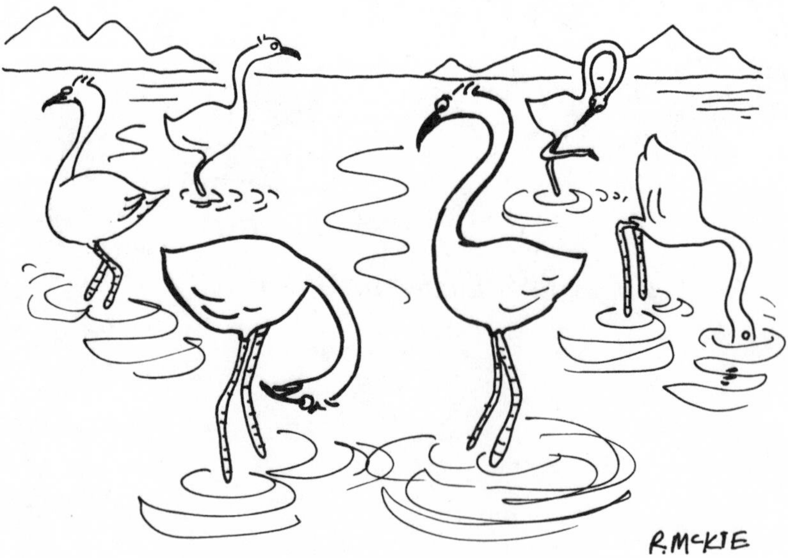

"Oh my God, I've got weird back-bendy legs too."

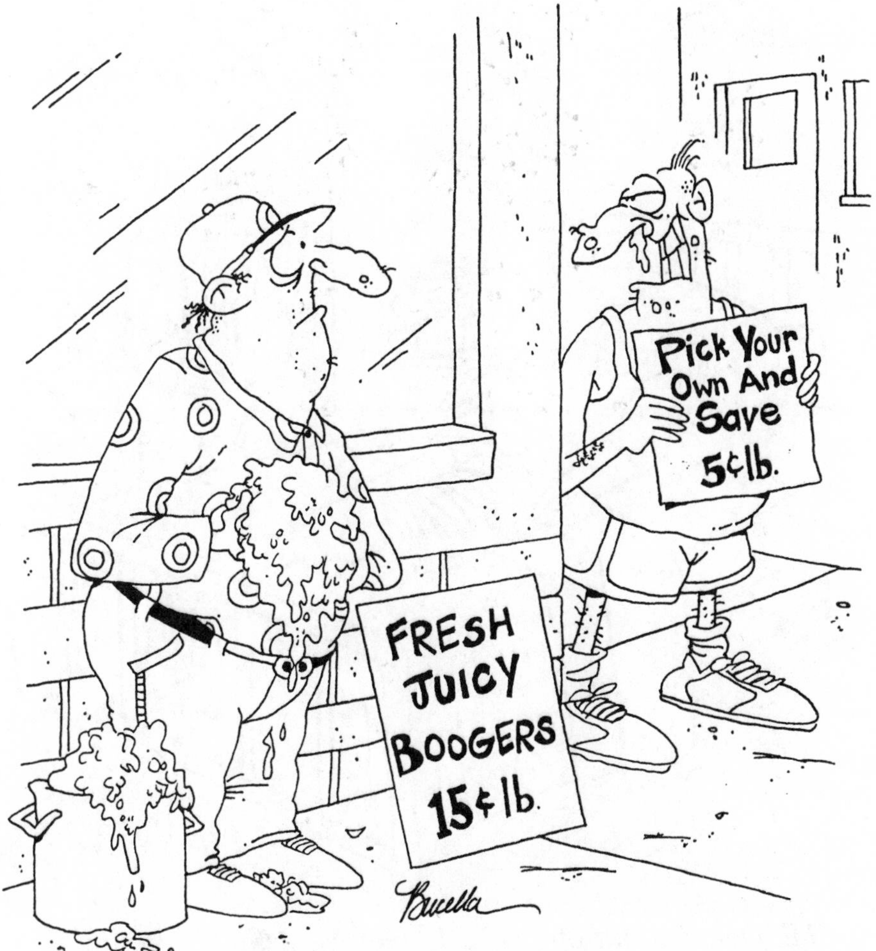
Pick Your Own And Save 5¢ lb.
FRESH JUICY BOOGERS 15¢ lb.
Bucella

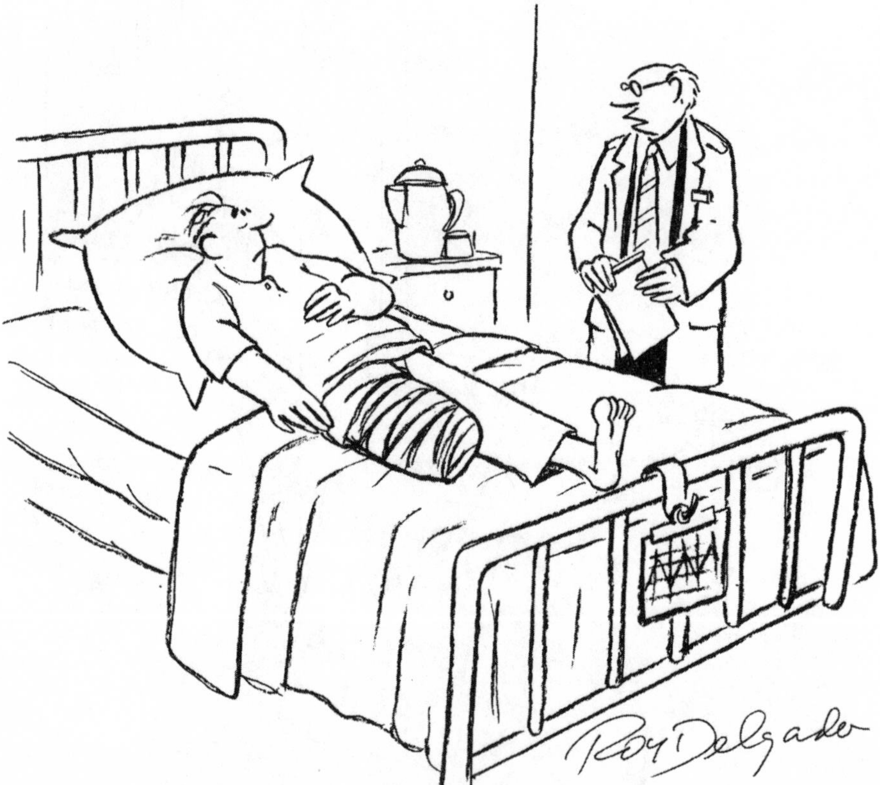
Roy Delgado

"I'll have you out of bed and up on your foot in no time."

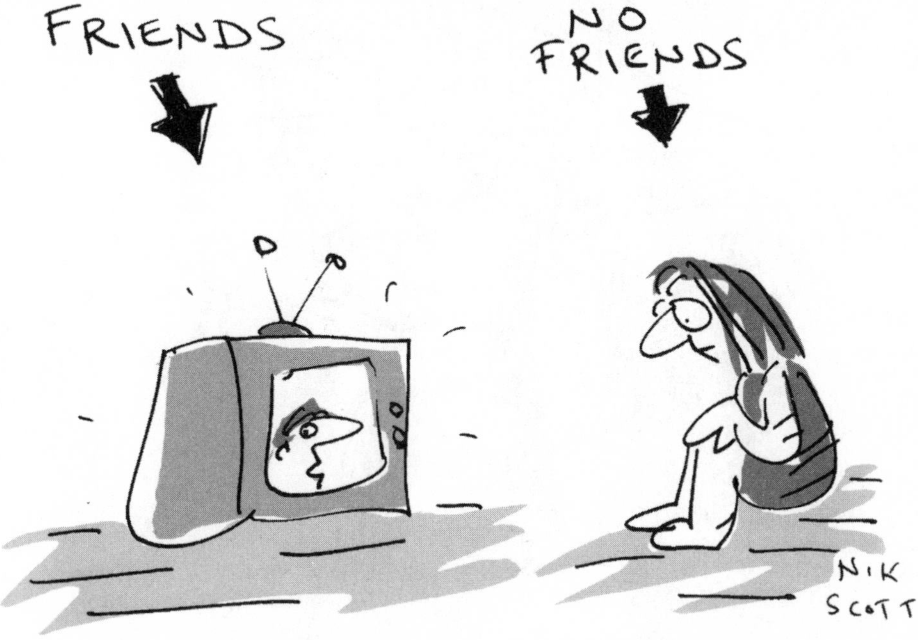
FRIENDS
NO FRIENDS
NIK SCOTT

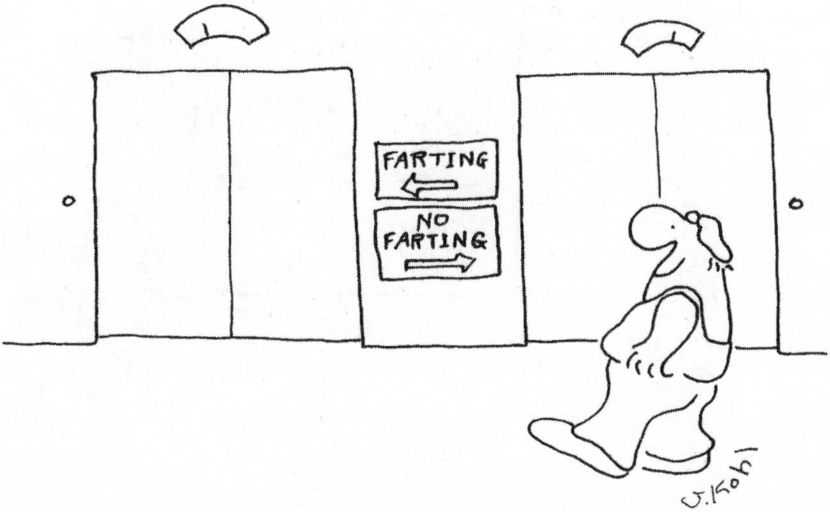
FARTING
NO FARTING

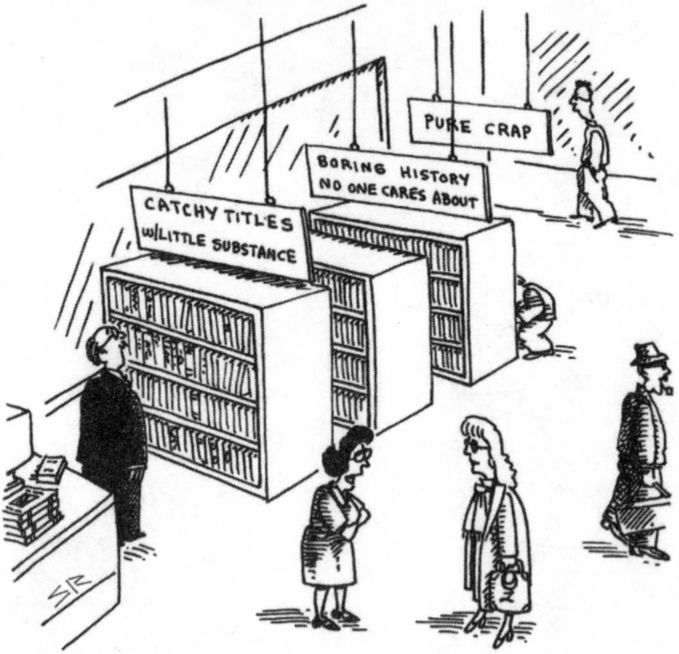
PURE CRAP
BORING HISTORY NO ONE CARES ABOUT
CATCHY TITLES w/LITTLE SUBSTANCE
SR

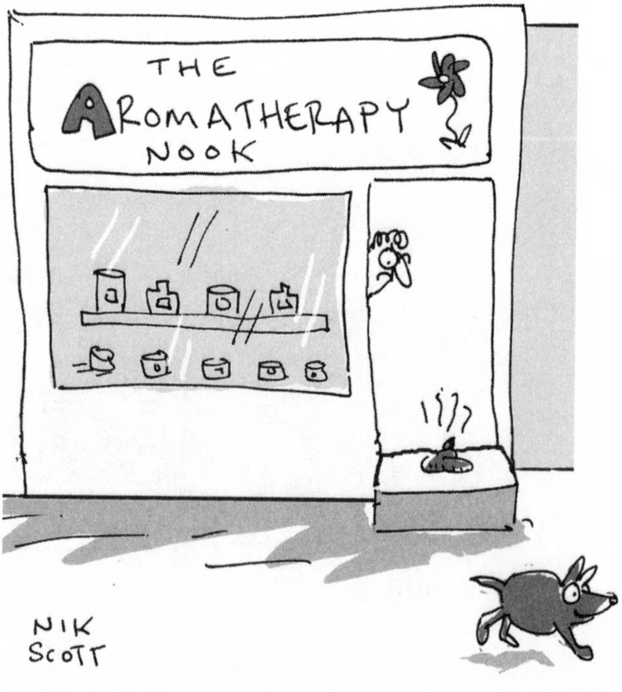
THE AROMATHERAPY NOOK
NIK SCOTT

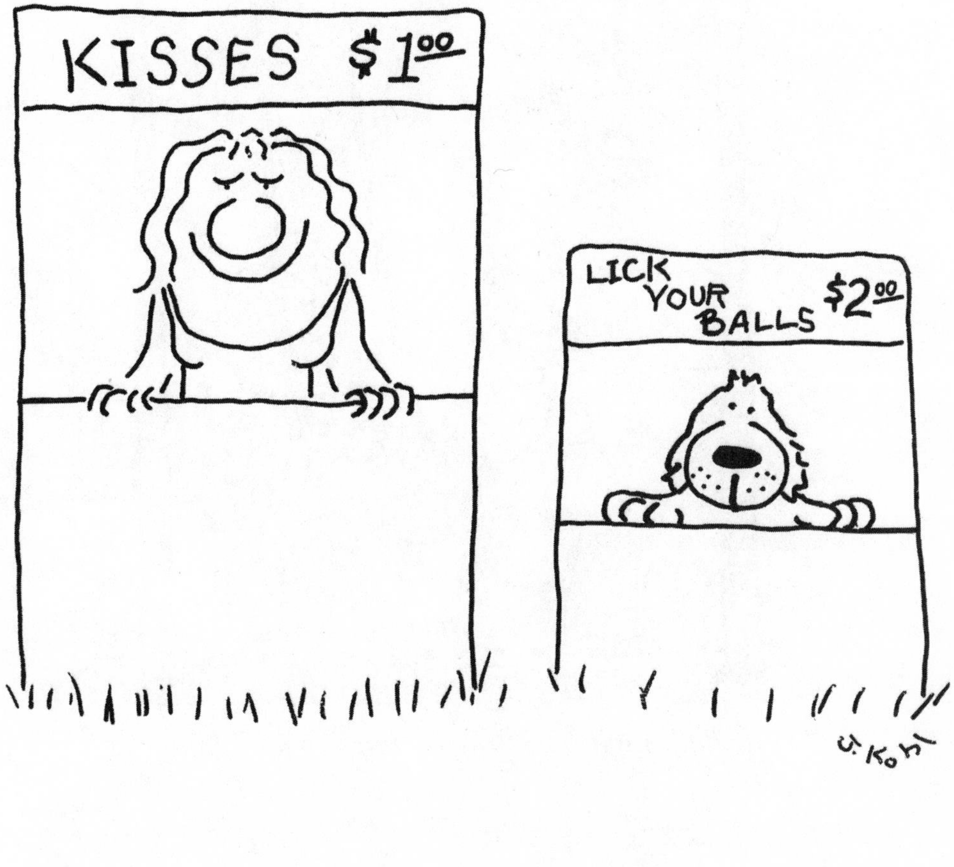
KISSES $1.00
LICK YOUR BALLS $2.00
J. Kohl

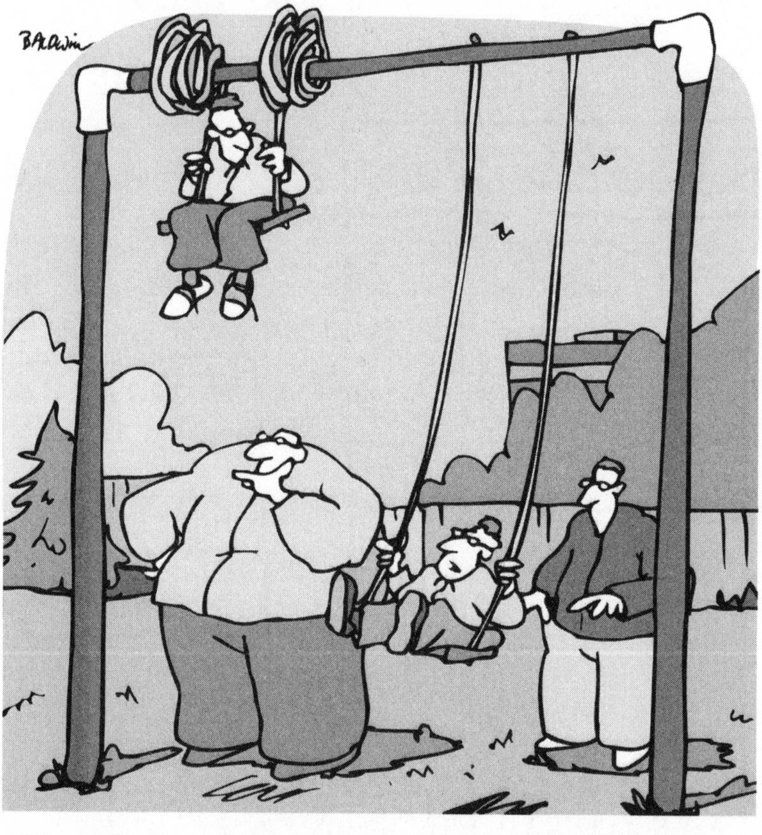
BALDWIN

"Your dad might be stronger, but my dad's smarter."

"Here's a little number I wrote after strangling my 18th and 19th victims and dismembering and cannibalizing their remains."

"Nice tits! Are they real?"

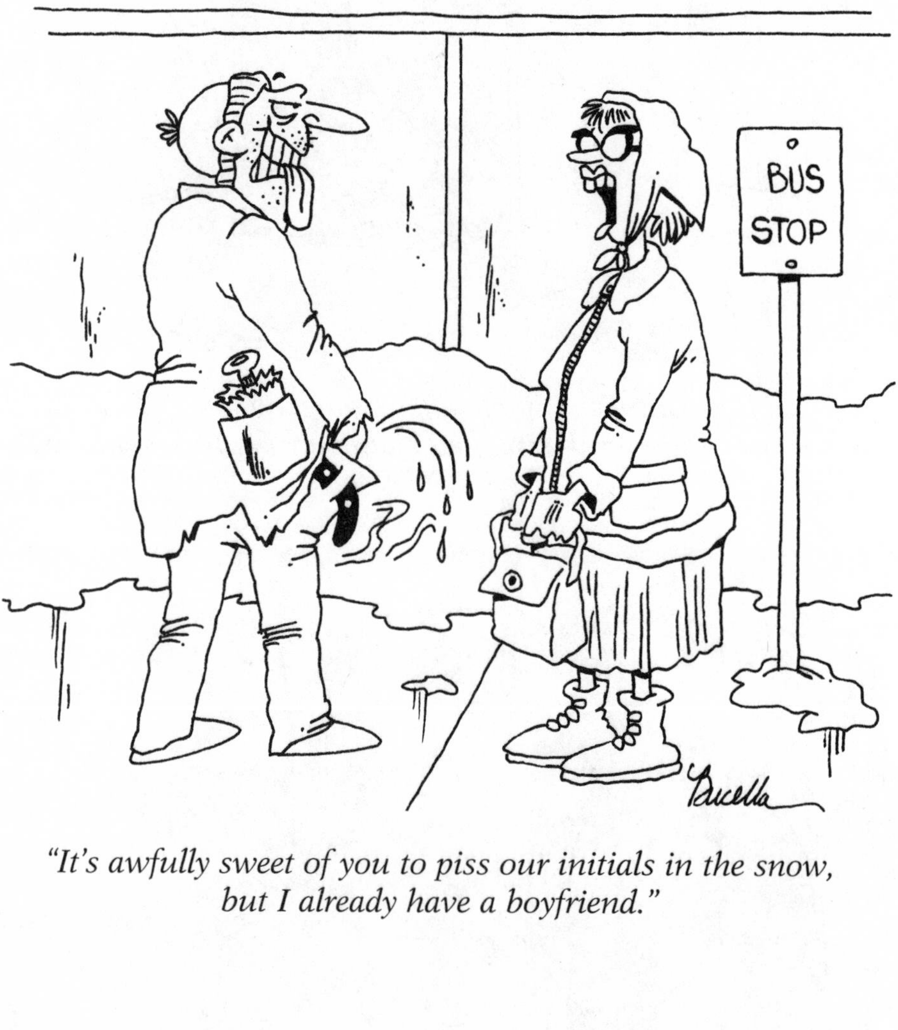
BUS
STOP
Bucella

"It's awfully sweet of you to piss our initials in the snow, but I already have a boyfriend."

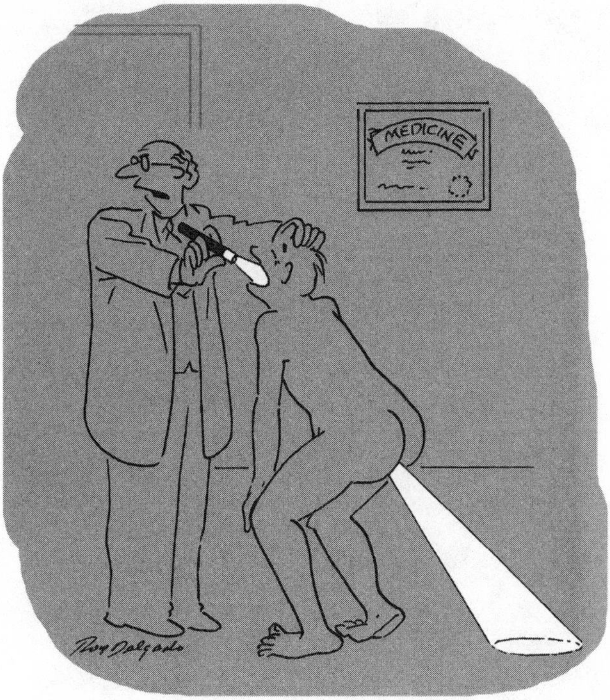
MEDICINE

"Nurse Cromwell... Forget the enema."

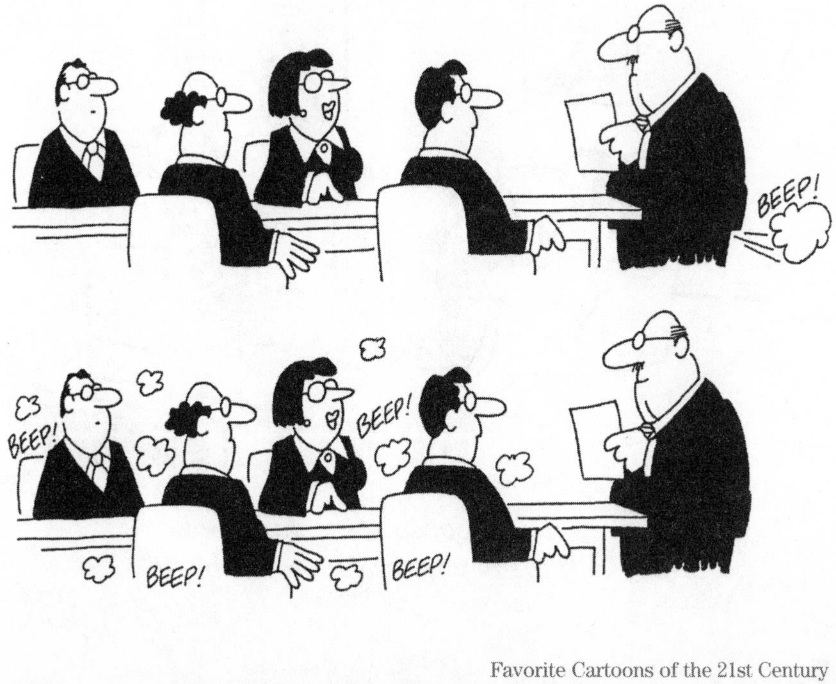
BEEP!
BEEP!
BEEP!
BEEP!
BEEP!

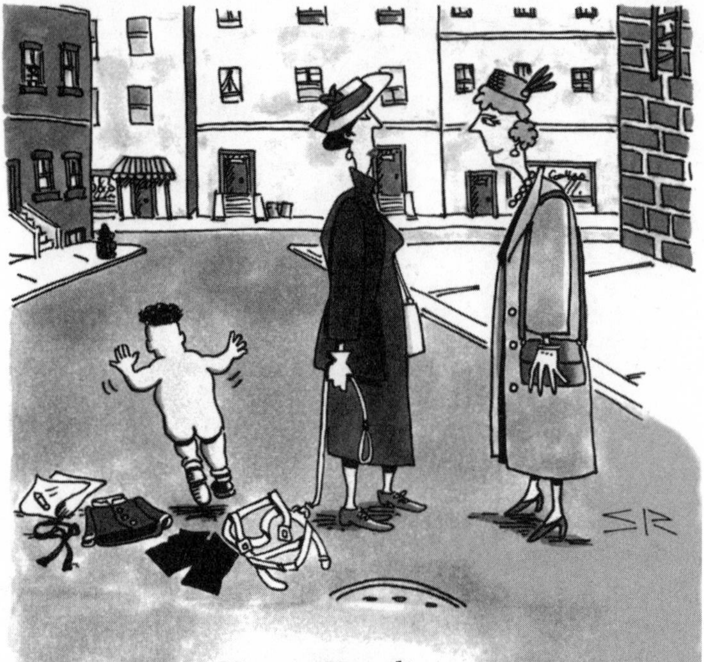

Young Houdini

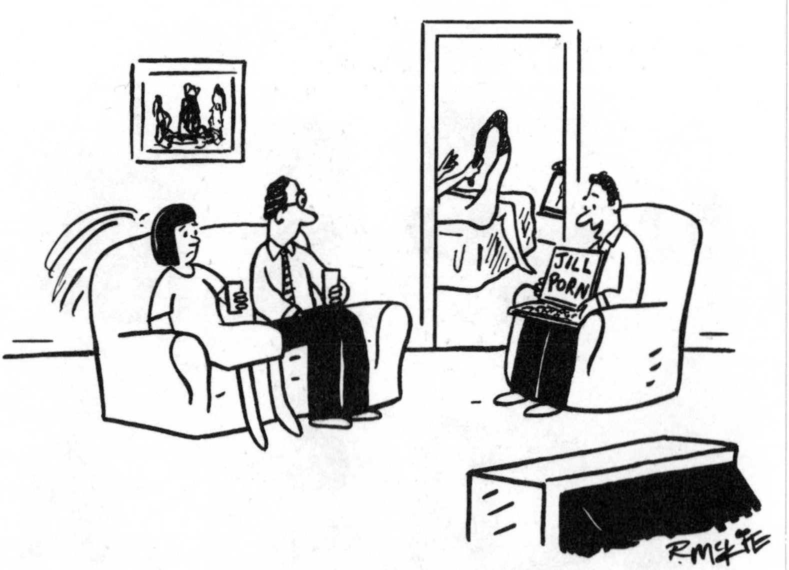
JILL PORN

"I'm a complete technophobe, but my wife has her own blog."

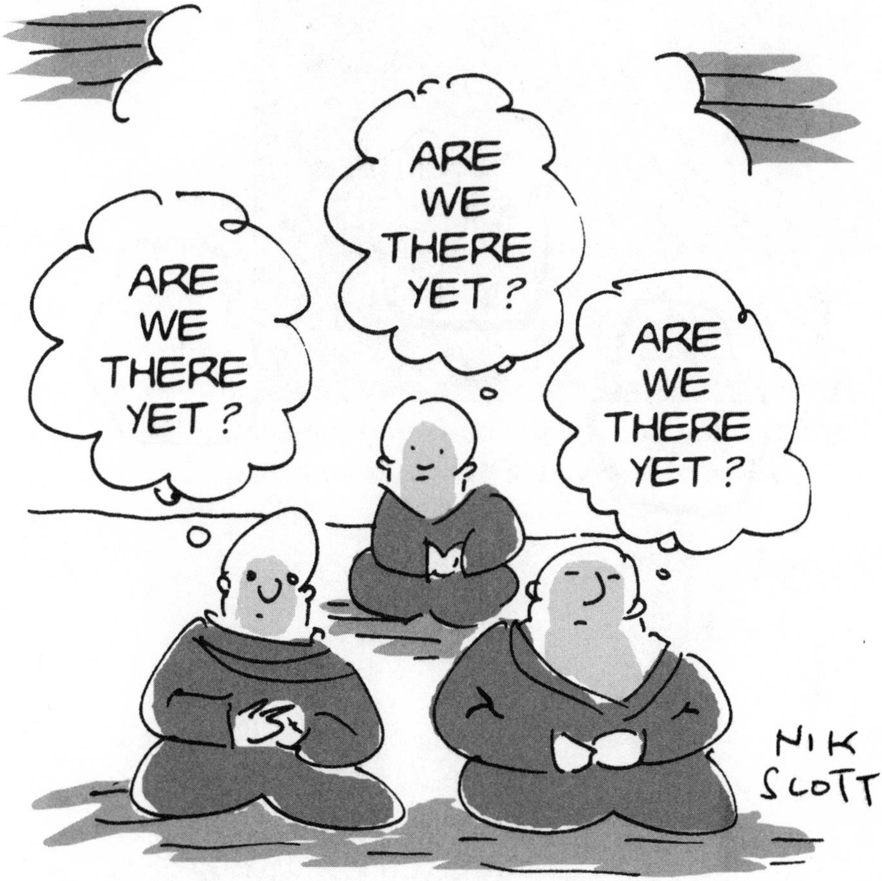
ARE WE THERE YET ?
ARE WE THERE YET ?
ARE WE THERE YET ?
NIK SCOTT

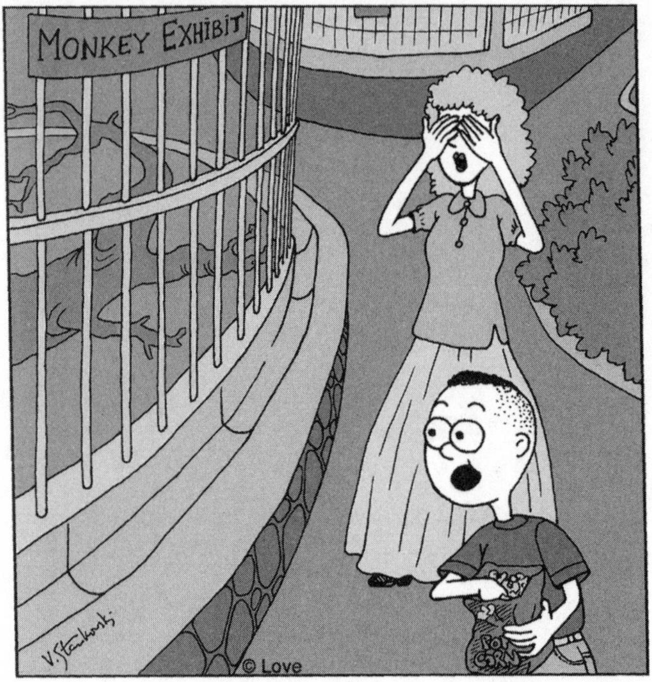
MONKEY EXHIBIT
POP CORN
V. Stankovski
© Love

Bobby never understood the birds and the bees,
but the monkeys made perfect sense.

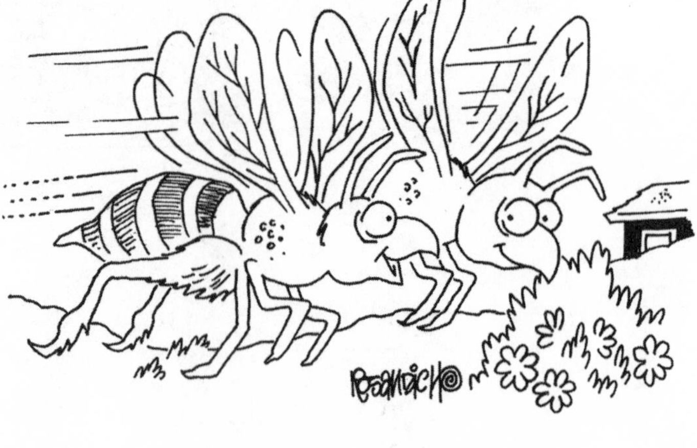
BOSANDICKO

"Let's go gangbang the queen!"

"He is a jealous God..."

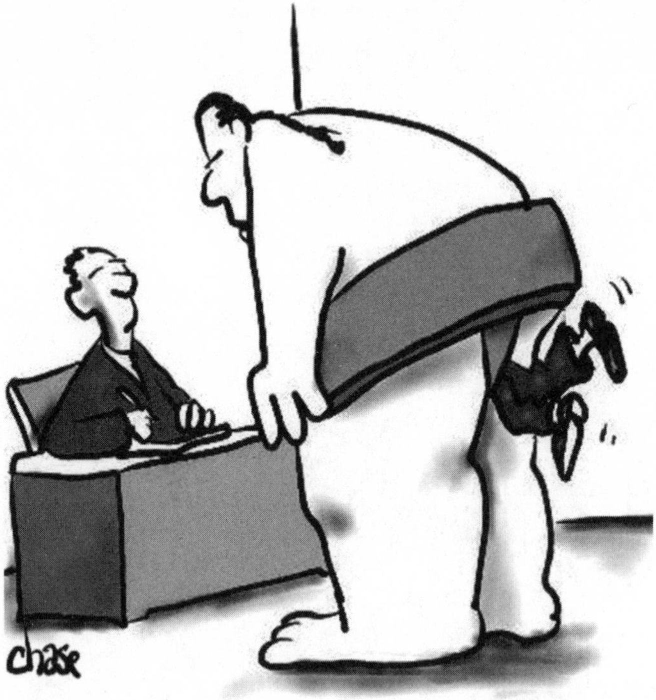
chase

"I seem to have misplaced my trainer."

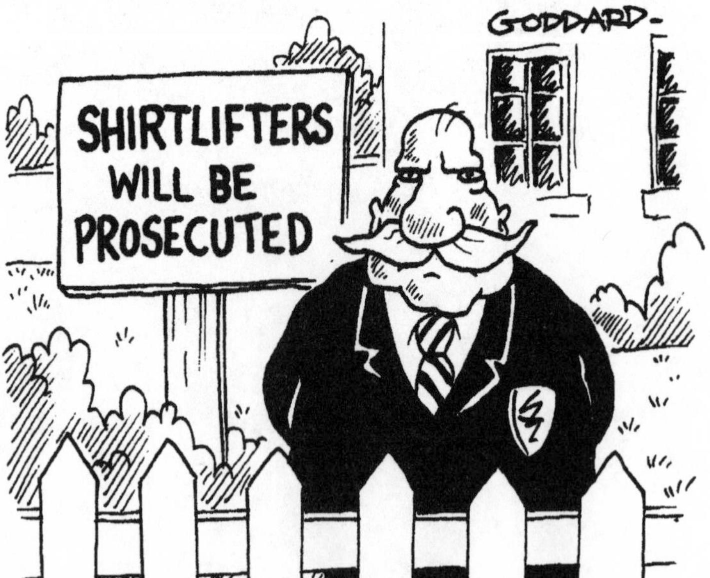
GODDARD-
SHIRTLIFTERS
WILL BE
PROSECUTED

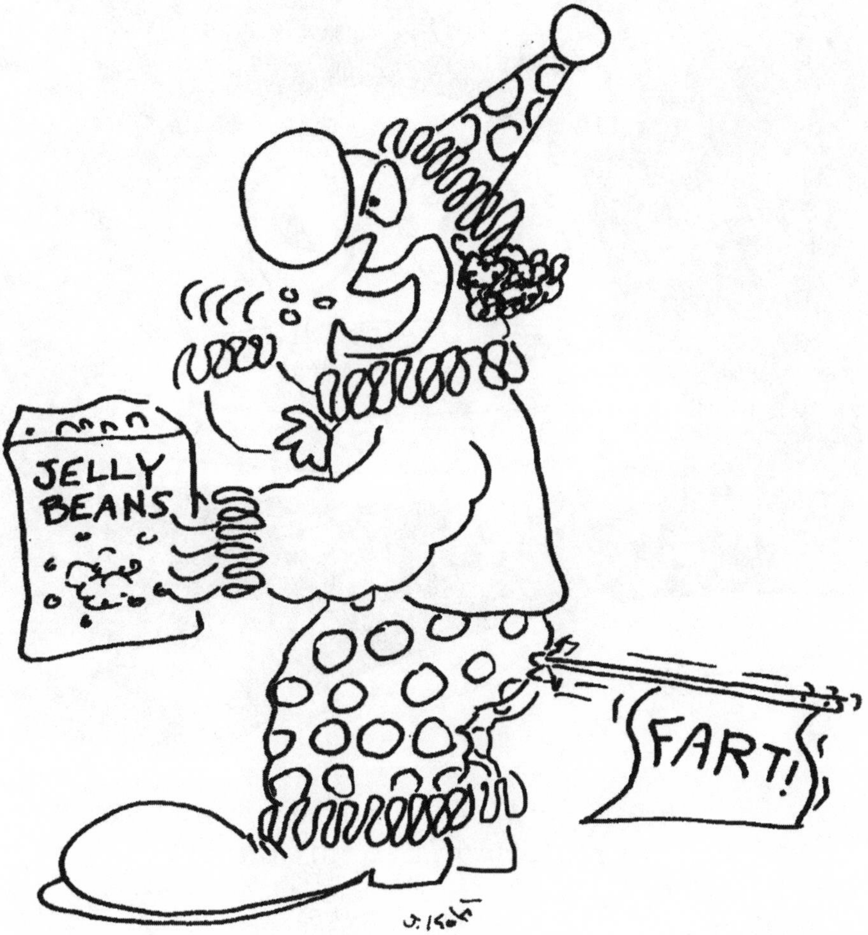
JELLY BEANS
FART!

"The rule is: Whoever uses the anal probe last
is the one who has to clean it."

"I got 397 dead birds and the mayor breathing down my neck. So, is this our perp or just another copycat?"

"Not now Pinocchio, can't you see I'm busy?"

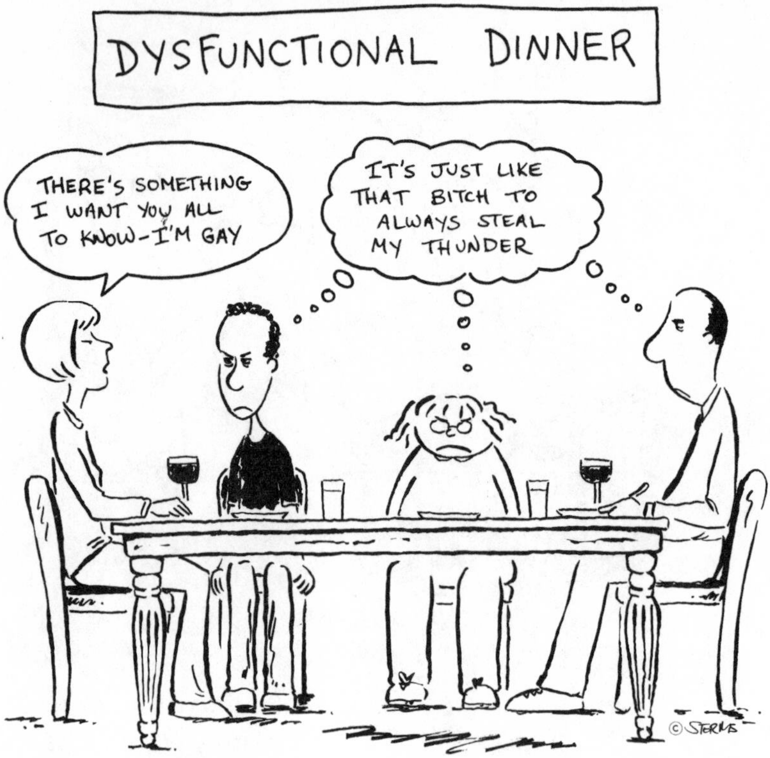
DYSFUNCTIONAL DINNER
THERE'S SOMETHING I WANT YOU ALL TO KNOW—I'M GAY
IT'S JUST LIKE THAT BITCH TO ALWAYS STEAL MY THUNDER
© STERNS

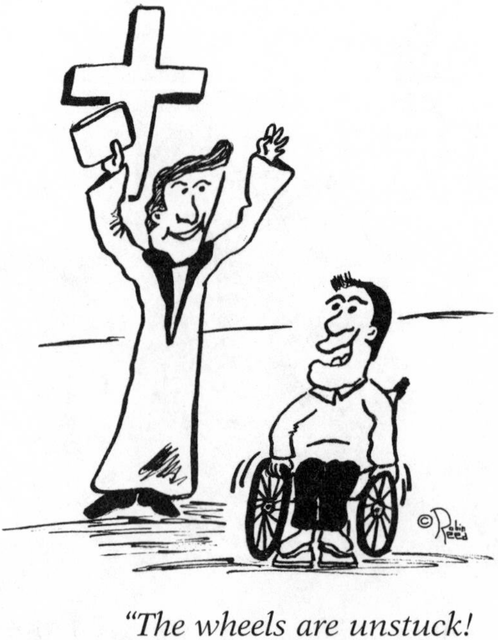
© Robin Reed

"The wheels are unstuck! The wheels are unstuck!"

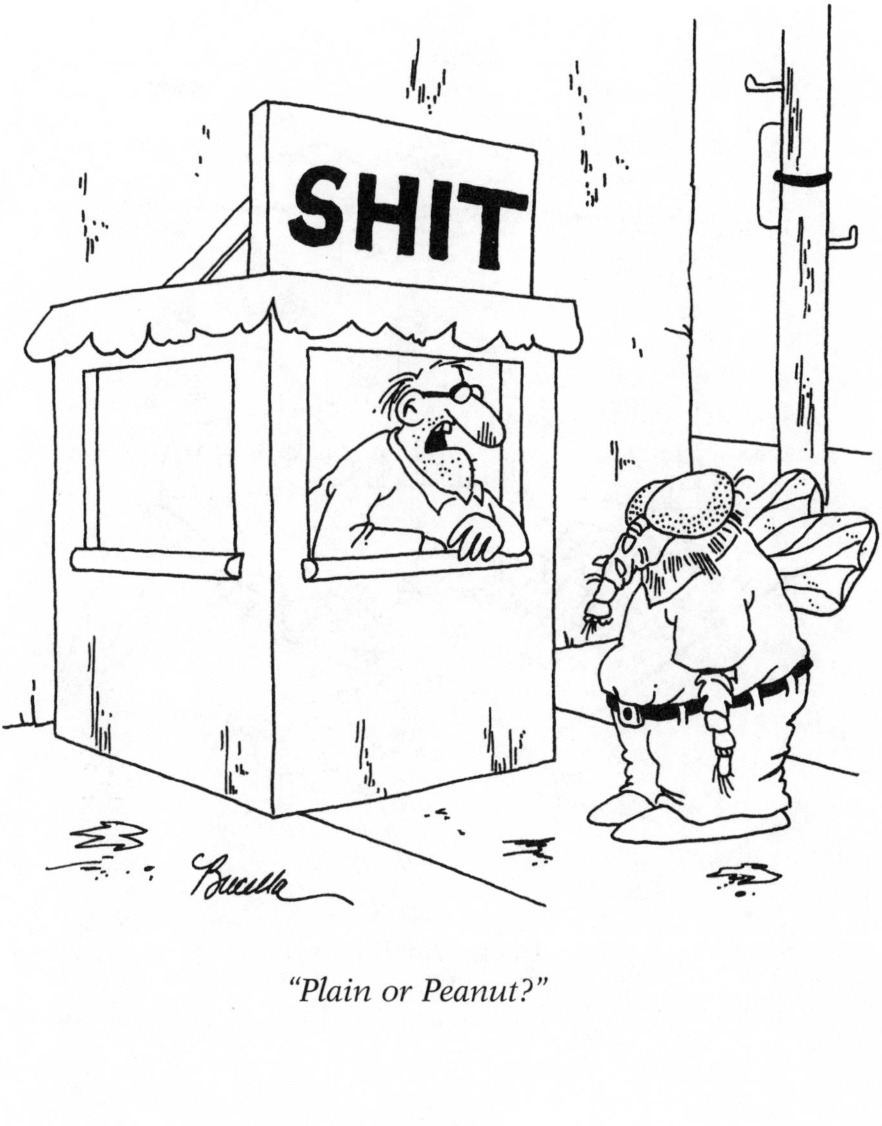
SHIT

"Plain or Peanut?"

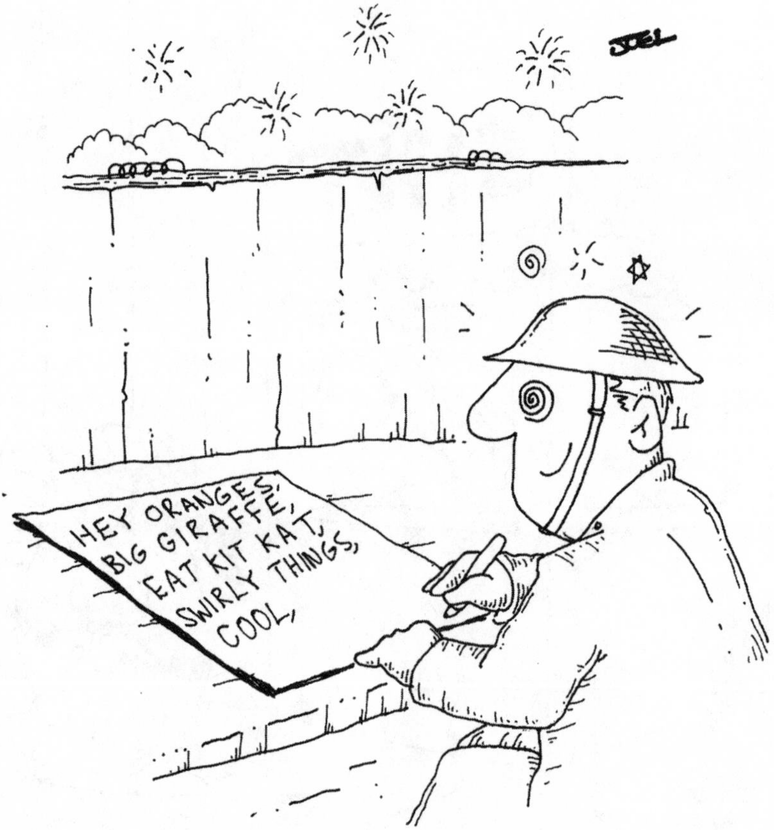
JOEL
HEY ORANGES,
BIG GIRAFFE,
EAT KIT KAT,
SWIRLY THINGS,
COOL,

Drug War Poet

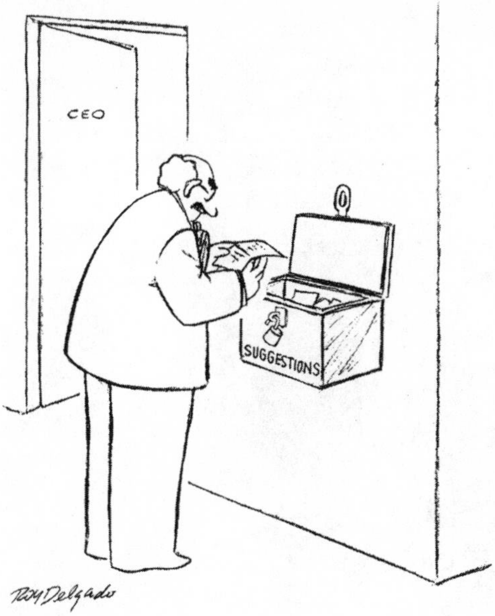
CEO
SUGGESTIONS
Roy Delgado

"Take suggestion box off wall. Coat it with Vaseline. Take pants down..."

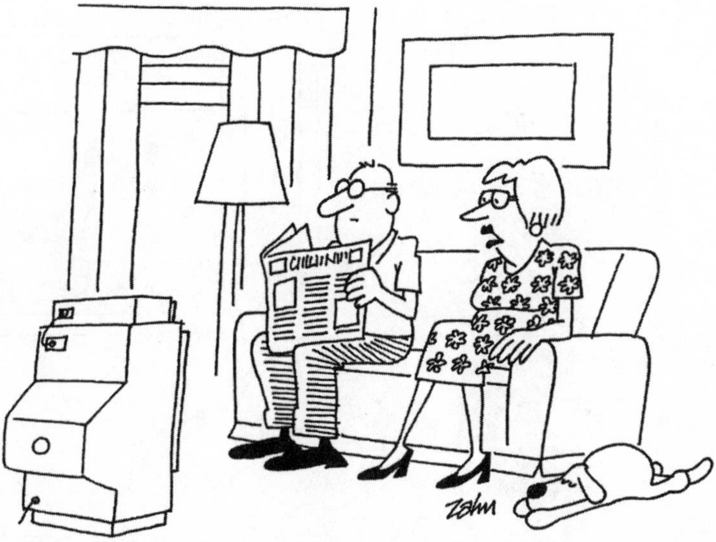
Zahn

"They're playing our song... in a diarrhea commercial!"

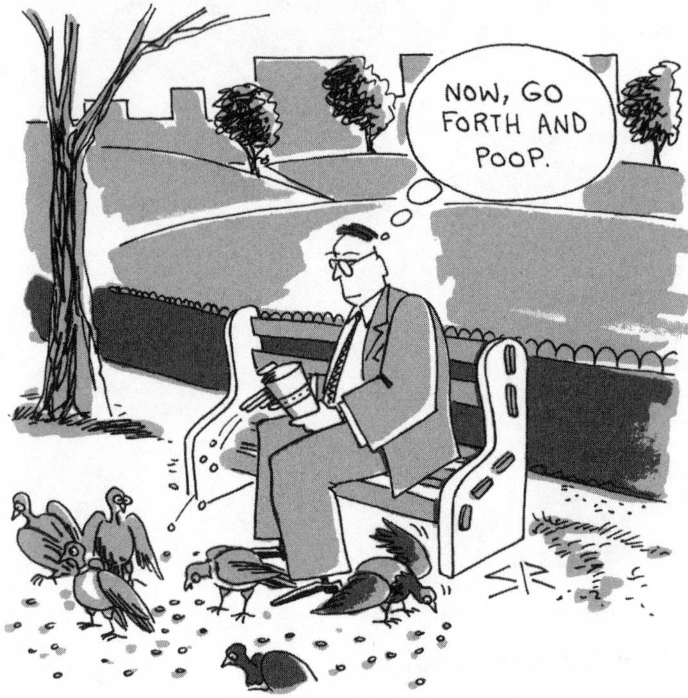
NOW, GO FORTH AND POOP.
SR

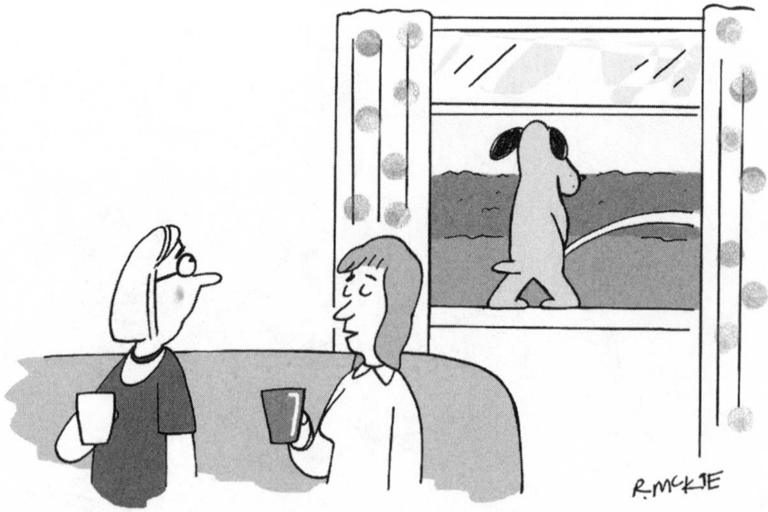
R.MCKIE

"It took a while, but we finally got him house-trained."

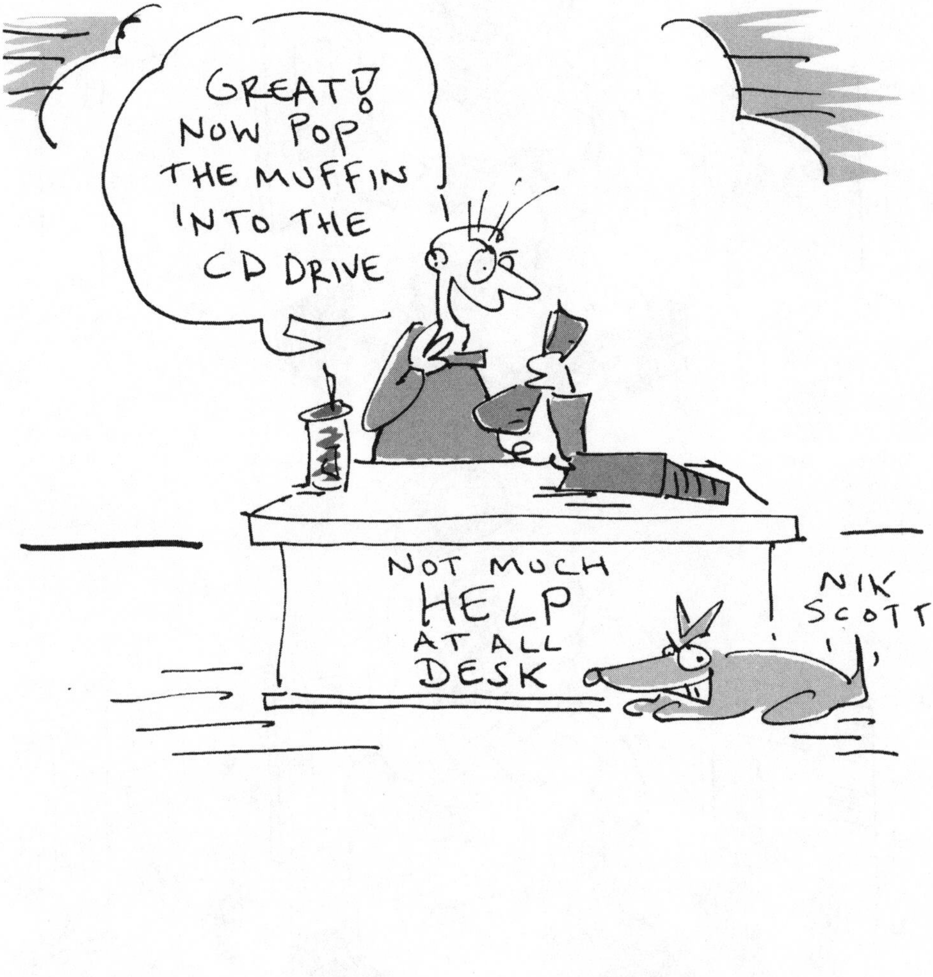
GREAT! NOW POP THE MUFFIN INTO THE CD DRIVE
NOT MUCH HELP AT ALL DESK
NIK SCOTT

1.

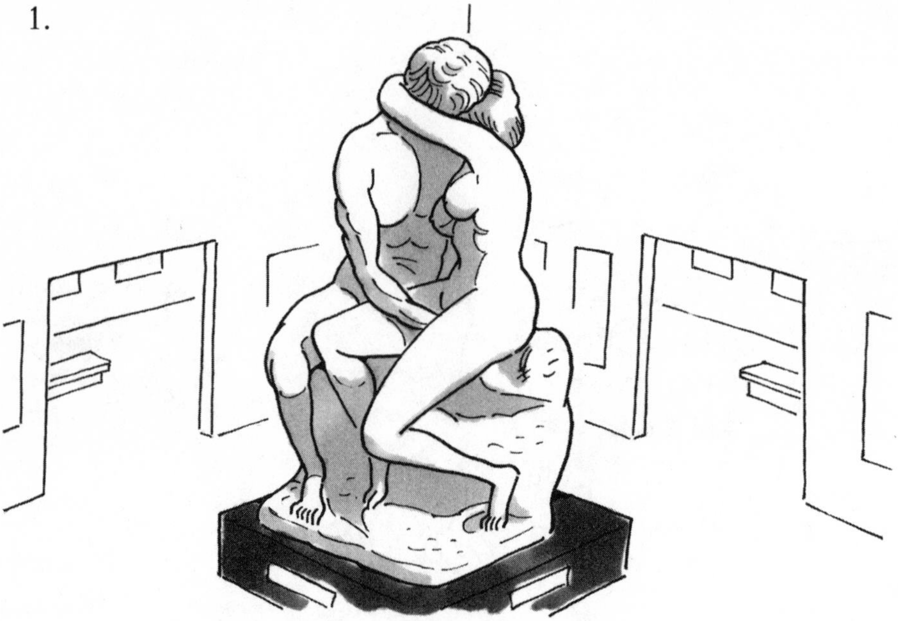

2.

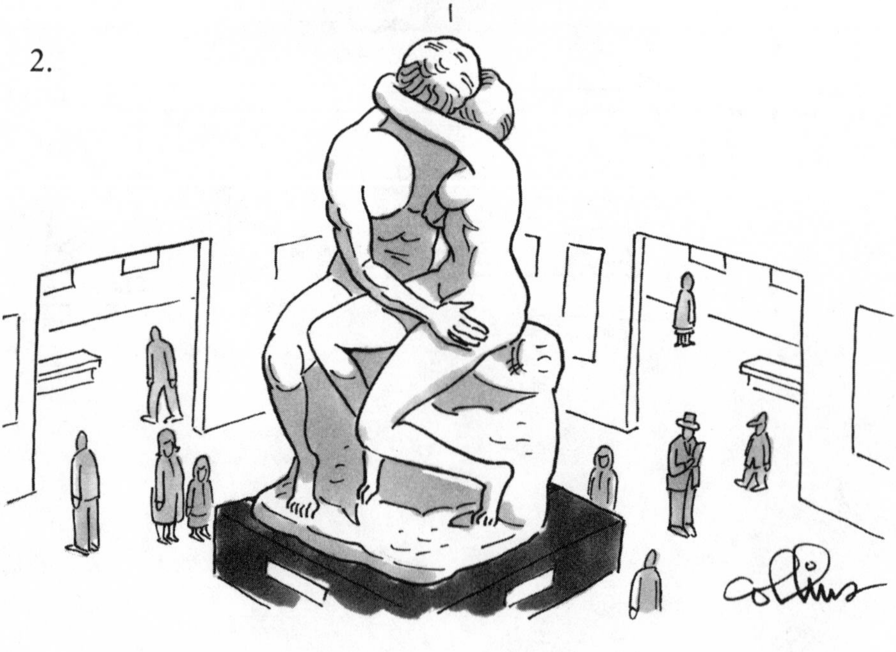

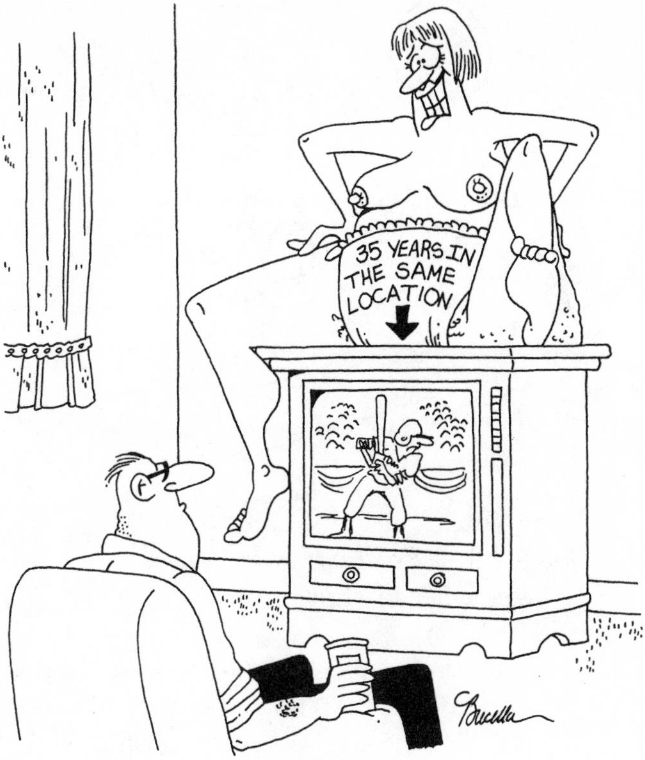
35 YEARS IN THE SAME LOCATION

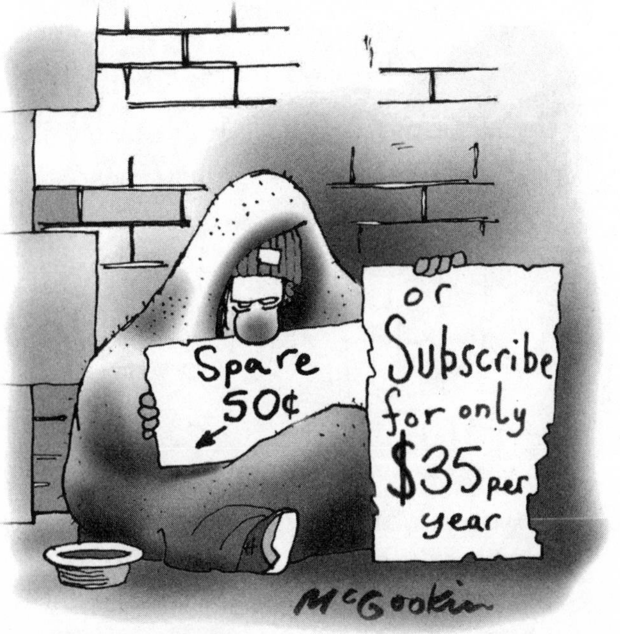
Spare 50¢
or Subscribe for only $35 per year

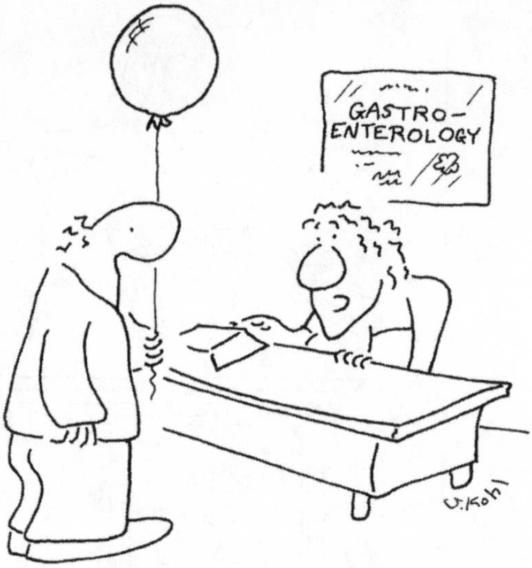
GASTRO-
ENTEROLOGY
U. Kohl

"Doctor, Mr. Freebish is here to see you with his fart sample.

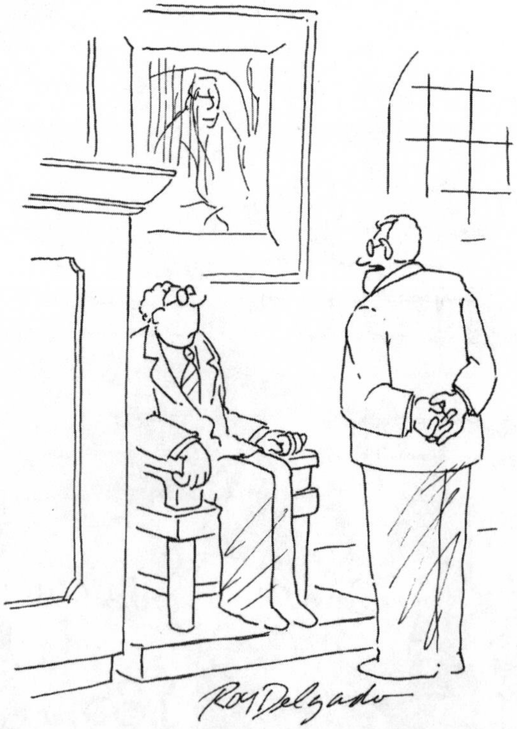
Roy Delgado

"Then you admit you went into the Mexican restaurant and said to the waitress, 'Baby, I'd like to nibble on your taco'."

Nothing's quite as painful as spotting your wife out on the town with your so-called "best friend."

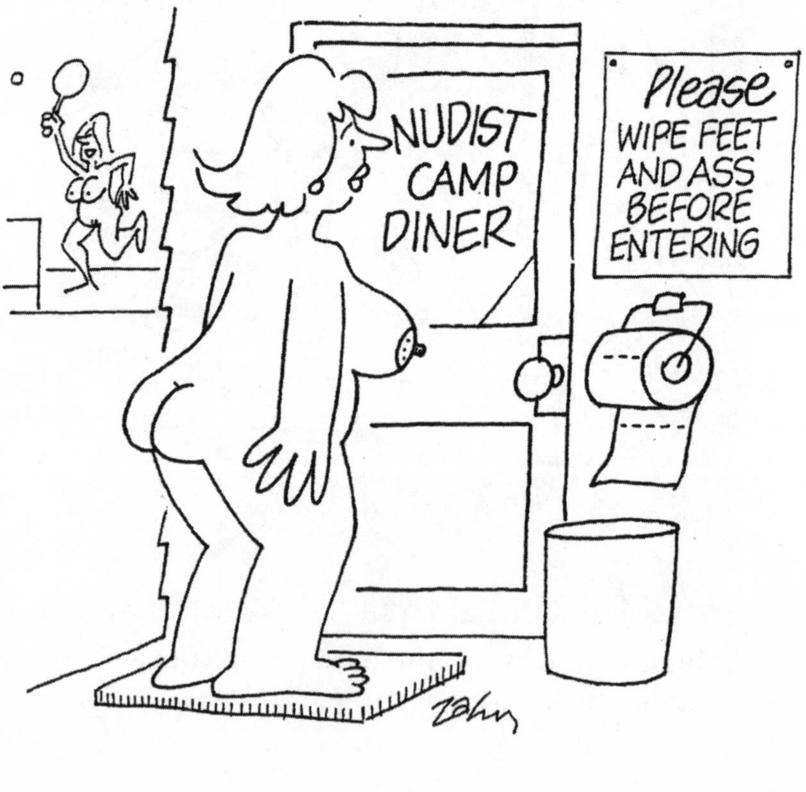
NUDIST
CAMP
DINER
Please
WIPE FEET
AND ASS
BEFORE
ENTERING

"Can I lick your balls? I can't find mine."

*"I'll see you in **HELL**, my friend."*

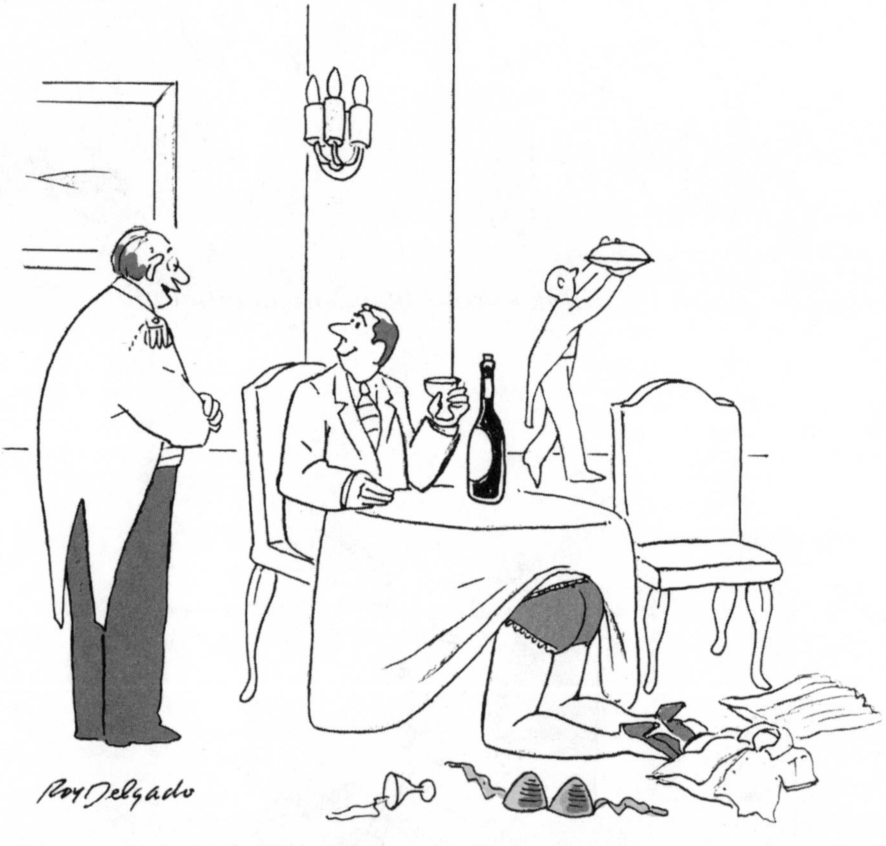
Roy Delgado

"You were right... two drinks and she's under the table."

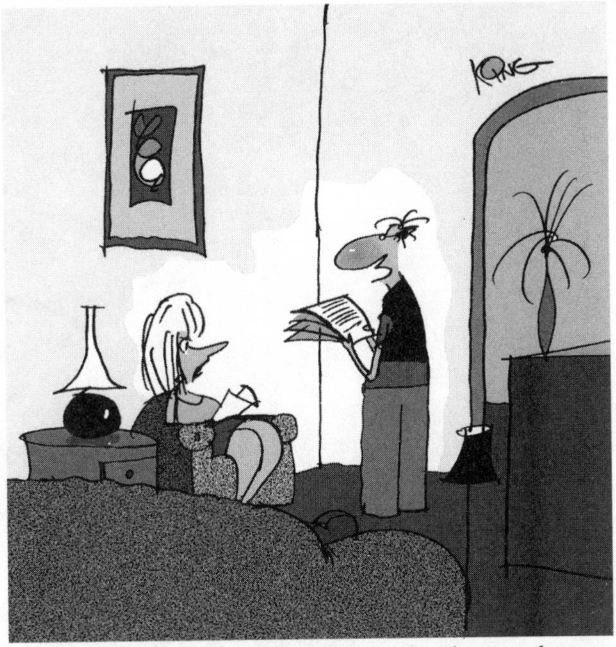

"You asked me what those chicks in those biker magazines have that you don't... well, I made a list. Number one..."

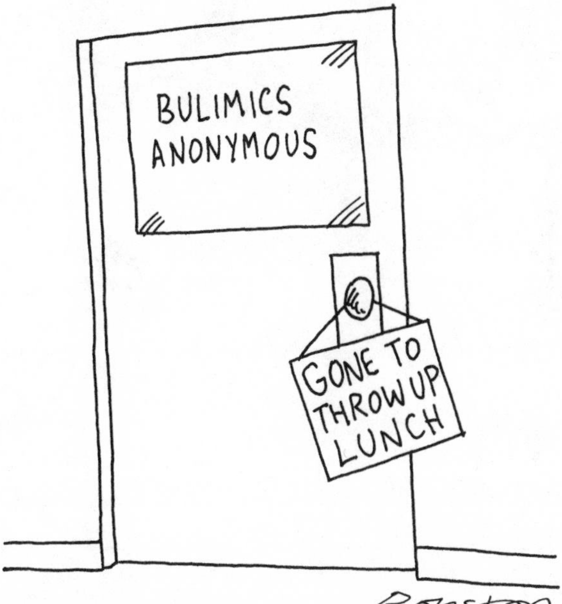
BULIMICS
ANONYMOUS
GONE TO
THROW UP
LUNCH

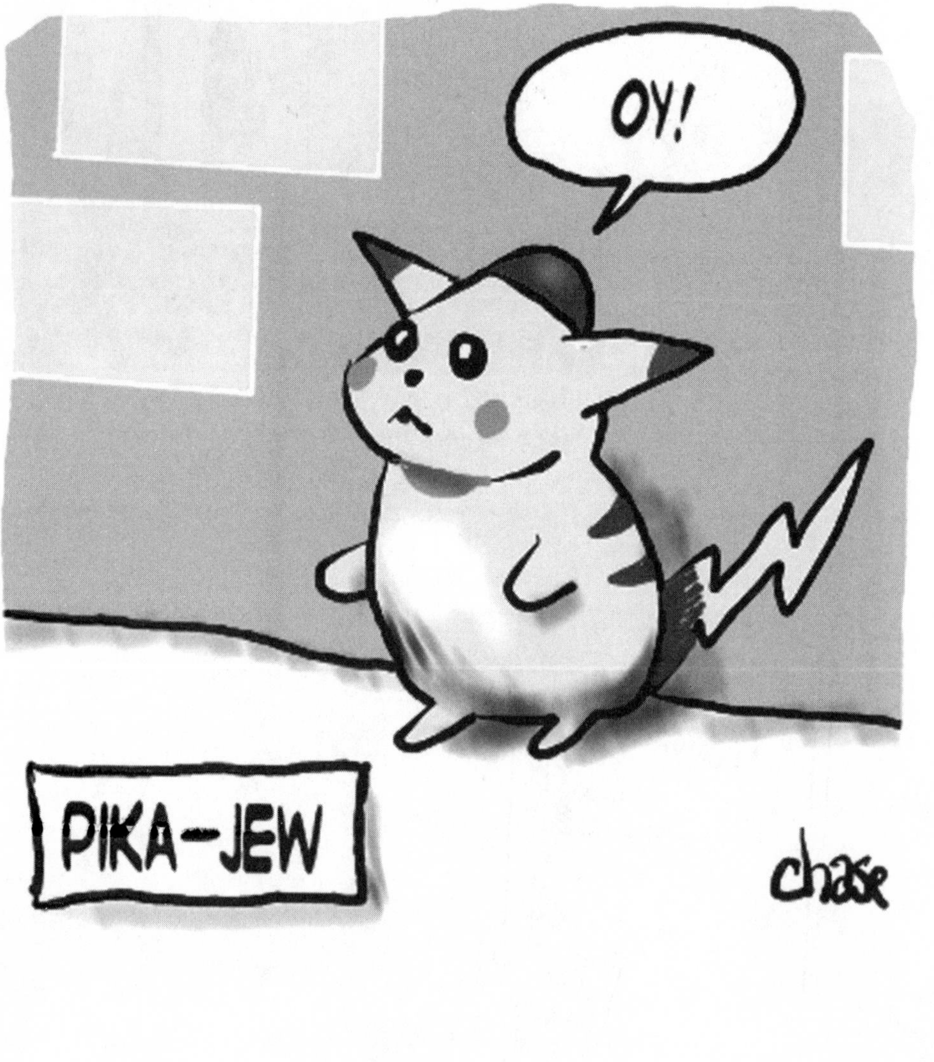
OY!
PIKA-JEW
chase

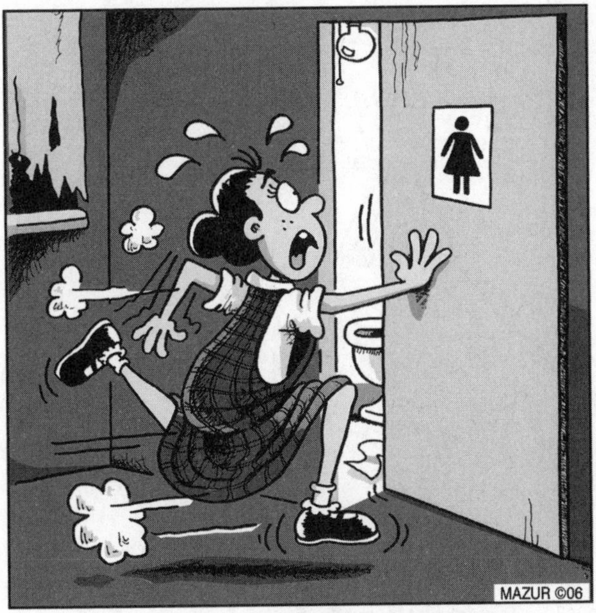
MAZUR ©06

The Diarrhea Of Anne Frank

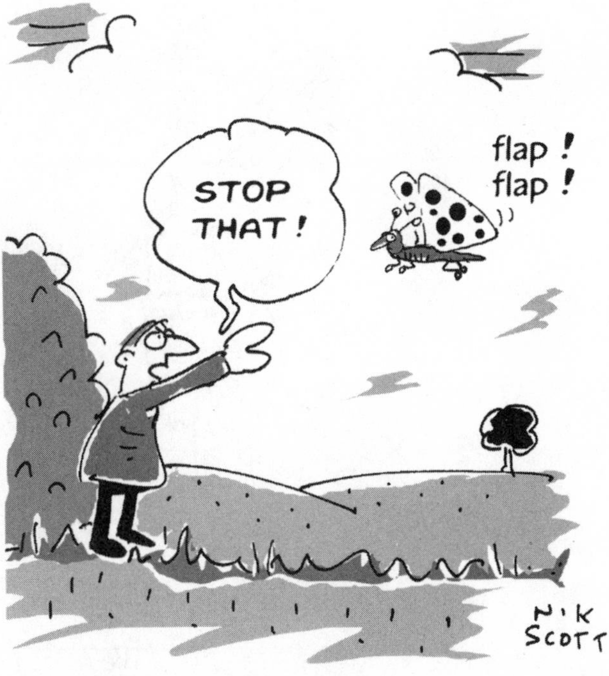
STOP THAT!
flap! flap!
NIK SCOTT

Chaos Theory

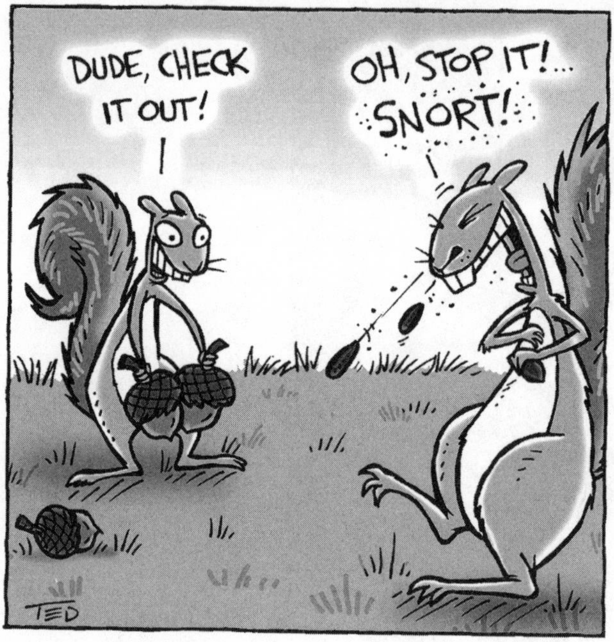
DUDE, CHECK IT OUT!
OH, STOP IT!... SNORT!
TED

Virgil loves to make sunflower seeds come out of Carlo's nose.

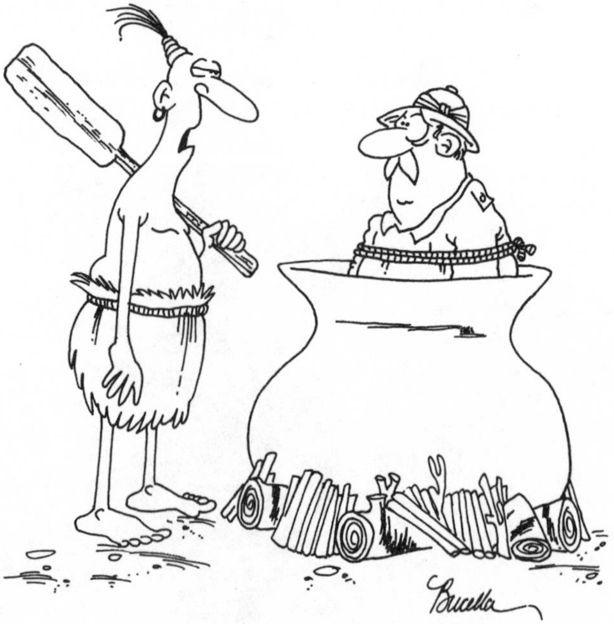
Bucella

"We're out of salt. Would you mind sweating?"

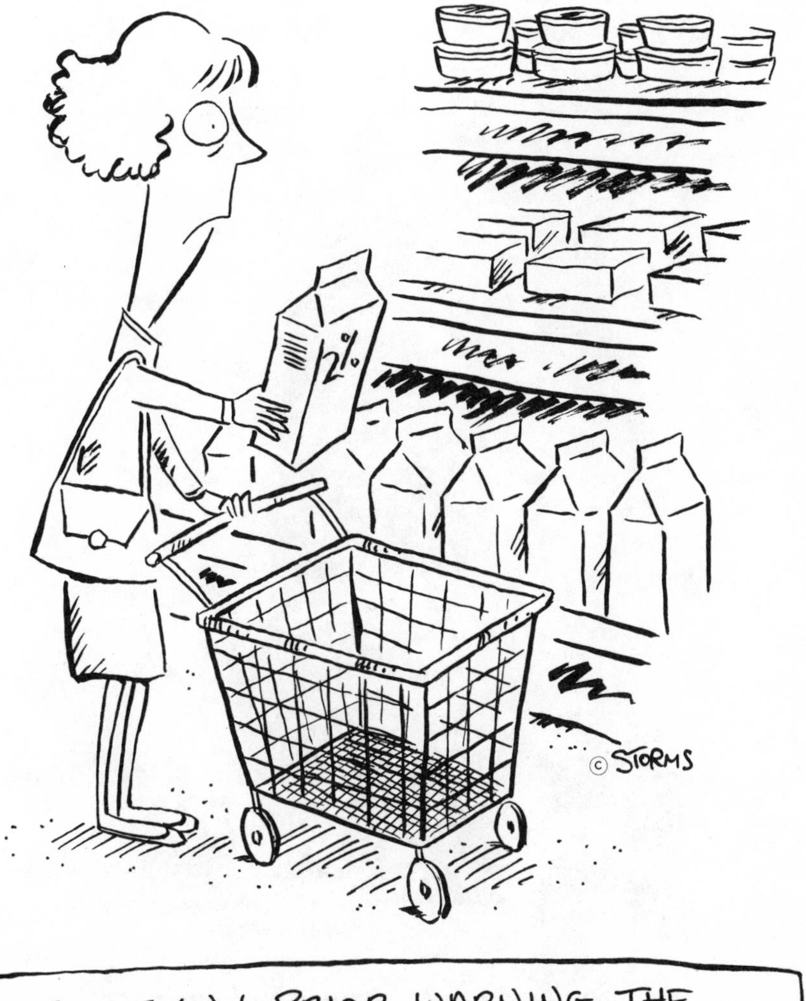
2%
© STORMS

WITHOUT ANY PRIOR WARNING, THE WARRANTY ON DOROTHY'S THONG EXPIRED.

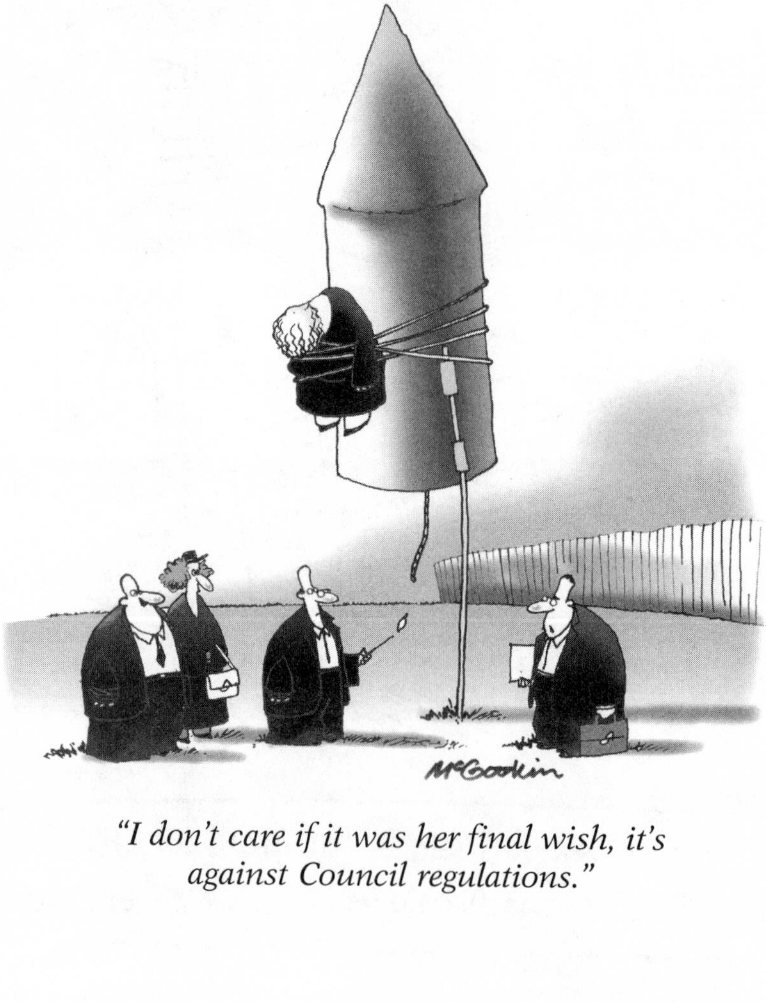
McGookin

"I don't care if it was her final wish, it's against Council regulations."

"Fuck you too, Grabowski!"

*"Since I've been using this hot tub of yours,
those festering boils on my genitals have cleared up!"*

*"You are charged with being the sort of person
who just pisses people off!"*

"Try again bitch, I've got an airbag!"

"That settles it! I need professional help."

"Boy, I have a
hard stool."

"I know the feeling."

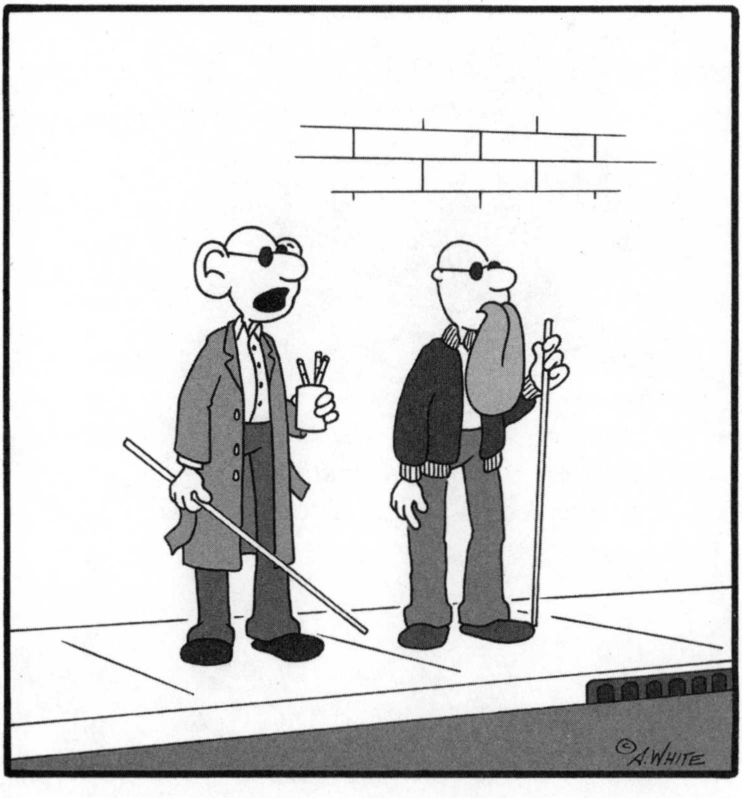
©A.WHITE

"Ever notice how, when you lose one sense, another sense seems to make up for it?"

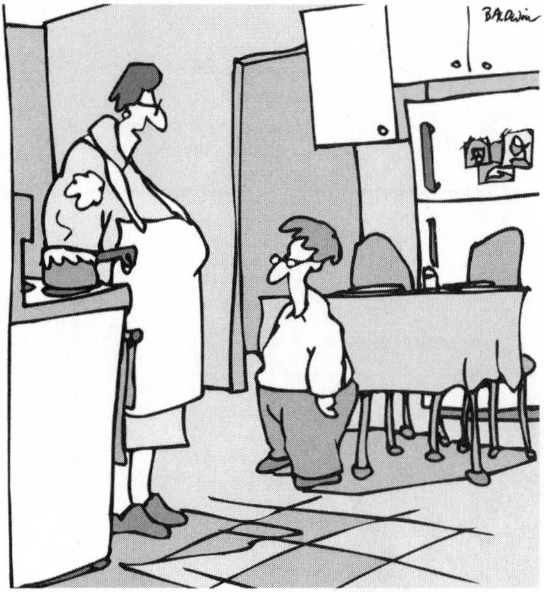

"Sure, you have a father. It's just that when you were born, I decided to stay at home and he decided to stay at work."

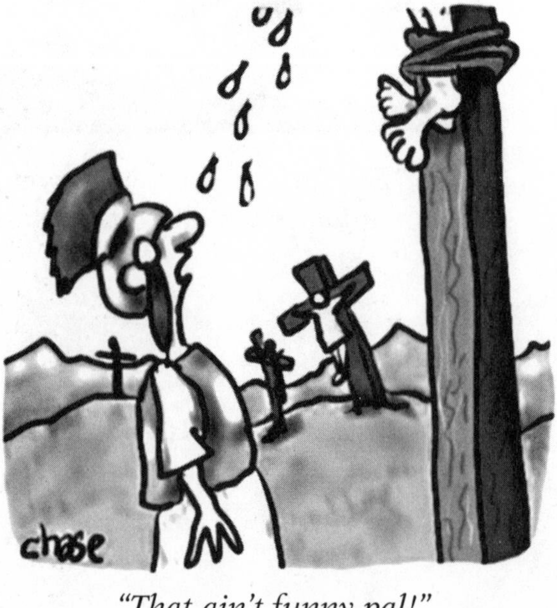
chase

"That ain't funny pal!"

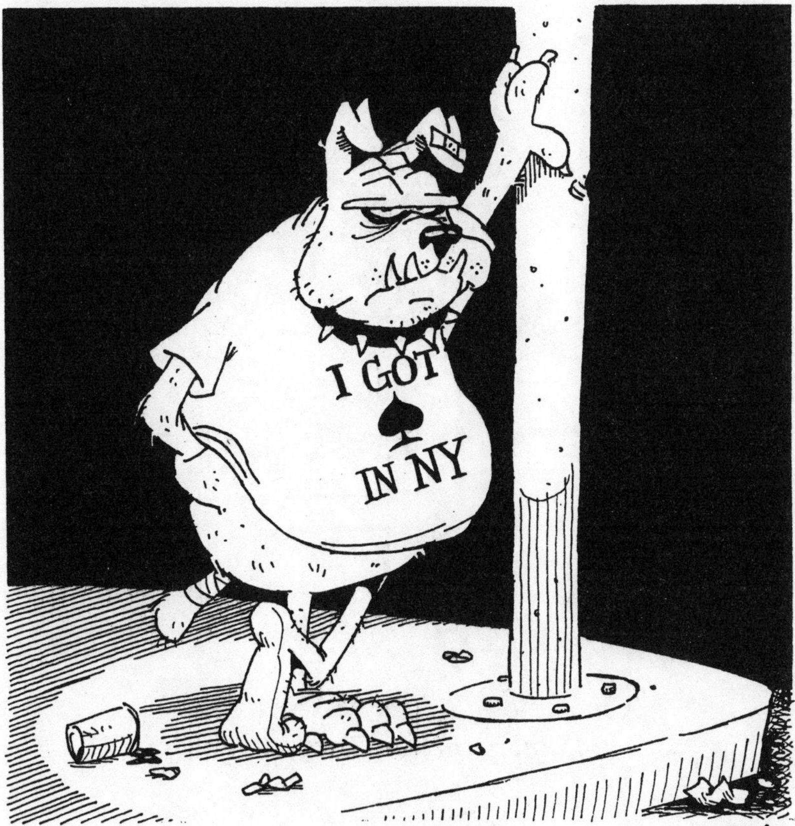
I GOT
IN NY
VIER/
JONES

"Very well, I'll allow this witness,
but you're on very thin ice..."

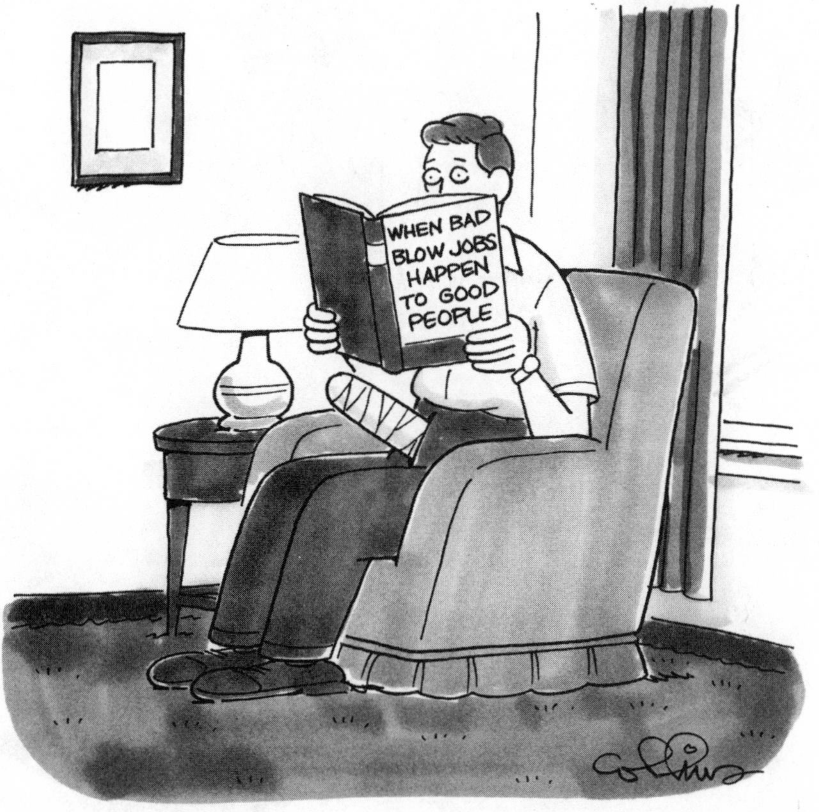
WHEN BAD
BLOW JOBS
HAPPEN
TO GOOD
PEOPLE

*"...and when you kiss me,
can you play with my ass?"*

...what happens when you kick a magician.

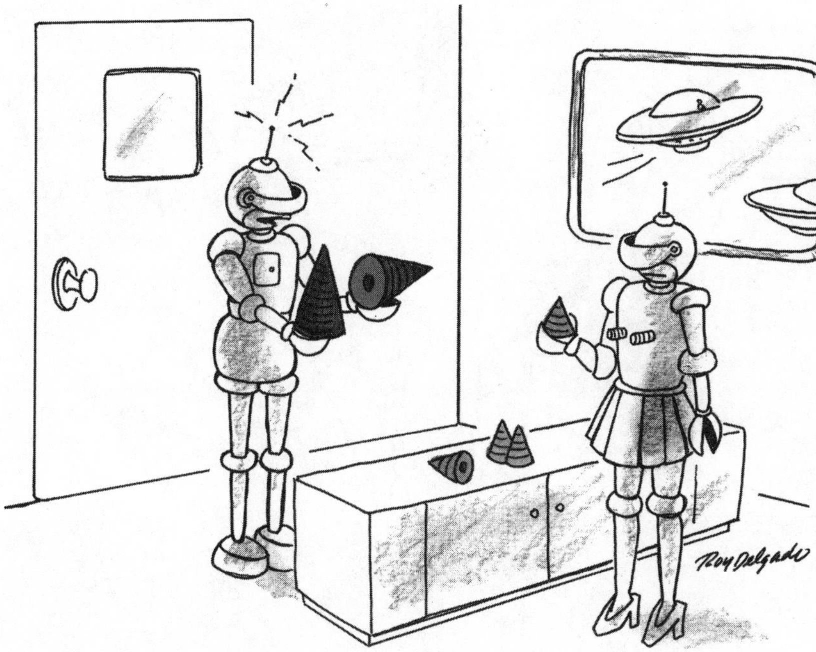
Roy Delgado

"Screw on the big tits, Gloria.
I want to make the Smiths jealous."

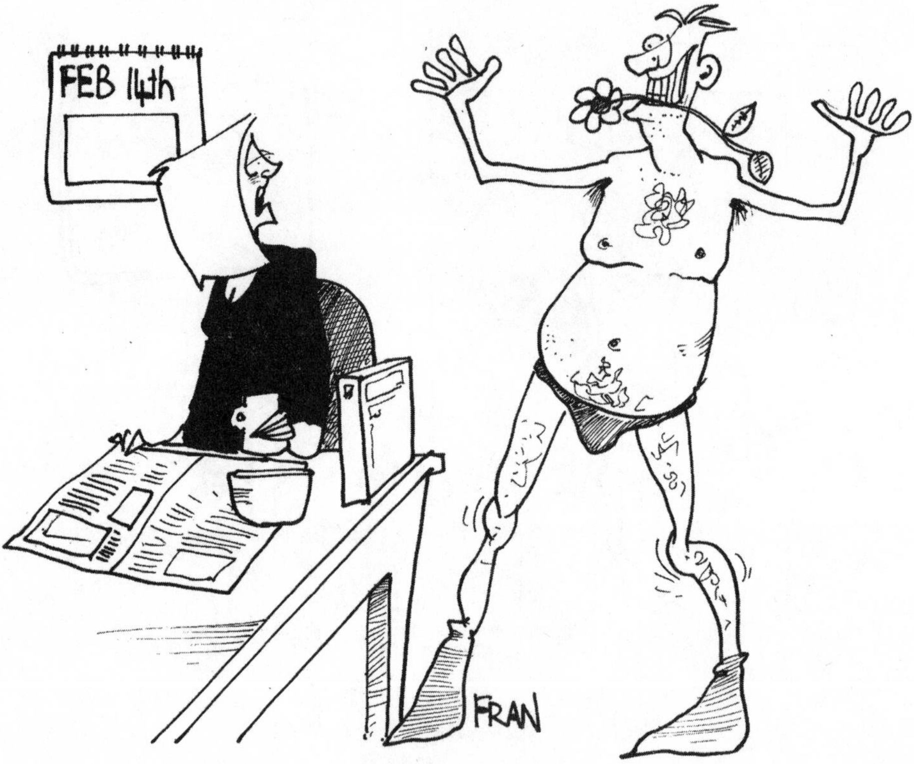
FEB 14th
FRAN

"Couldn't I just have chocolates this year?!"

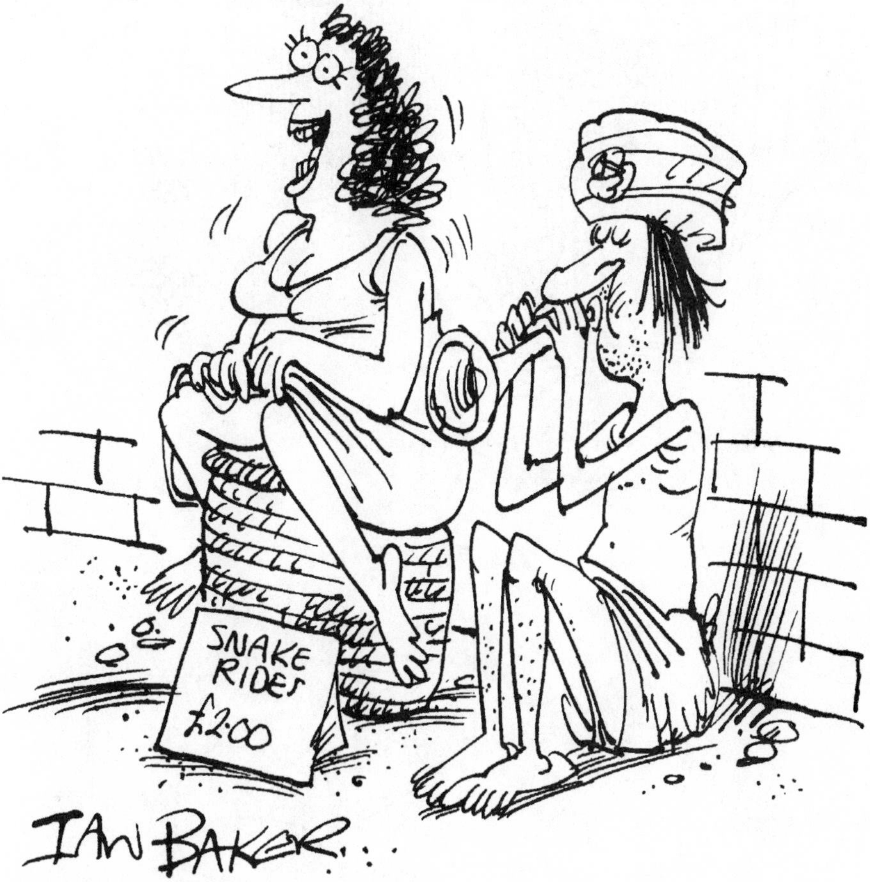
SNAKE
RIDES
£2·00
IAN BAKER

"I don't care if this does work.
It's still embarrassing!"

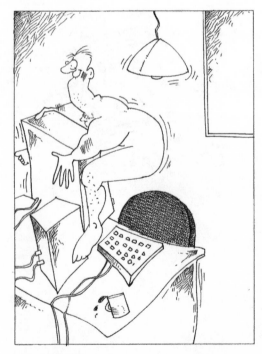

Tom's first attempt at cybersex
failed to live up to expectations.

"Wow, are those tits real?"

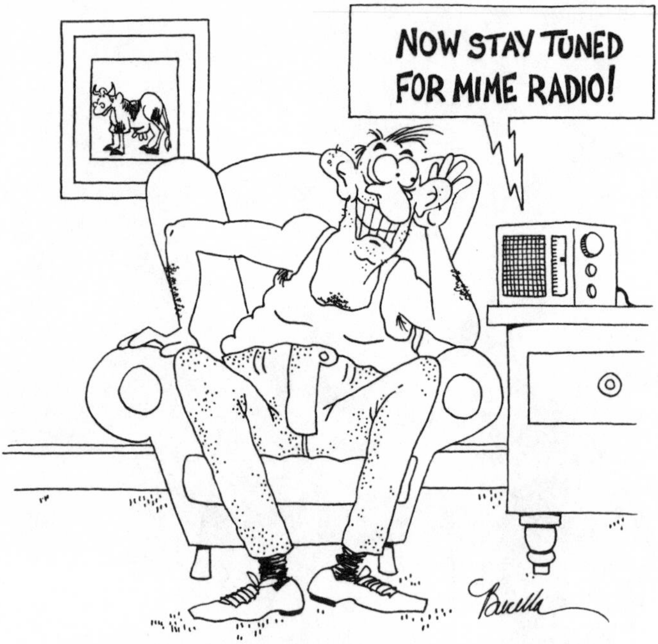
NOW STAY TUNED
FOR MIME RADIO!

POLAND'S TOP-RATED RADIO SHOW

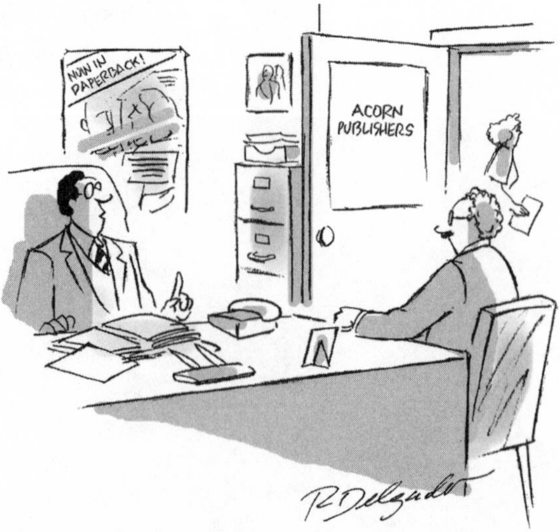
NOW IN
PAPERBACK!
ACORN
PUBLISHERS

"Spice it up a bit. For every 300 words, you're allowed one 'asshole'... for each 500 words, one 'cunt'... for every 1000 words, a 'fuck.' And for every 5000, a 'motherfucker'..."

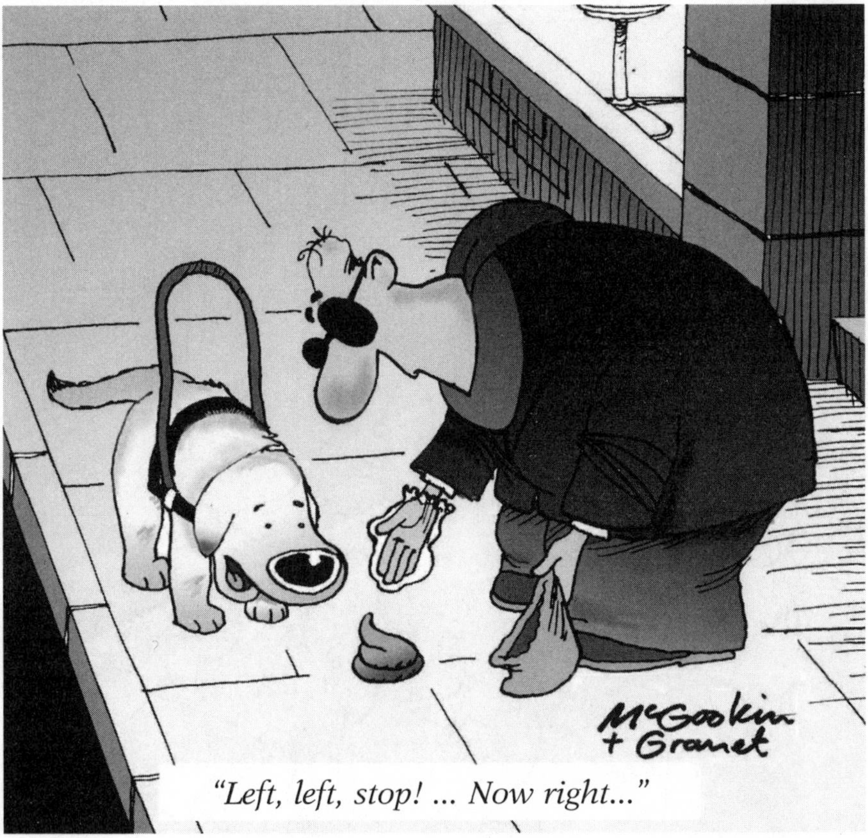
McGookin
+ Granet

"Left, left, stop! ... Now right..."

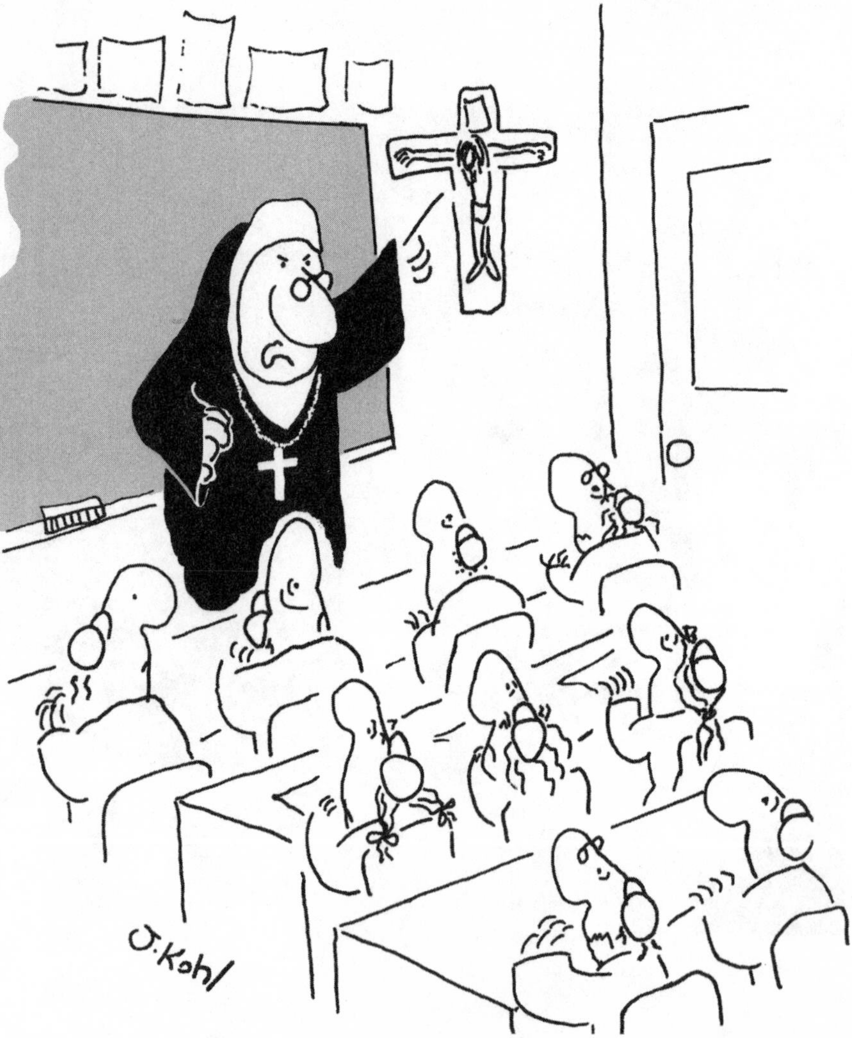
J. Kohl

"THAT'S what happens if you don't do your homework!"

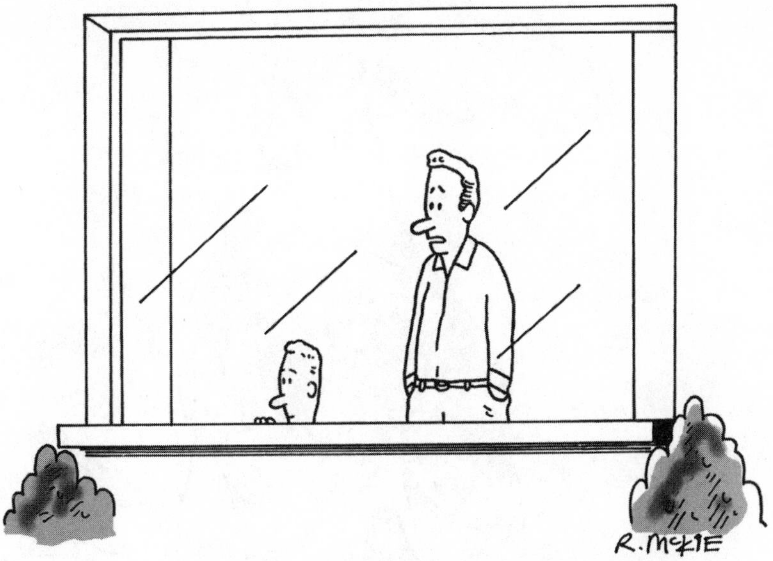
R. McKIE

"There's a big, wide world of opportunity out there, lad ... at first glance."

Ben liked his new supervisor

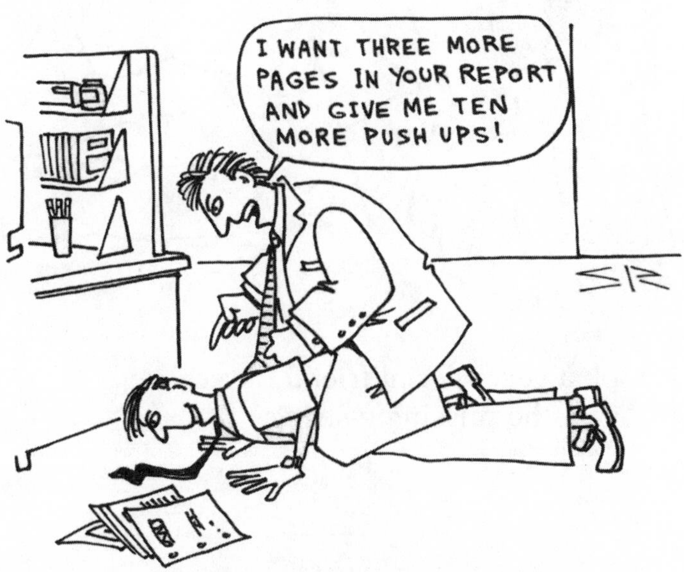
I WANT THREE MORE PAGES IN YOUR REPORT AND GIVE ME TEN MORE PUSH UPS!
SR

...but then, he was into abuse.

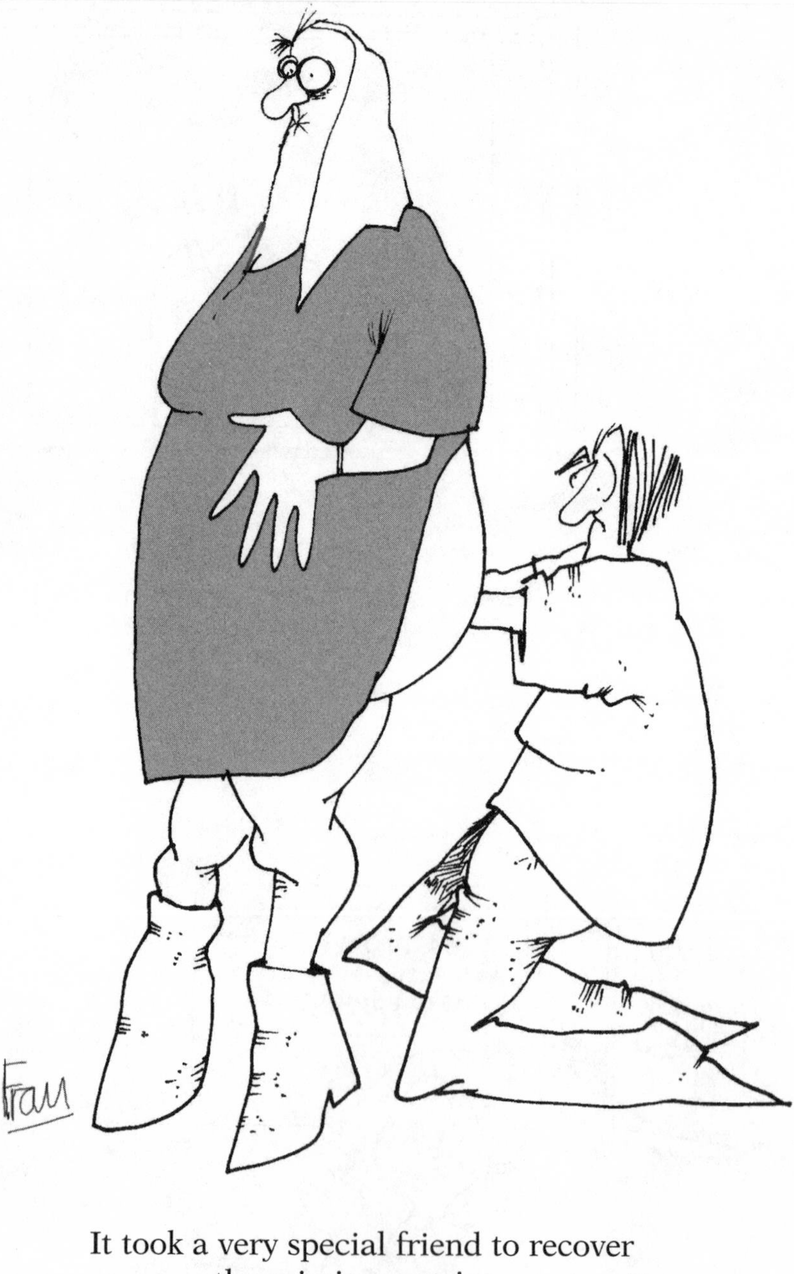
Fran

It took a very special friend to recover
the missing g-string.

*"Well, it certainly looks like your DNA.
How many times have I told you to wear
gloves before touching anything?"*

*"Hey, Babe! How about you
wear this fur?"*

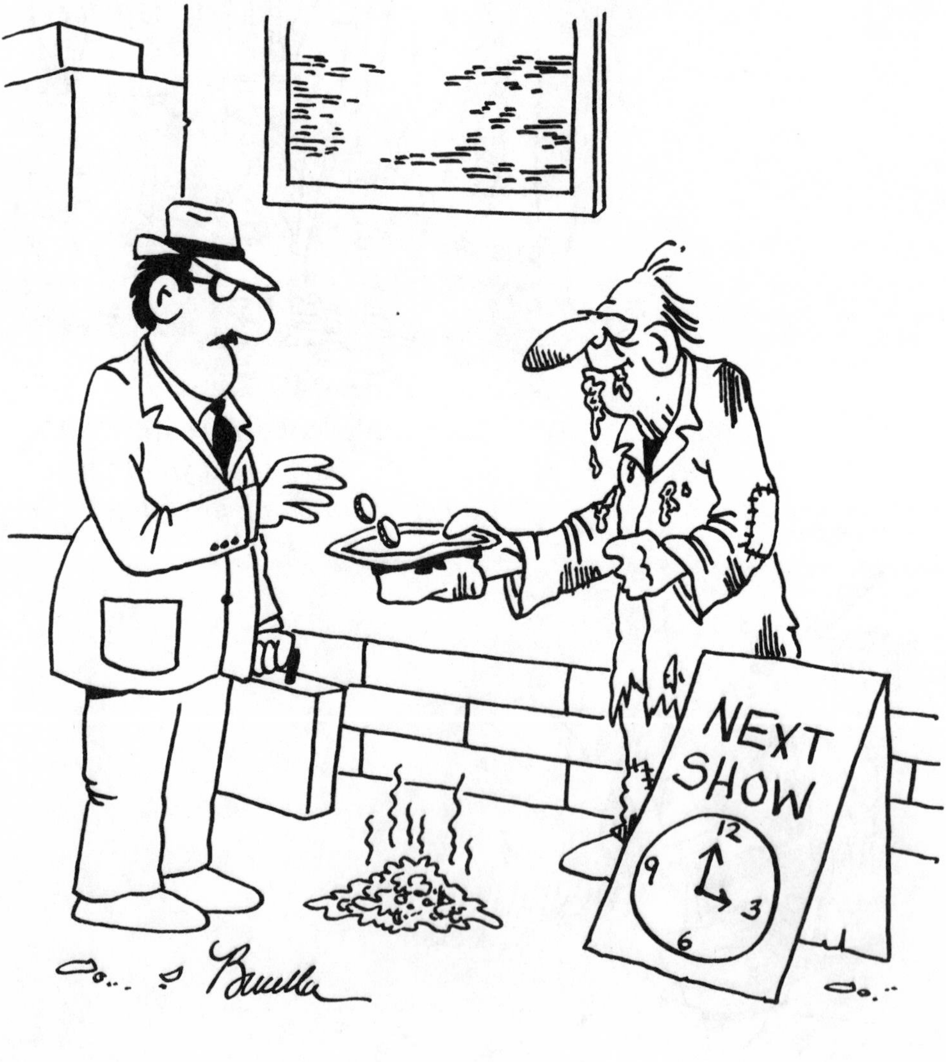
NEXT SHOW
12
9
3
6

"So, what's this I hear about you not liking artichokes?"

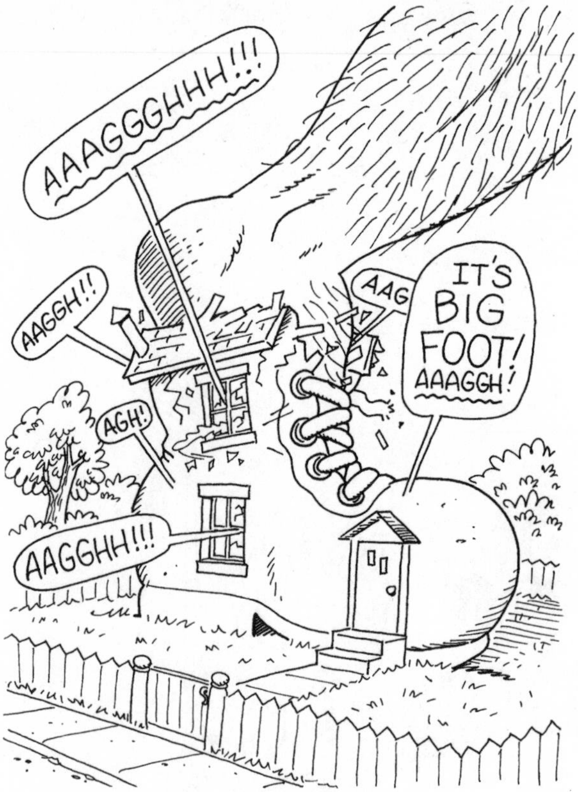
AAAGGGHHH!!!
AAGGH!!
AGH!
AAGGHH!!!
AAG
IT'S BIG FOOT! AAAGGH!

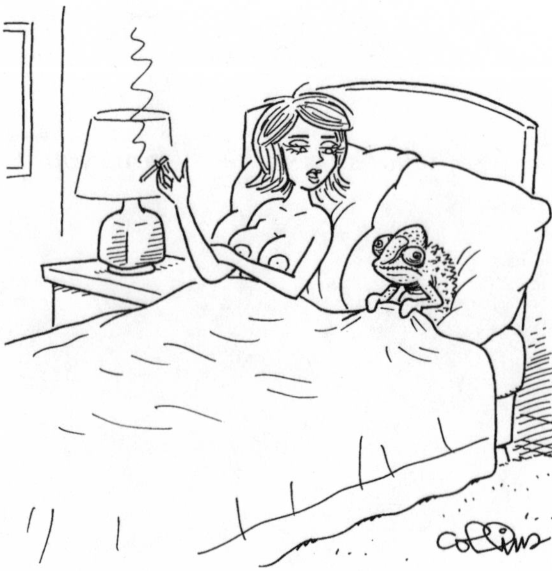

"Don't worry, it'll grow back."

"The Emperor has no clothes!
And he's masturbating!"

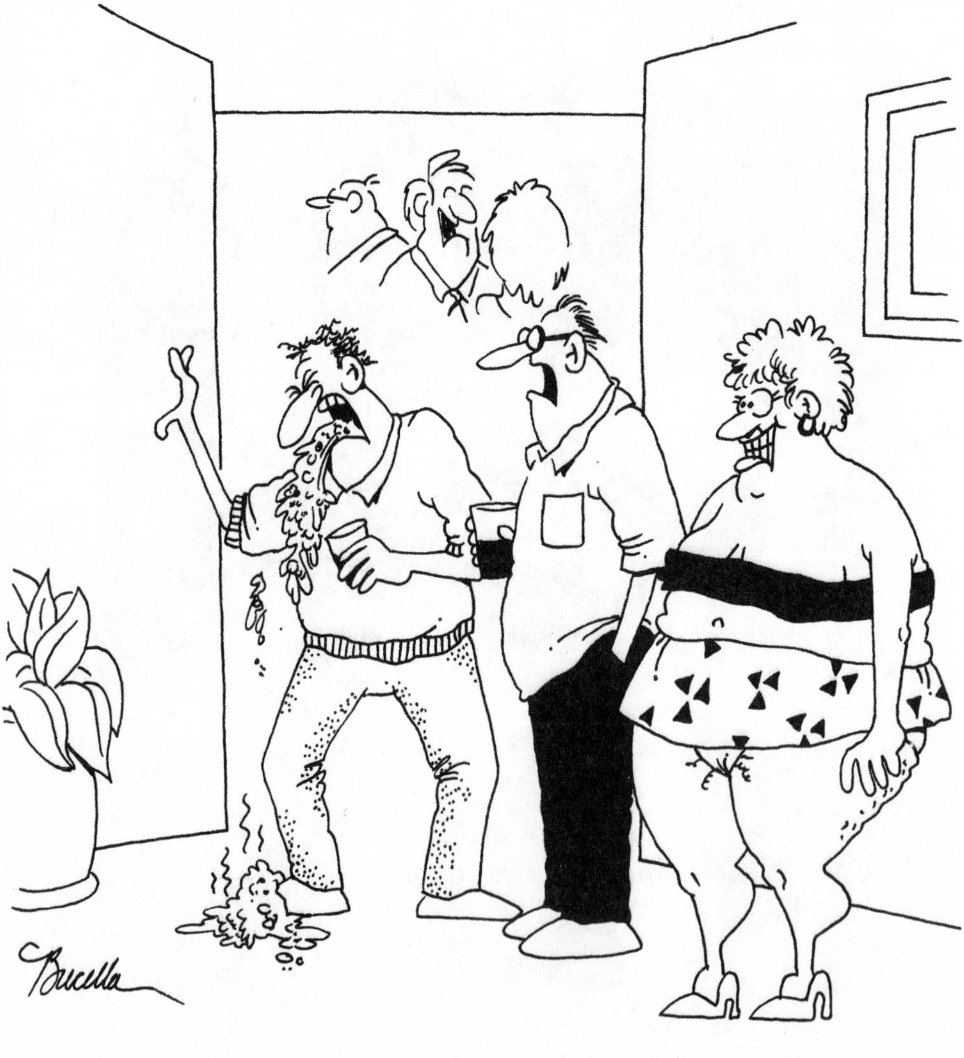
Bucella

"I see you've already met my wife."

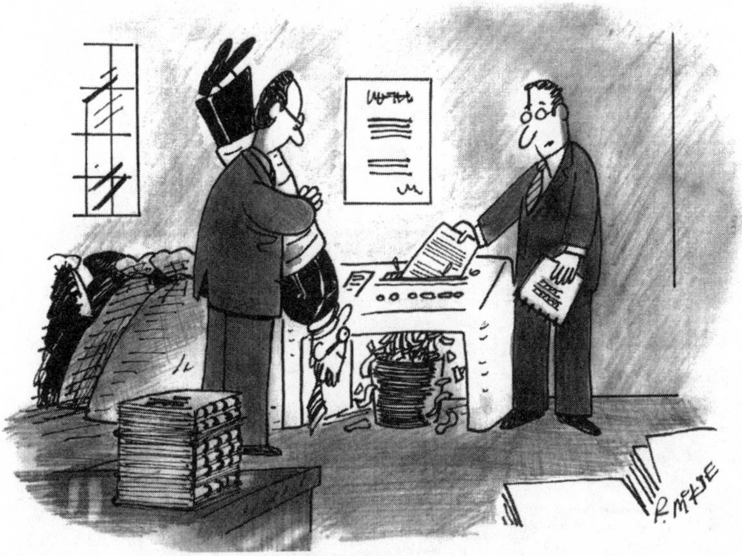

"Nothing personal, Simpkins, it's only business."

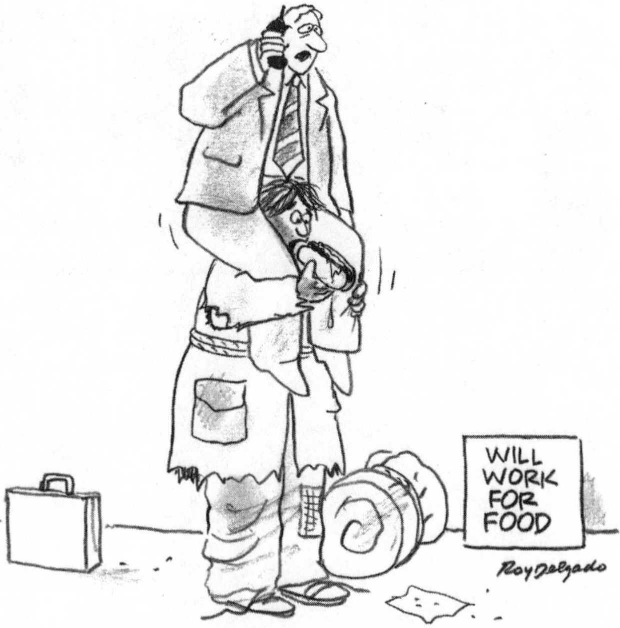
WILL WORK FOR FOOD
Roy Delgado

"Can you hear me now?"

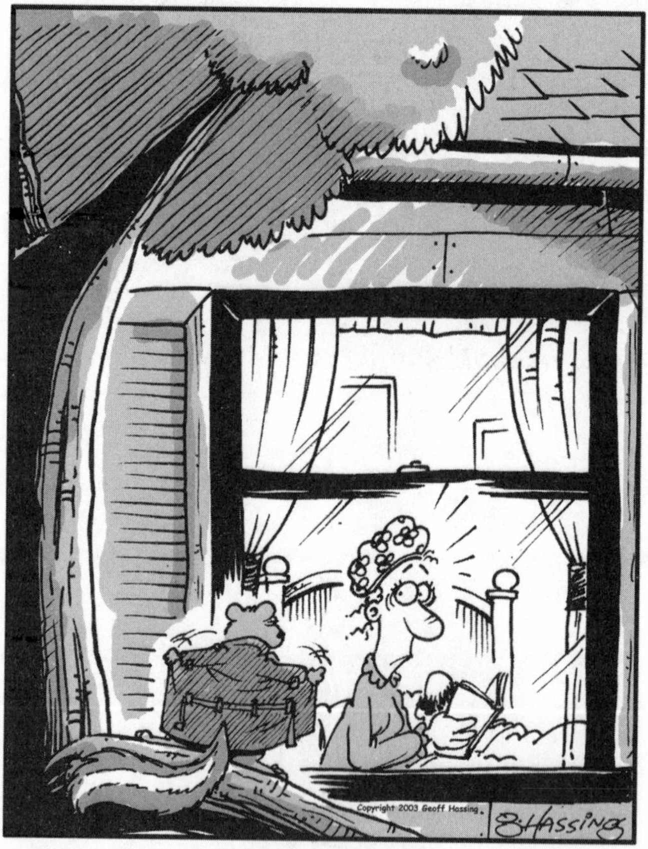
Copyright 2003 Geoff Hassing
HASSING

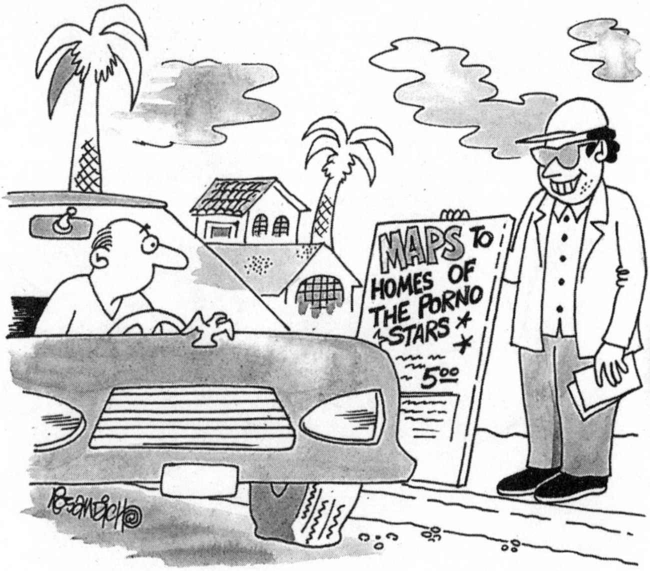
MAPS TO
HOMES OF
THE PORNO
STARS
5^{00}
ROSANDICH

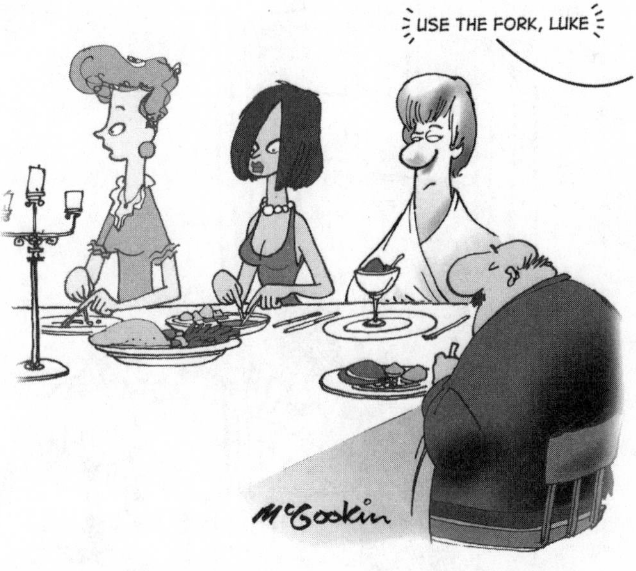
USE THE FORK, LUKE

Skywalker was beginning to find Obi-wan
a bit of a pain in the ass.

Brain Food

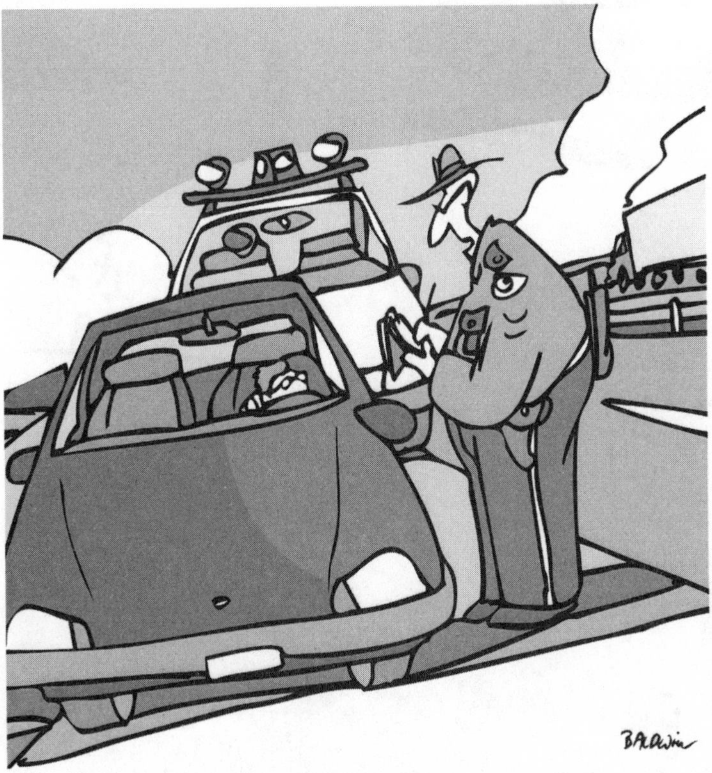
BALDWIN

"I've heard some lame excuses in my time, but 'I'm only 7' takes the cake."

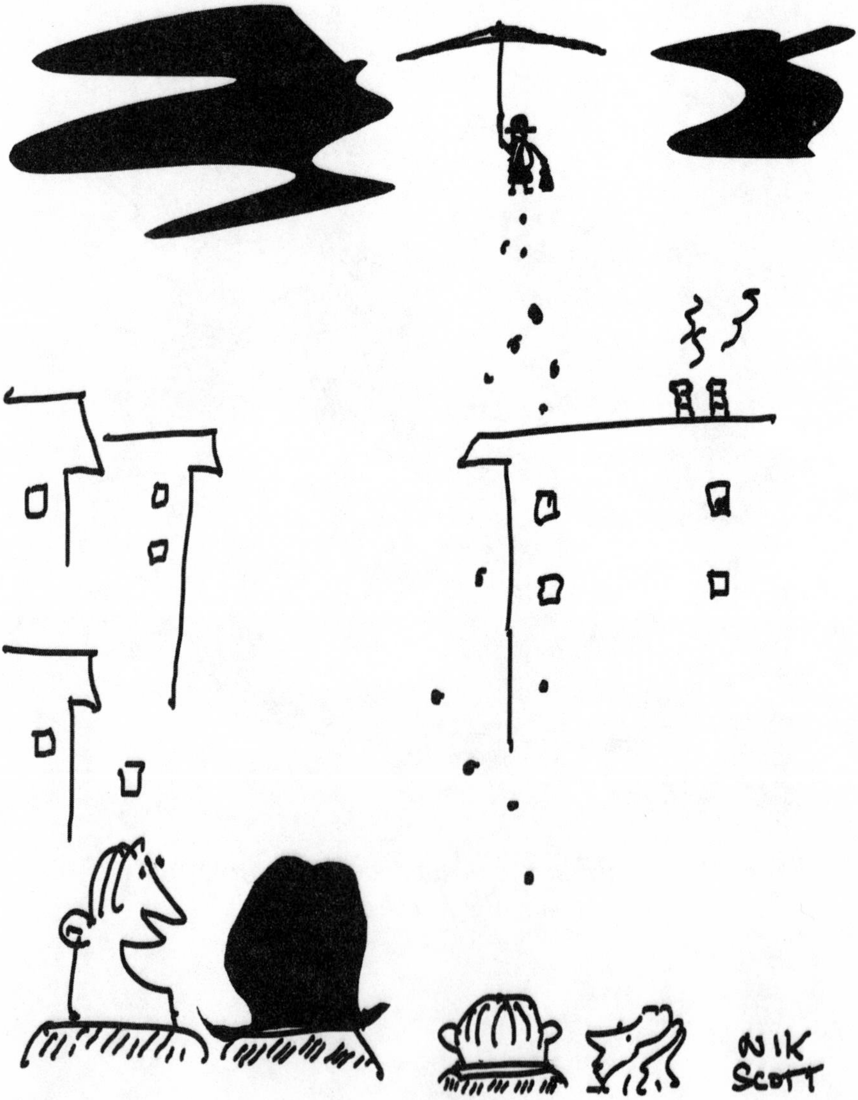
NIK
SCOTT

"Look children! It's Mary Poopins..."

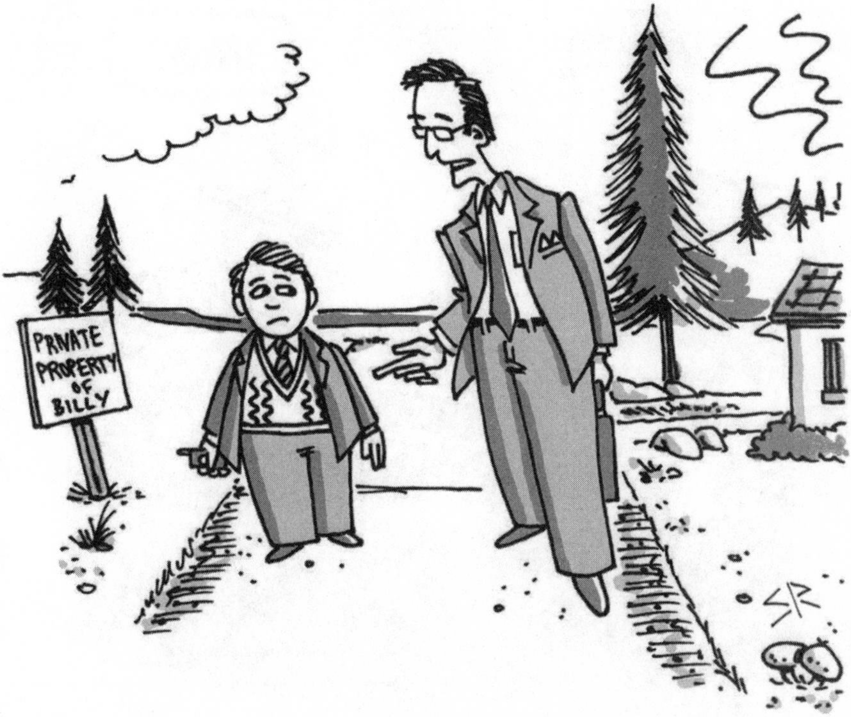
PRIVATE
PROPERTY
OF
BILLY

"Sure, you're a child prodigy. You're rich. You're a professor and you're my boss, but I'm still your father and you're grounded."

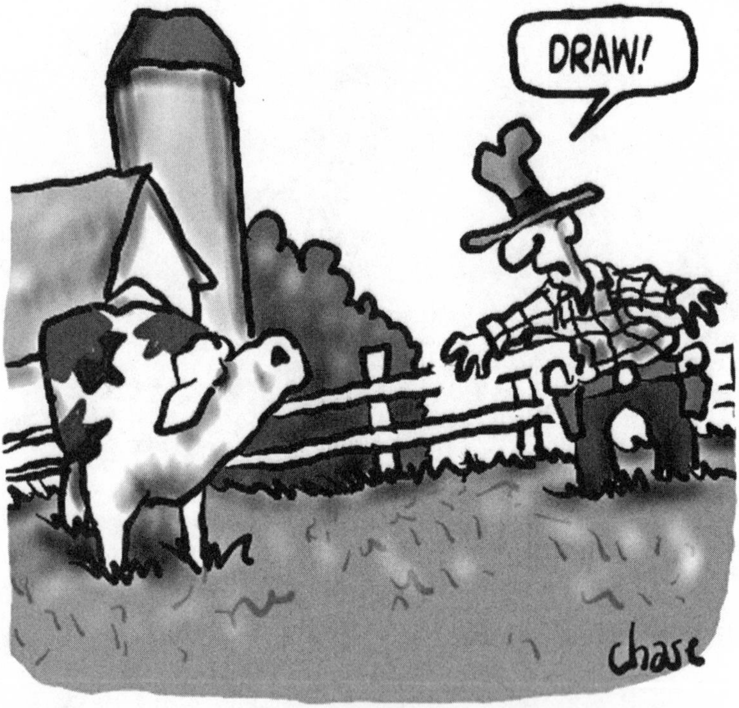
DRAW!
chase

Ed's goal was meager...
Fastest Draw in the Midwest

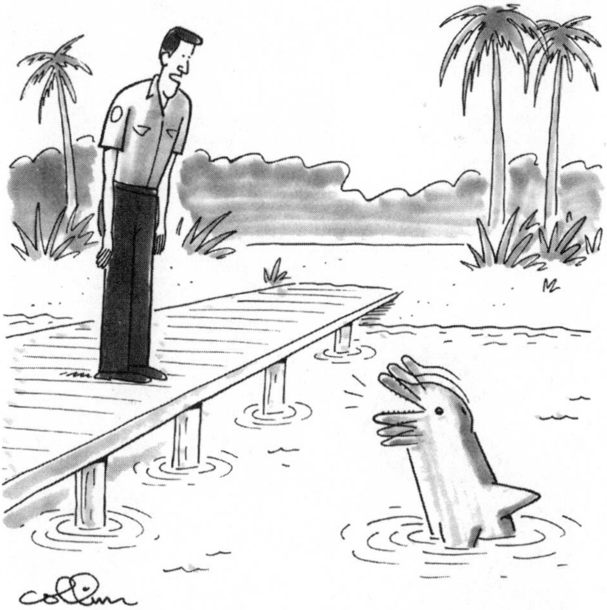

"What is it Flipper? Is it Bud? Is Bud in trouble? Is he drunk? Is he in town exposing himself to nuns? Is that it?"

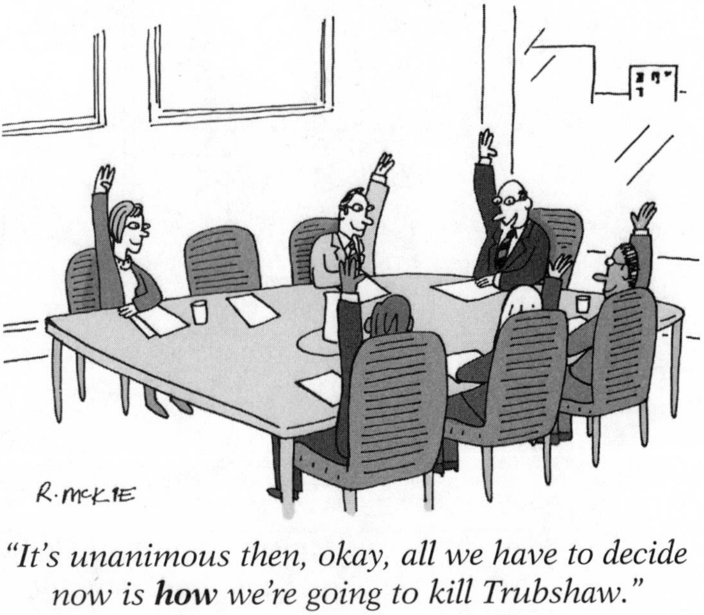
R. McKIE

*"It's unanimous then, okay, all we have to decide now is **how** we're going to kill Trubshaw."*

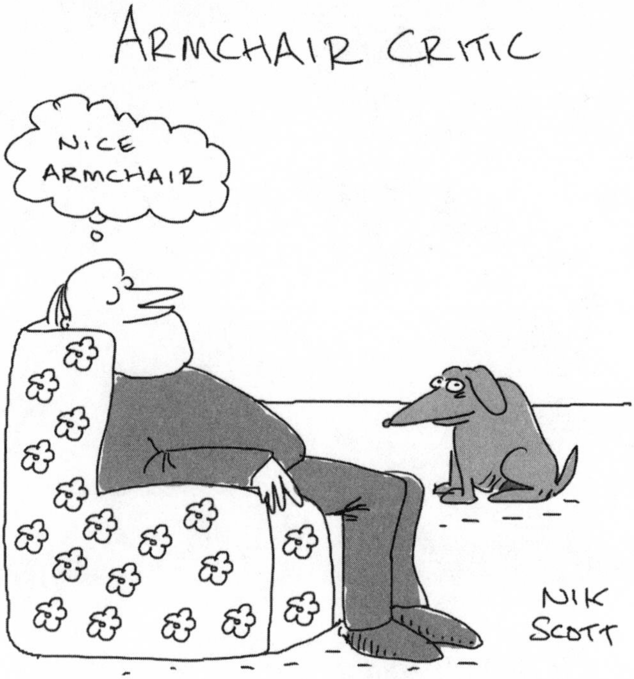
ARMCHAIR CRITIC
NICE ARMCHAIR
NIK SCOTT

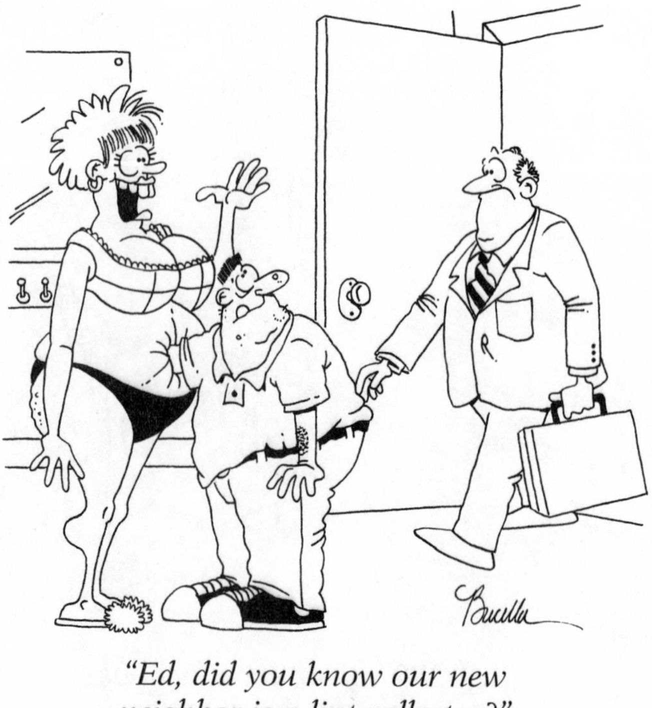
Bucella

"Ed, did you know our new neighbor is a lint collector?"

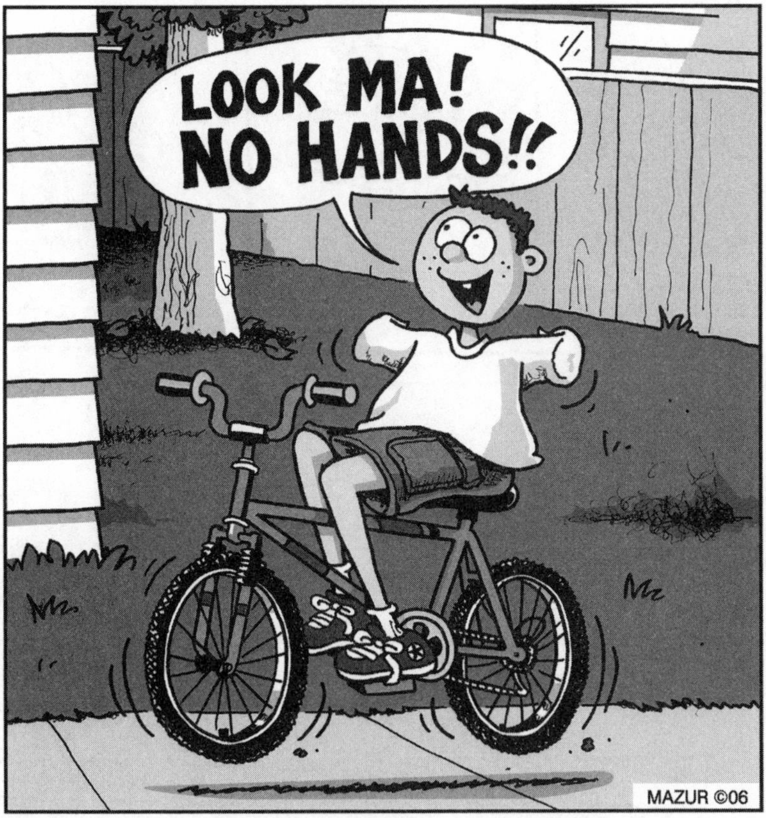
LOOK MA! NO HANDS!!
MAZUR ©06

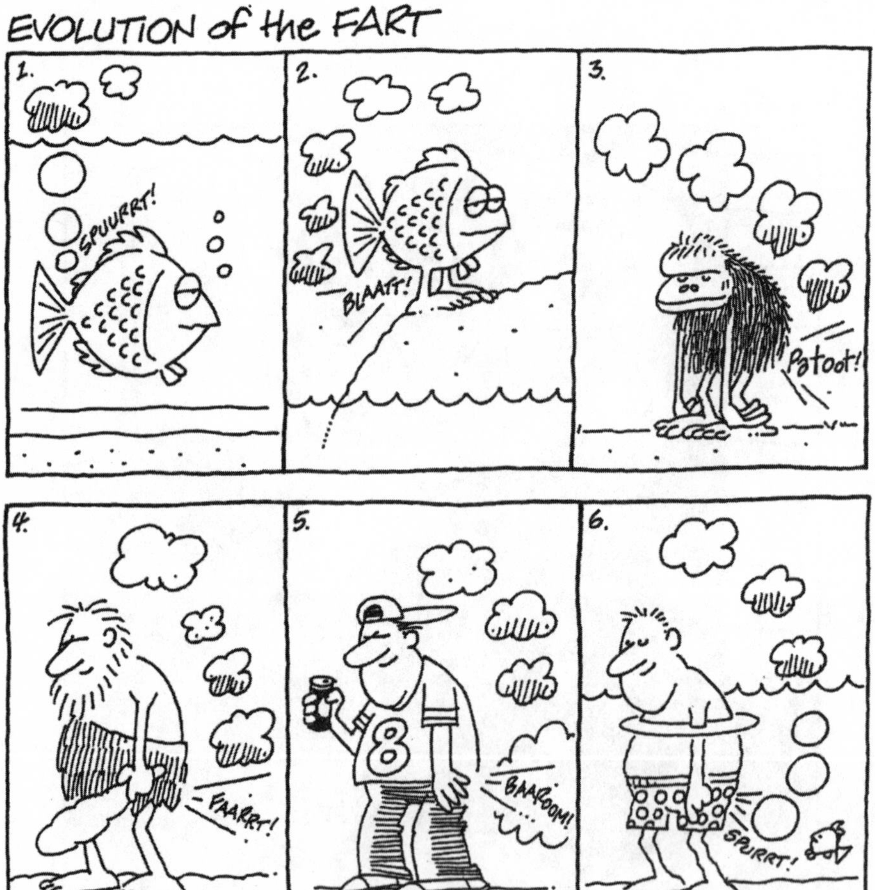
EVOLUTION of the FART
1.
SPUURRT!
2.
BLAATT!
3.
Patoot!
4.
FAARRT!
5.
8
BAAROOM!
6.
SPURRT!

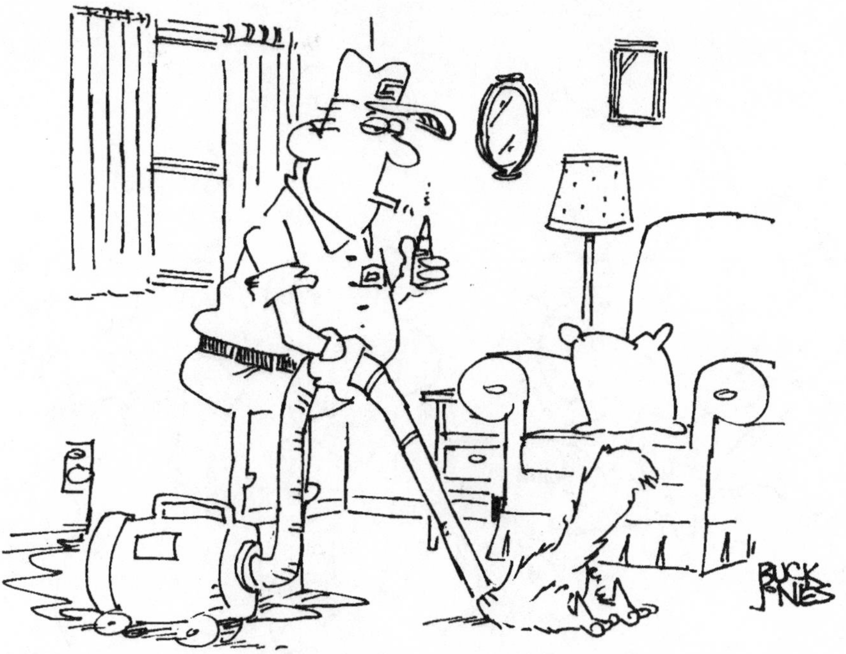
BUCK JONES

Semi-Professional Cat Hair Removal

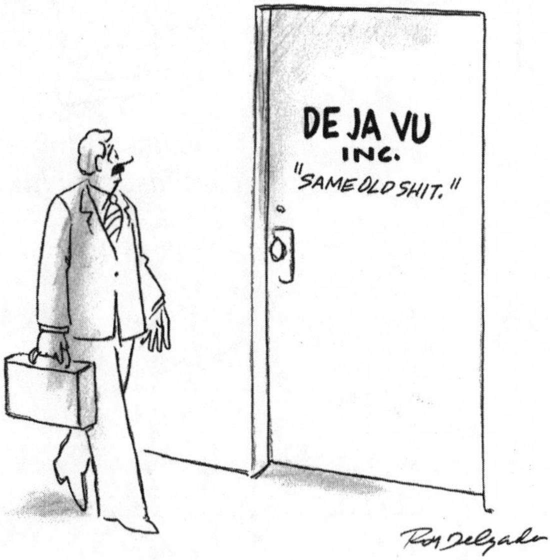
DE JA VU
INC.
"SAME OLD SHIT."

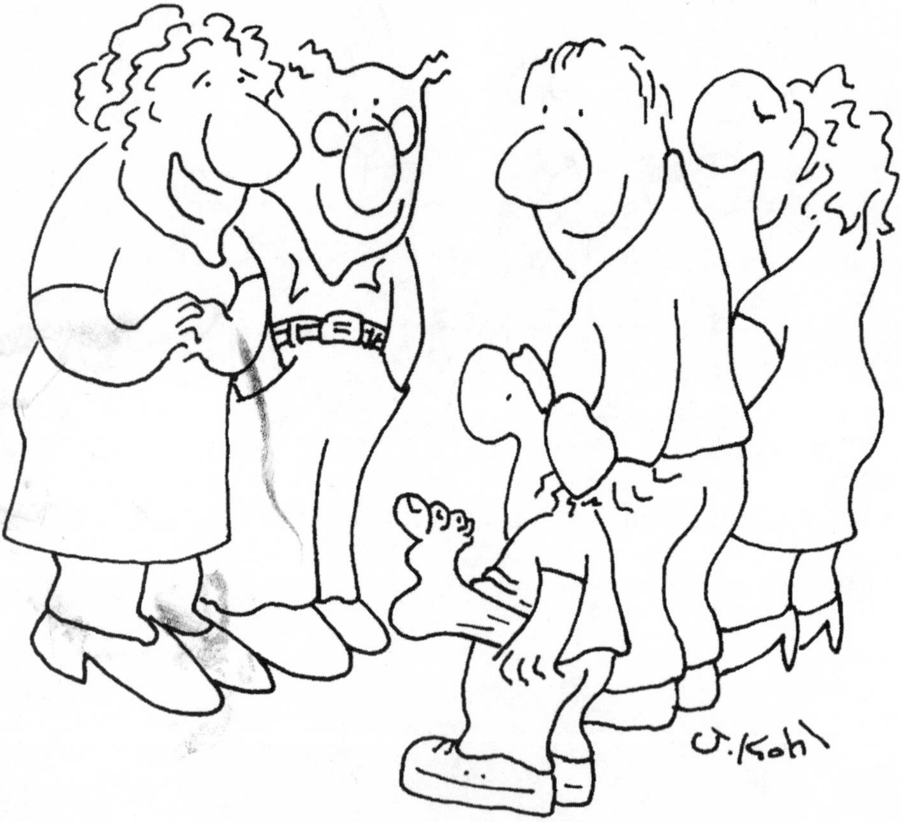
J. Kohl

"Seems like Willie has grown another foot since we last saw him!"

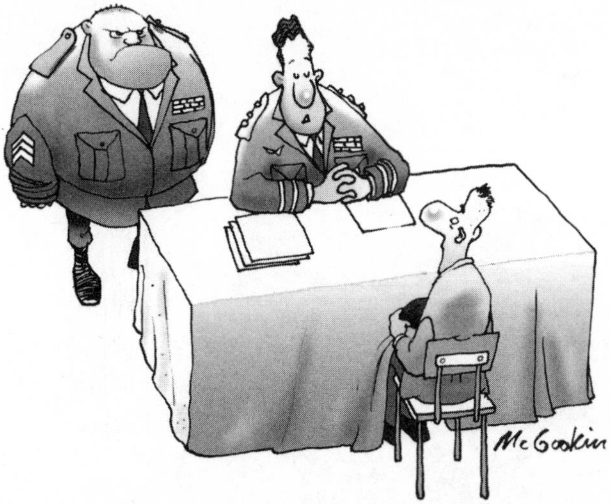
McGookin

"No, I don't know if having a dry scalp excludes you from serving in Iraq. Why don't we ask the sergeant here?"

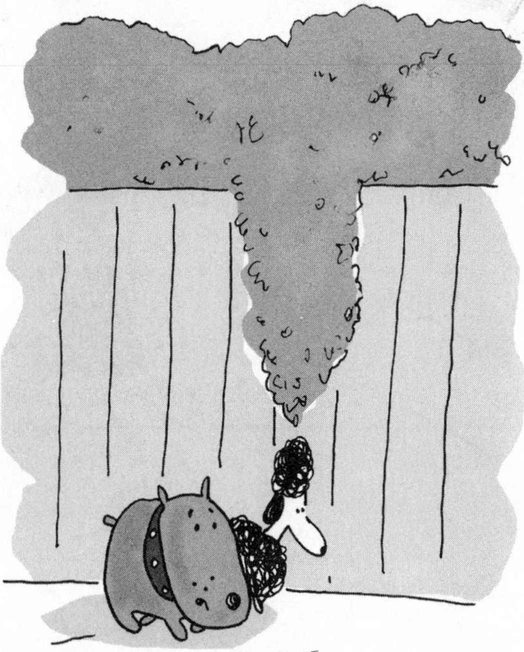
R. McKIE

"Of course it's easier for you to 'come out,' you're a poodle. Everybody expects poodles to be gay."

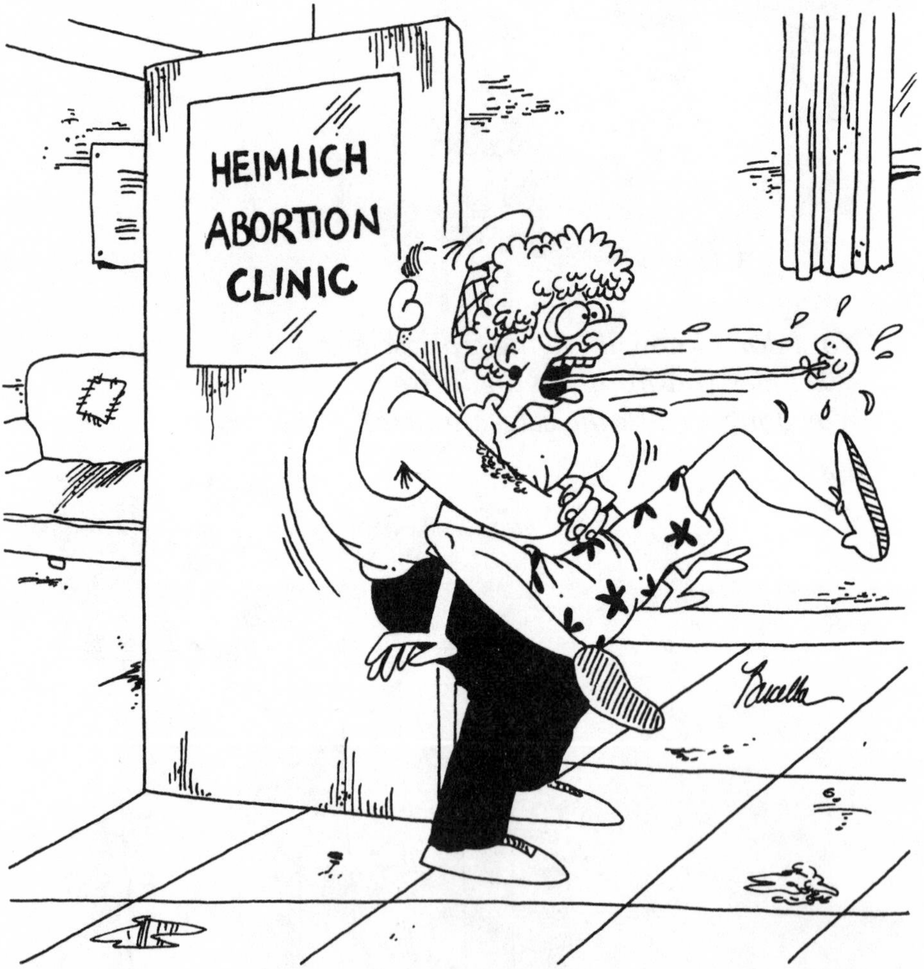
HEIMLICH
ABORTION
CLINIC

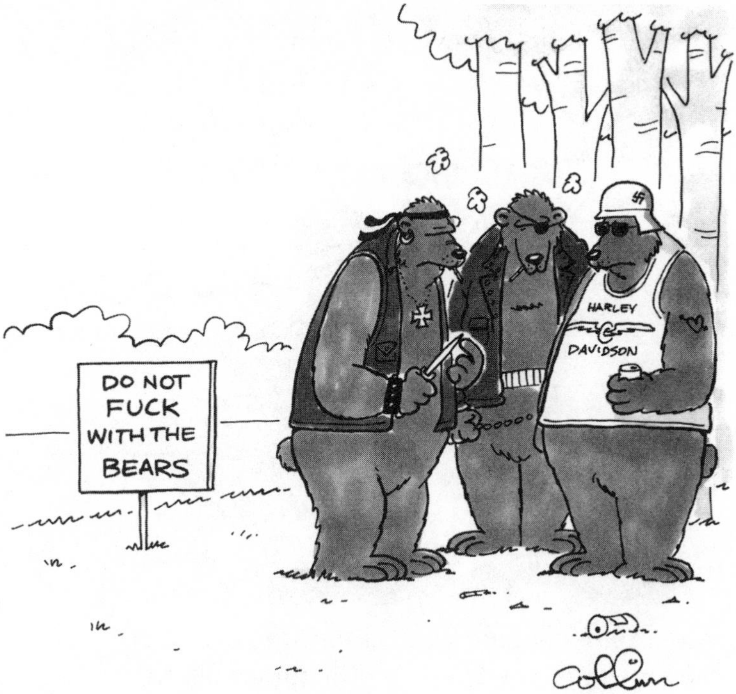
DO NOT
FUCK
WITH THE
BEARS
HARLEY
DAVIDSON

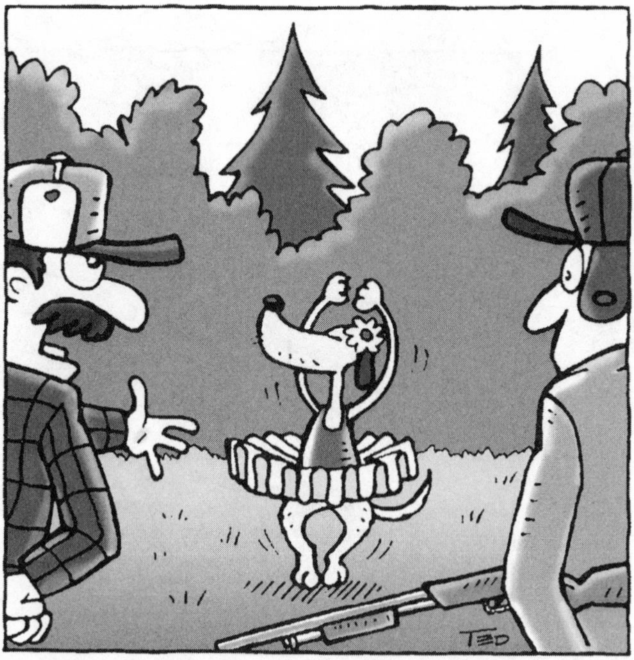

"Sorry, Joe, but that dog won't hunt."

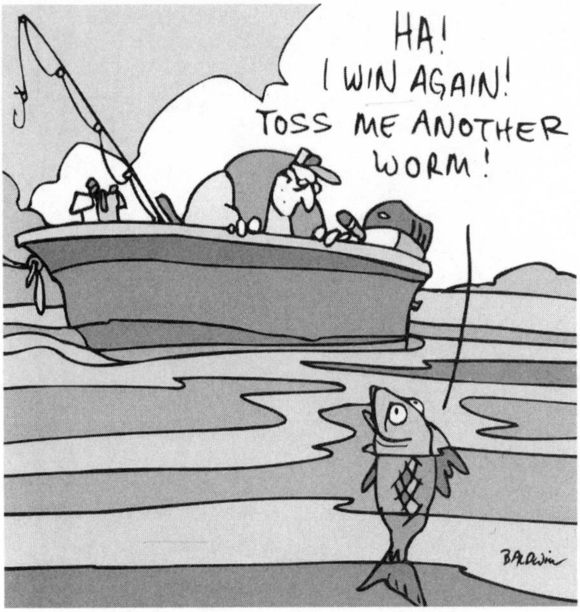
HA!
I WIN AGAIN!
TOSS ME ANOTHER
WORM!

Most experienced fishermen know better than to get involved in staring contests.

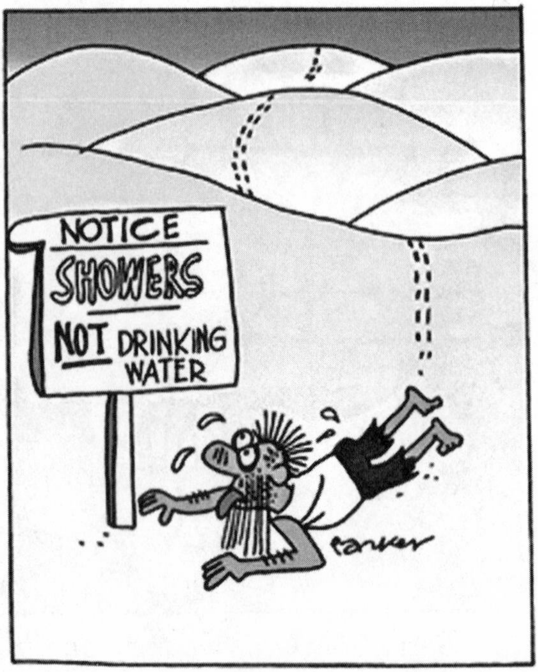
NOTICE
SHOWERS
NOT DRINKING
WATER

WHEN FORENSIC SCIENTISTS DINE IN RESTAURANTS
WAITER!! THERE'S A BLONDE HAIR, FEMALE, SMOKER, APPROXIMATELY 20 YEARS OLD IN MY SOUP!!
STORMS
©

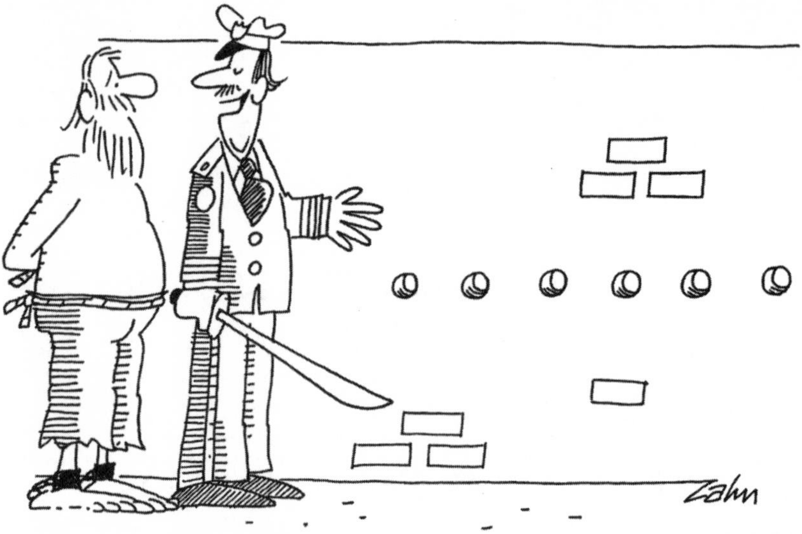
Zahn

"Behind that wall there are five cannibals and one gay guy."

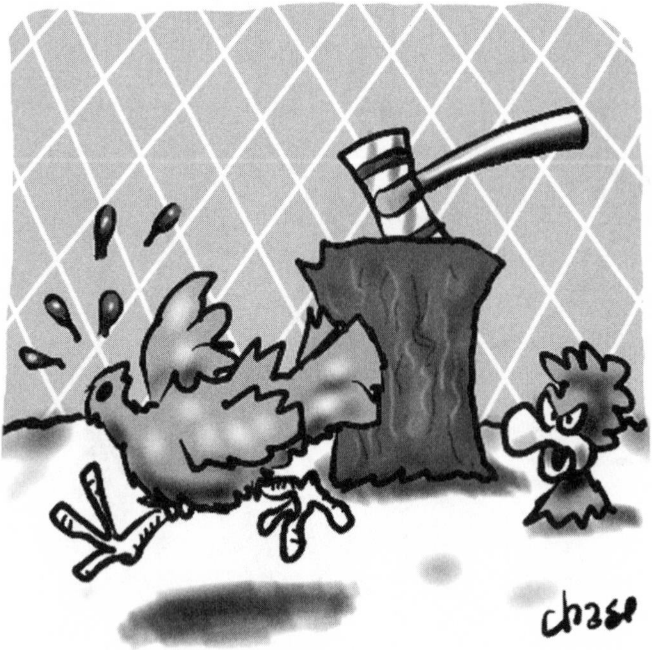
chase

"Oh, sure, now you run!!"

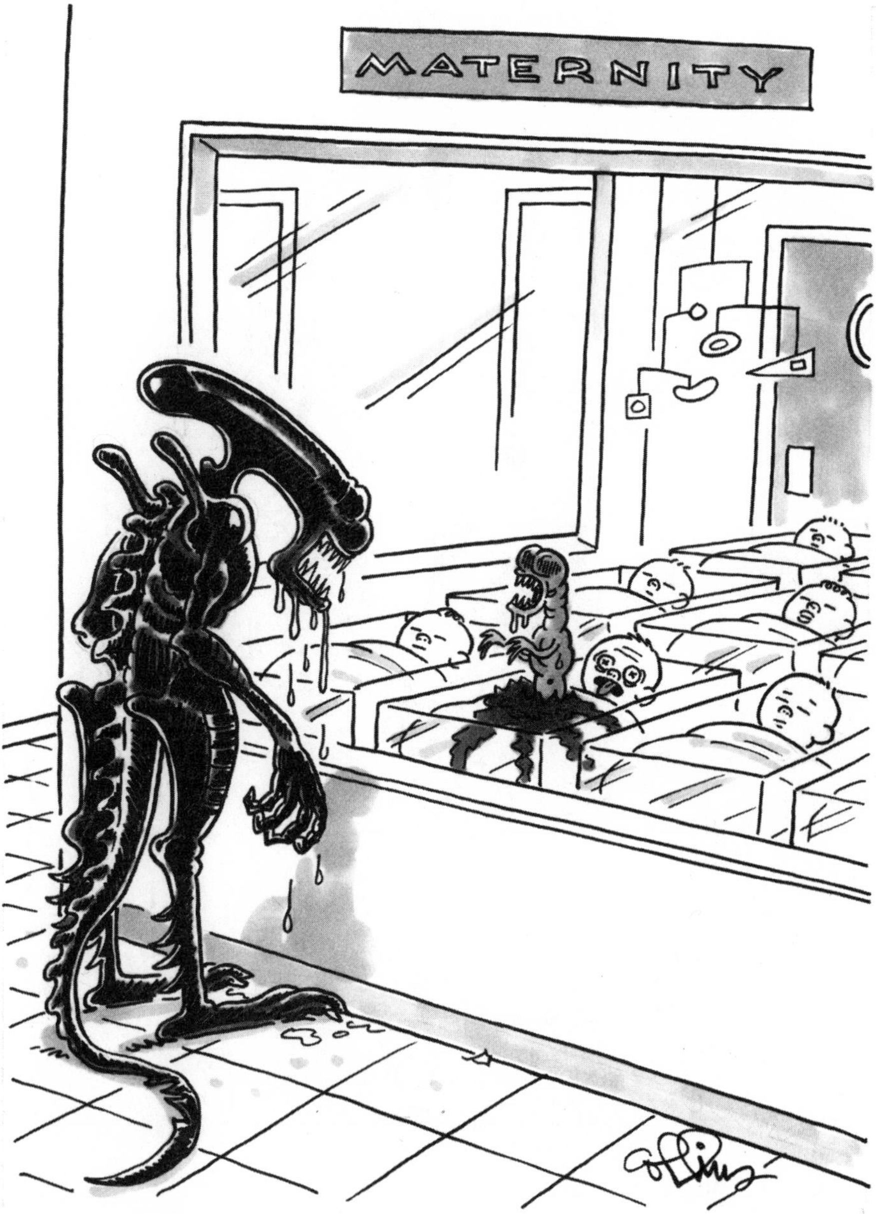
MATERNITY

The ladies were usually put off
by Bob's nose hare.

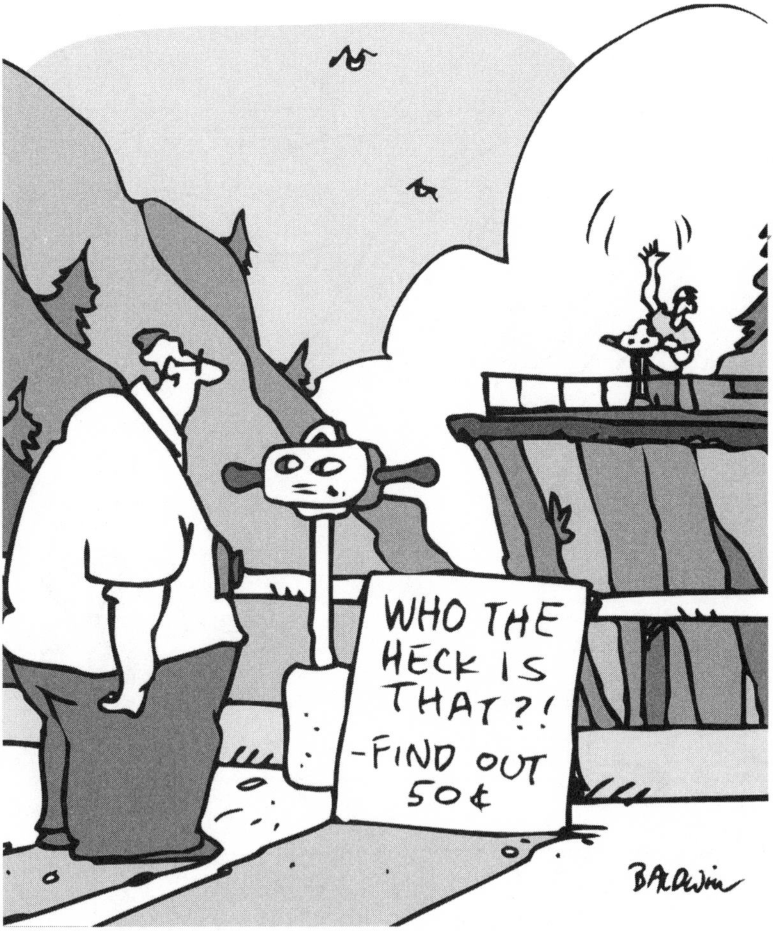
WHO THE
HECK IS
THAT?!
-FIND OUT
50¢
BALDWIN

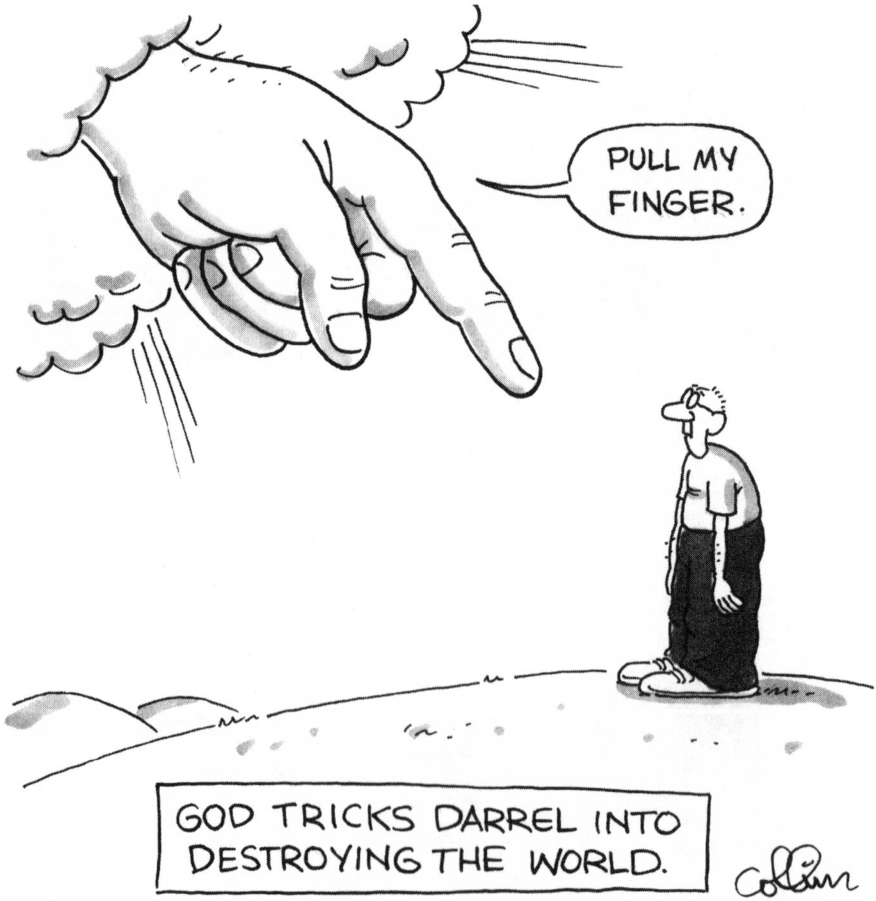
PULL MY FINGER.
GOD TRICKS DARREL INTO DESTROYING THE WORLD.
Collins

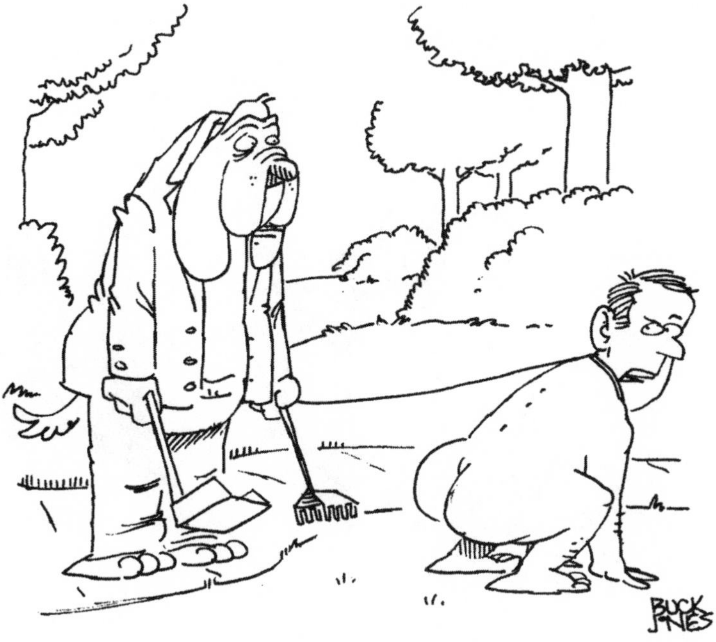
BUCK JONES

"Don't watch."

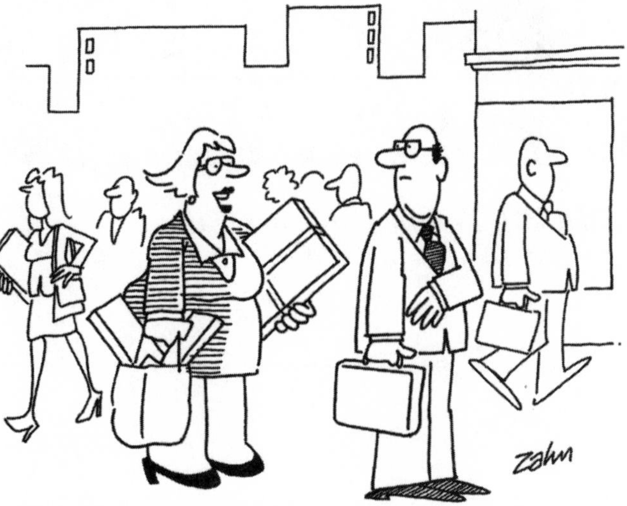
zahn

"Pardon me. I came into the city to shop and I ran out of money. How much would you pay me for a blow job?"

"Hi kid, I'm the pubic hair fairy."

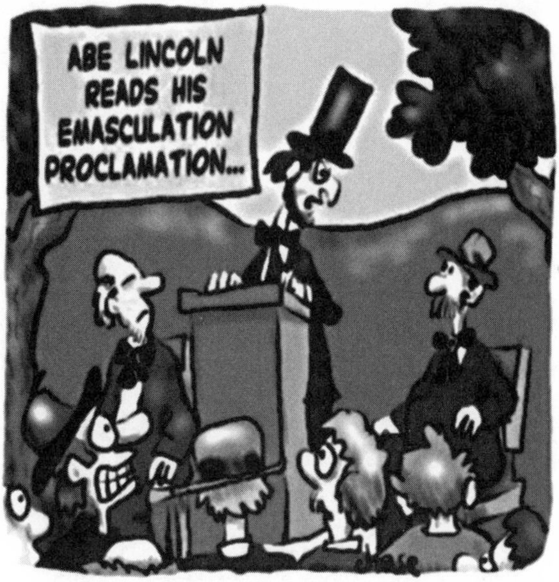
ABE LINCOLN
READS HIS
EMASCULATION
PROCLAMATION...

"Who the hell wrote this?"

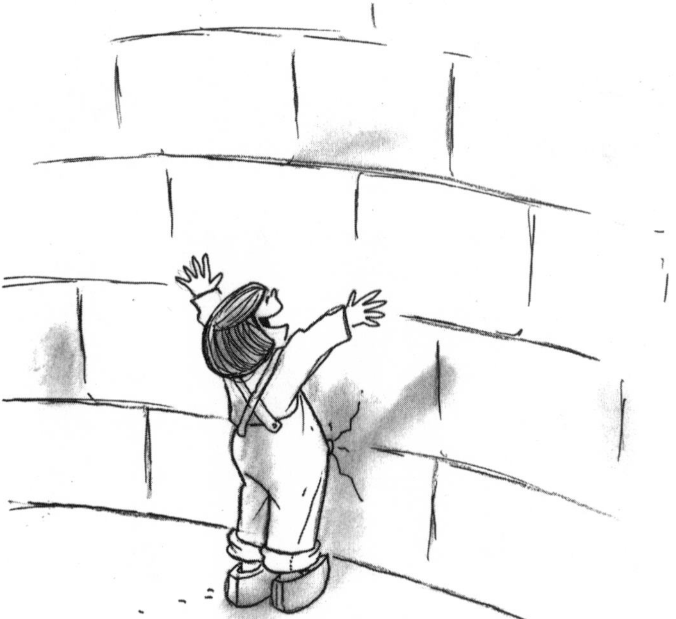

"Look, Ma! No hands!"

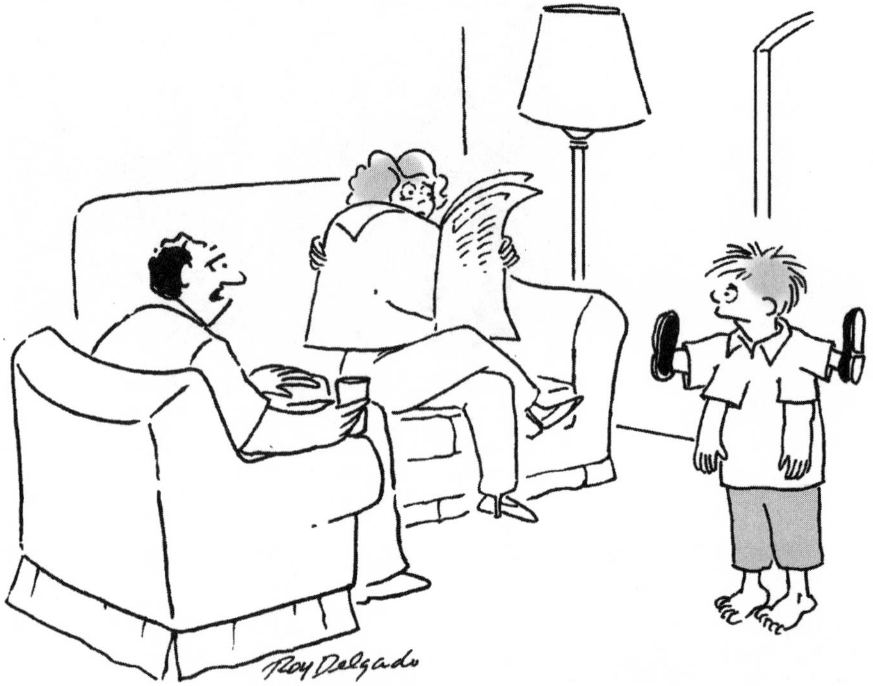
Roy Delgado

"He's got his shoes on the wrong feet again."

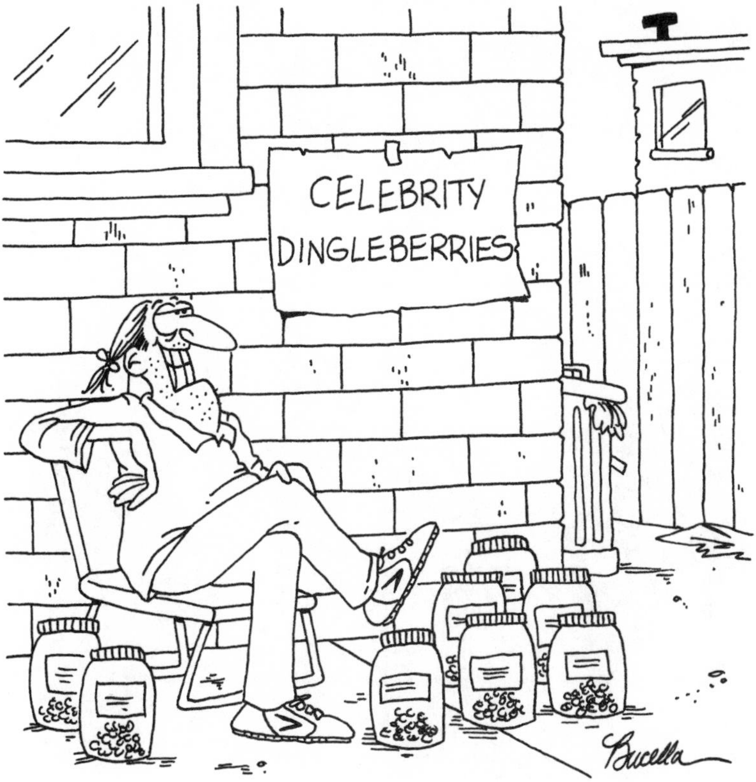
CELEBRITY DINGLEBERRIES

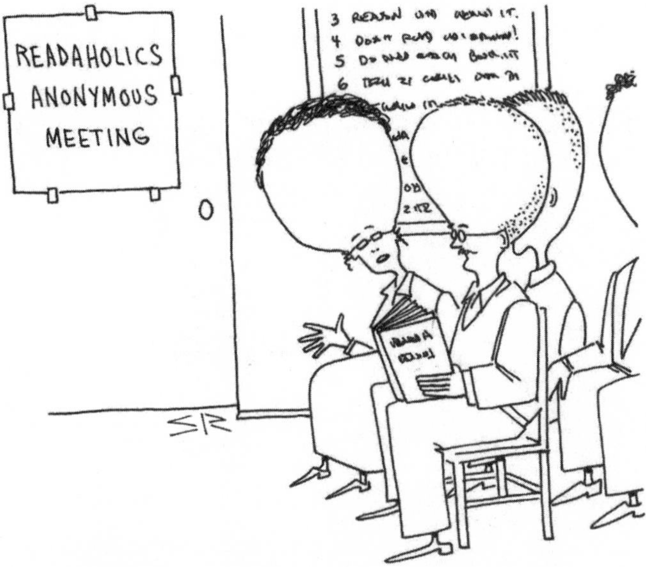
READAHOLICS ANONYMOUS MEETING

"Put the book down, Dennis. Put it down."

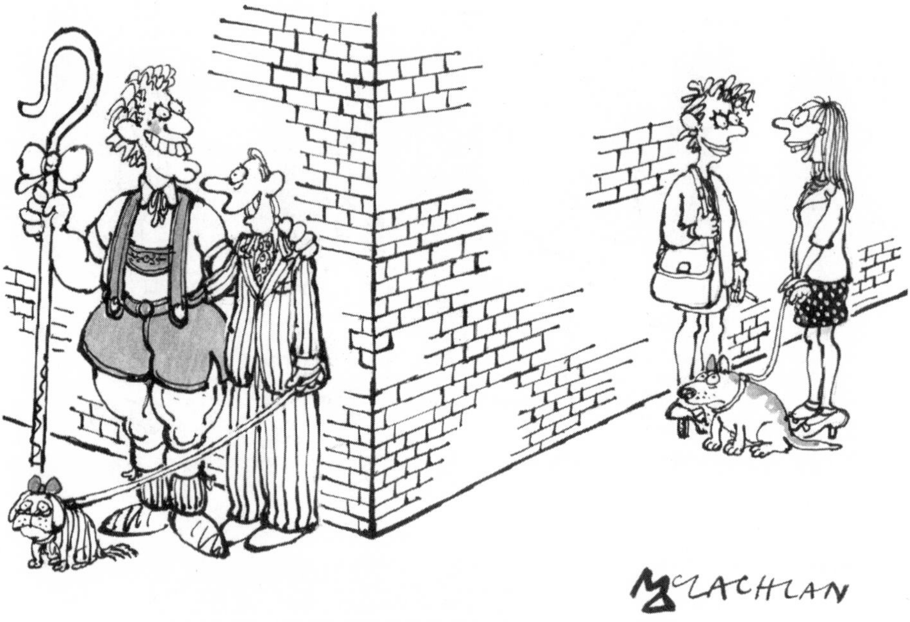
McLACHLAN

"I'm meeting my blind date. He's a dog lover and he has a young German Shepherd."

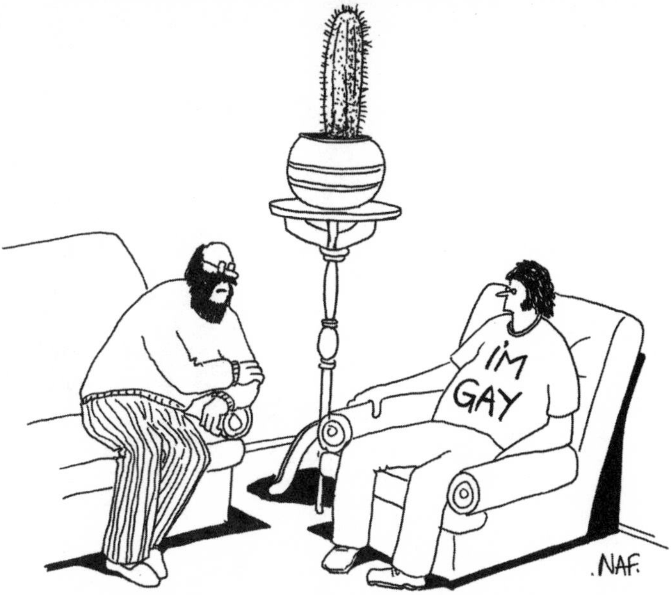
I'M
GAY
NAF.

"It's not the fact that you're gay that bothers me son, it's the fact you're so open about it."

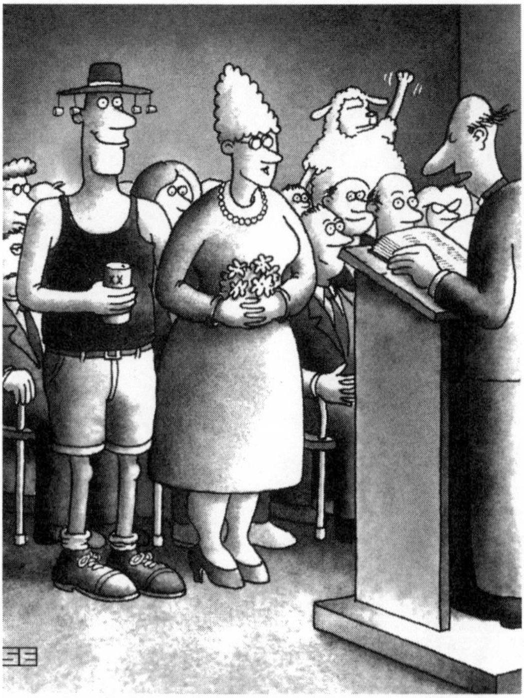

"If there's anybody here who knows why these two should not be wed..."

"This is one sick dog."

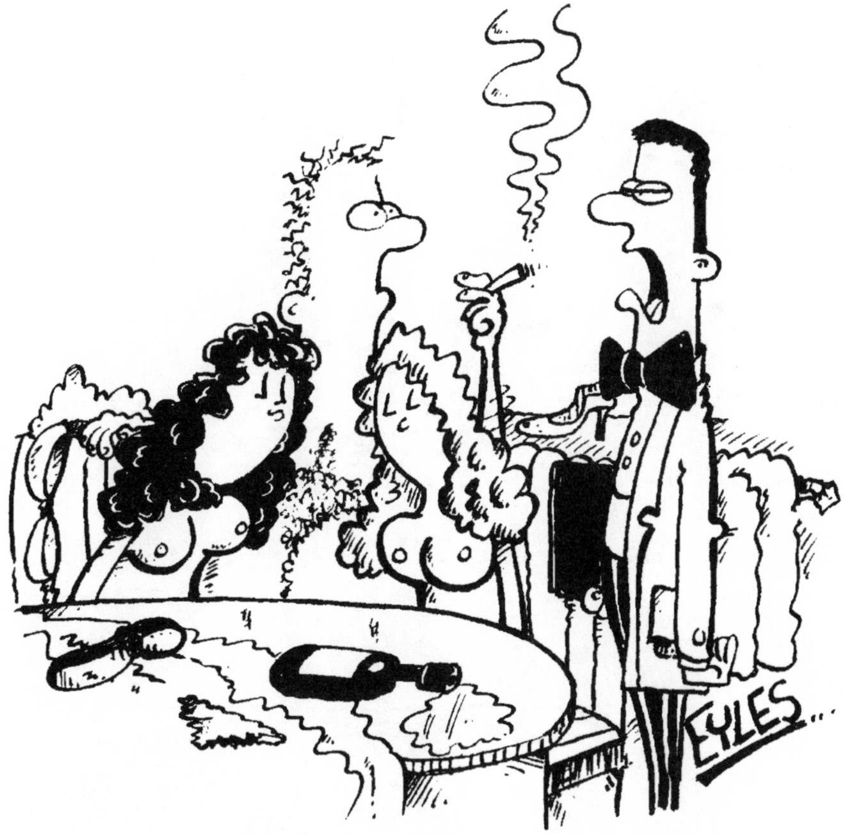
EYLES...

"Pardon Monsieur, the restaurant is non smoking."

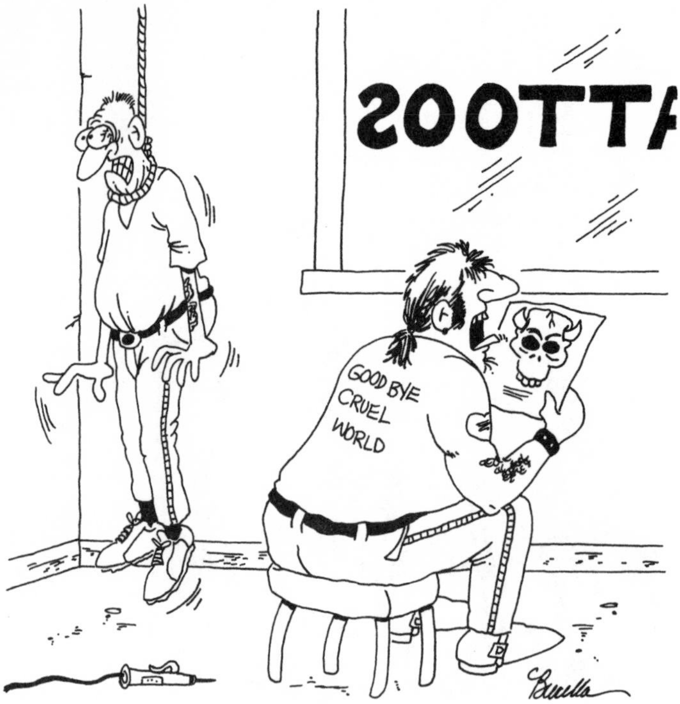
GOOD BYE
CRUEL
WORLD

"You done already?"

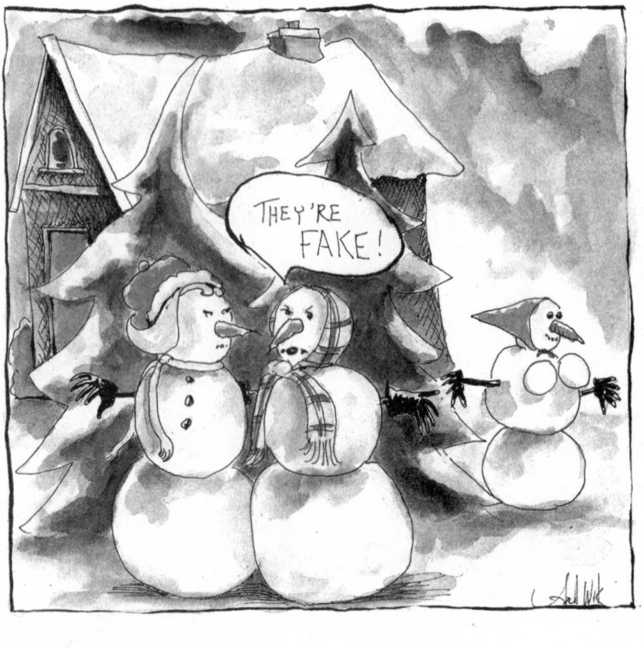
THEY'RE FAKE!

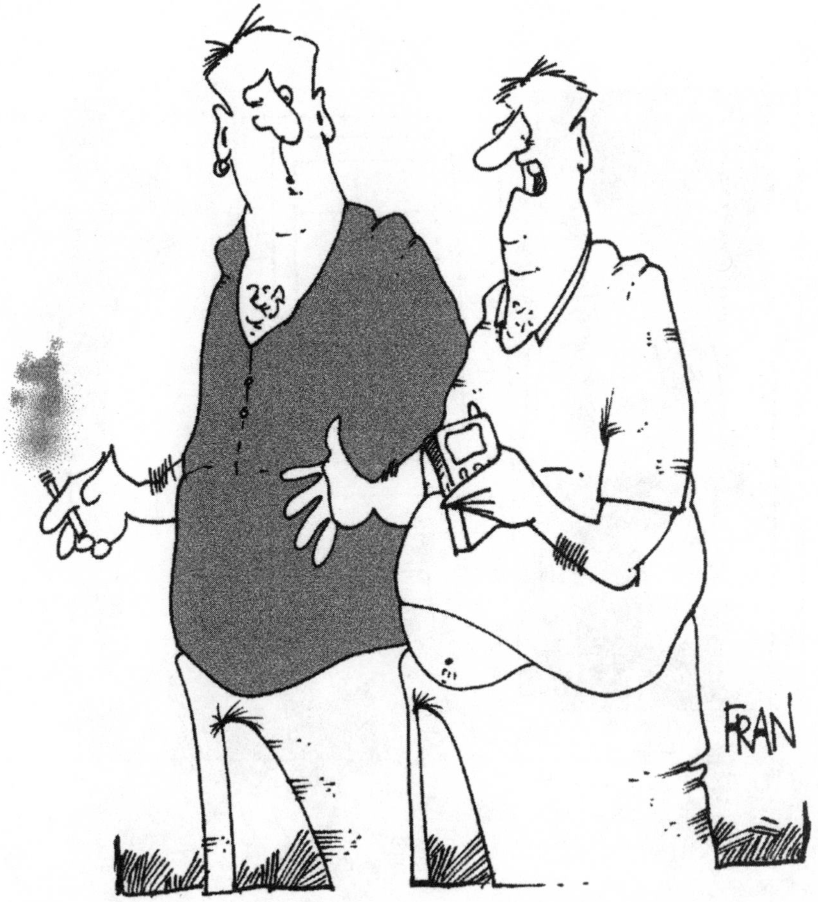
FRAN

"I mean, what is the point of getting the Internet on your mobile phone if you can only see one tit at a time?"

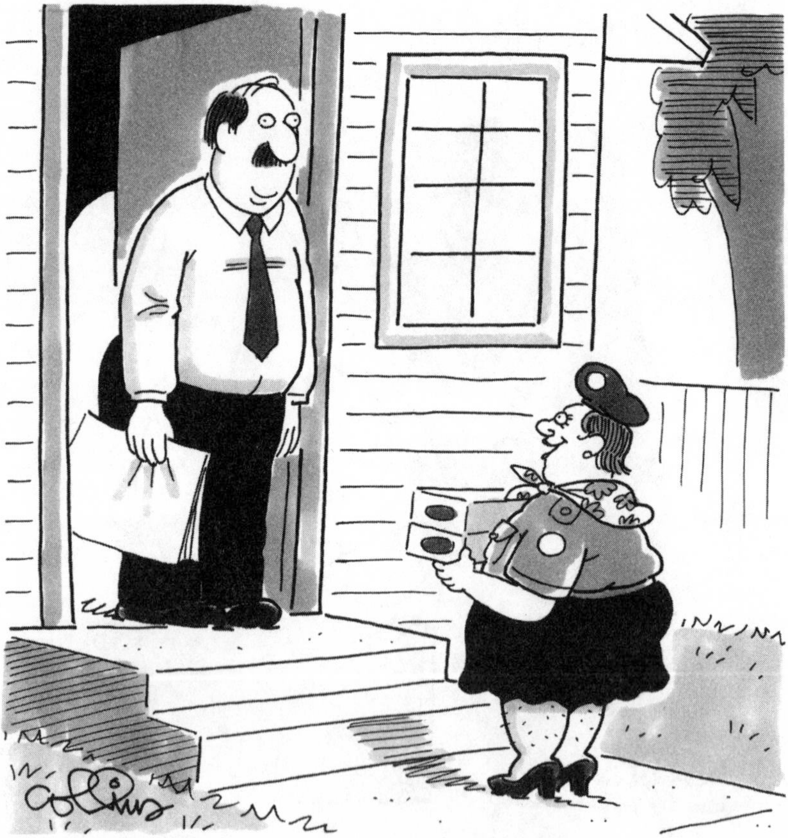
Collins

"Would you like to buy some gay scout cookies?"

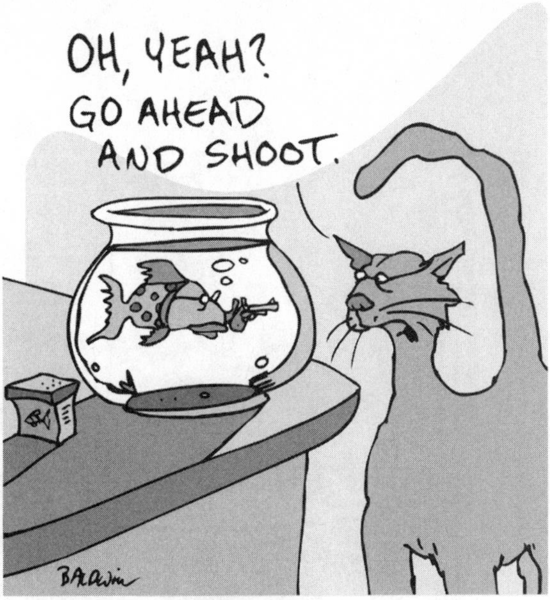
OH, YEAH?
GO AHEAD
AND SHOOT.

Bluffer Fish

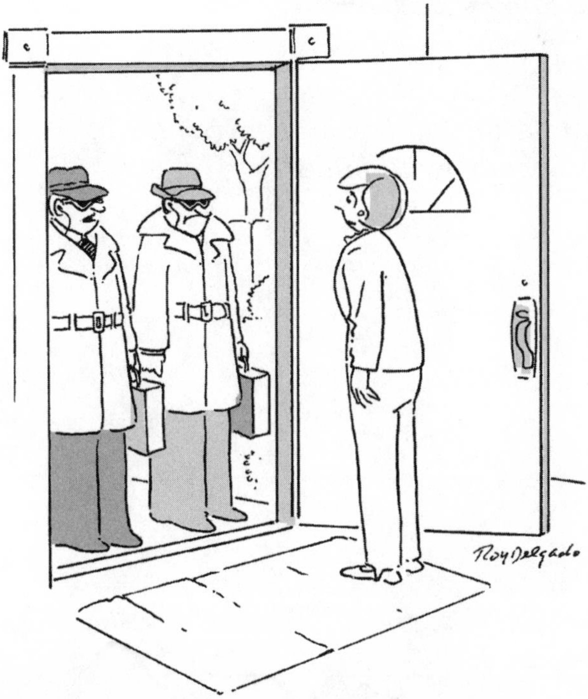

"We smelled middle-eastern cooking."

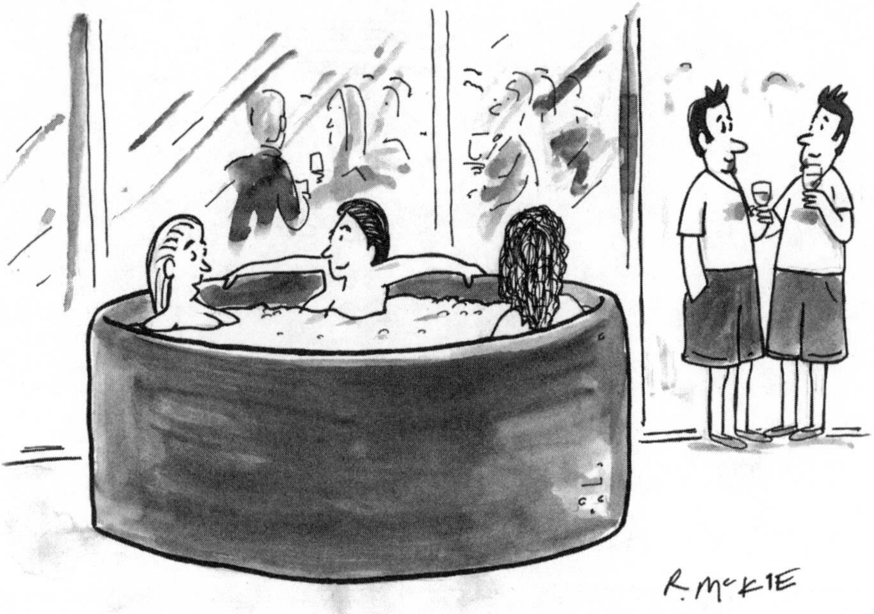
R. McKIE

"It is impossible to tell the difference between them, they're both awful in bed."

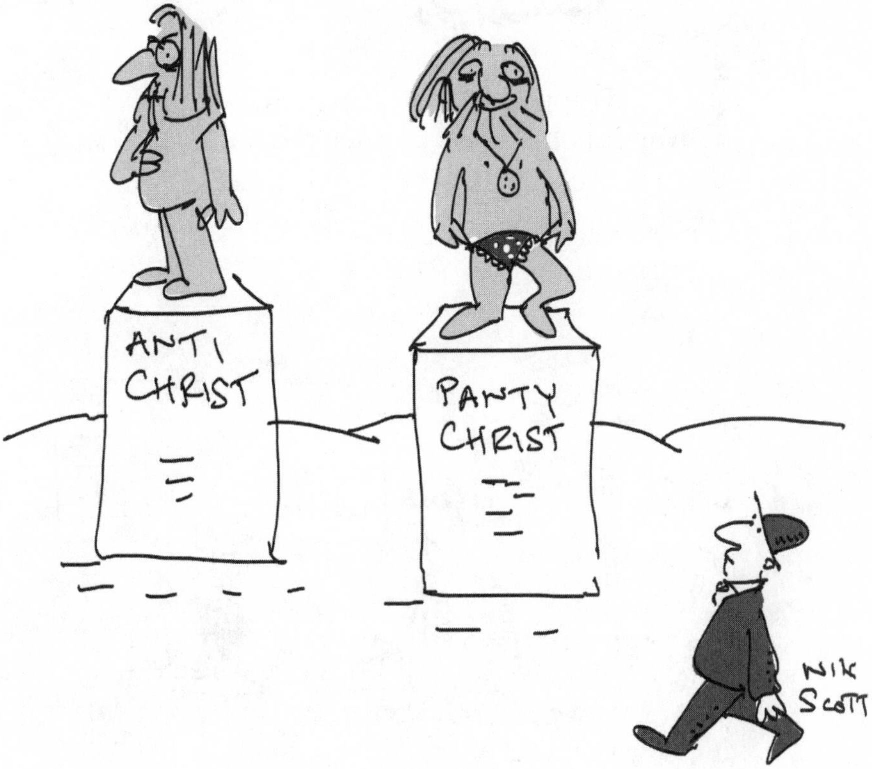
ANTI
CHRIST
PANTY
CHRIST
NIK
SCOTT

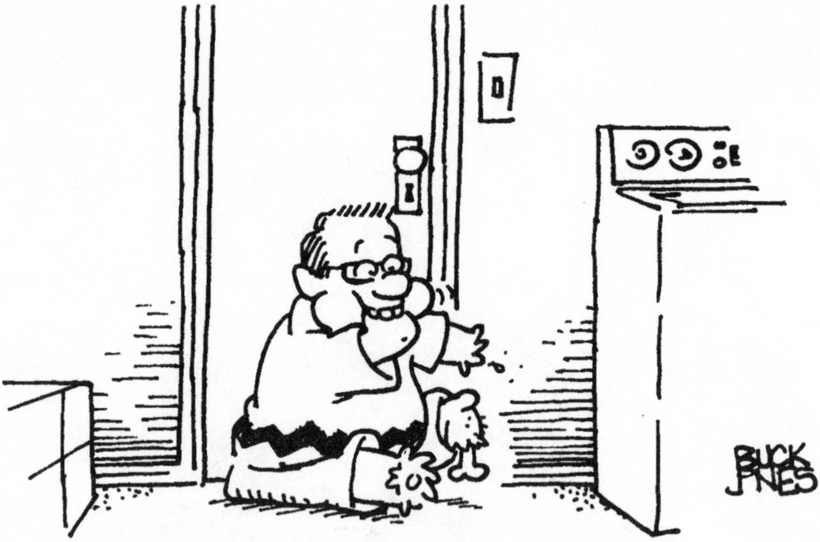
BUCK JONES

Trapped in his basement,
Oliver eats his arms and legs to survive.

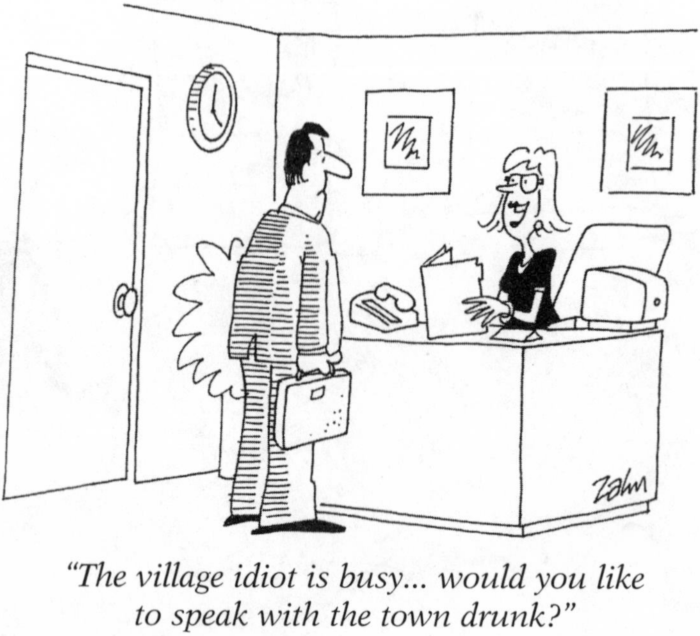
Zahn

"The village idiot is busy... would you like to speak with the town drunk?"

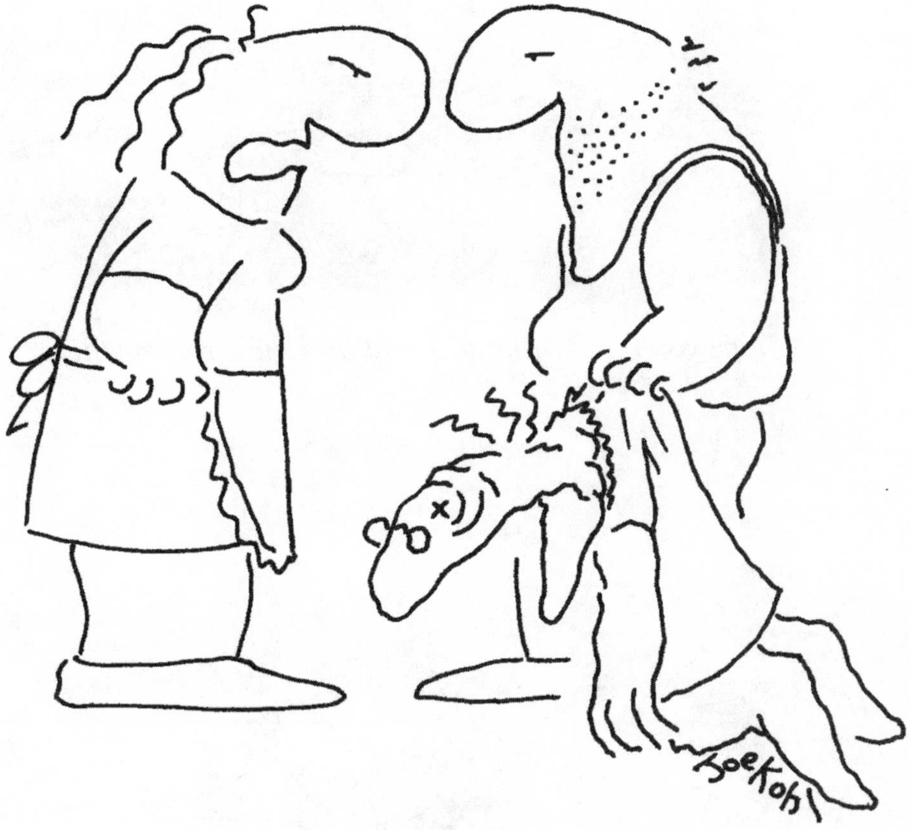
JoeKohl

"Every time we have an argument you gotta drag my mother into it!"

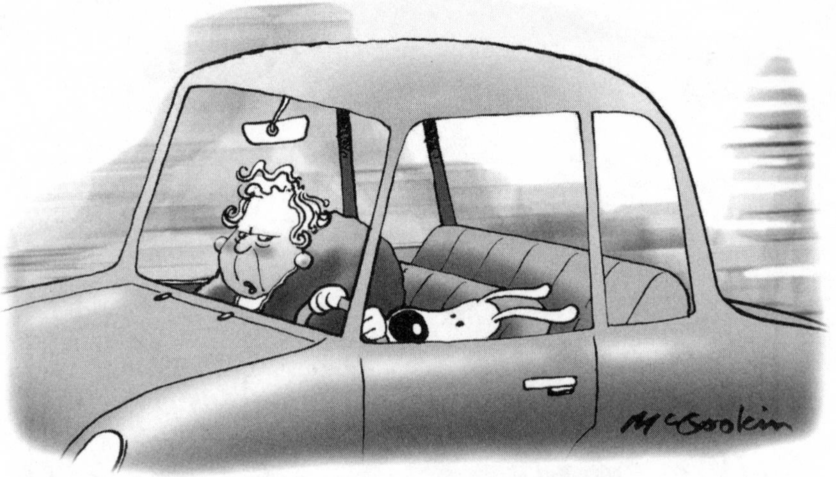

"I hope you don't think this will become a regular thing."

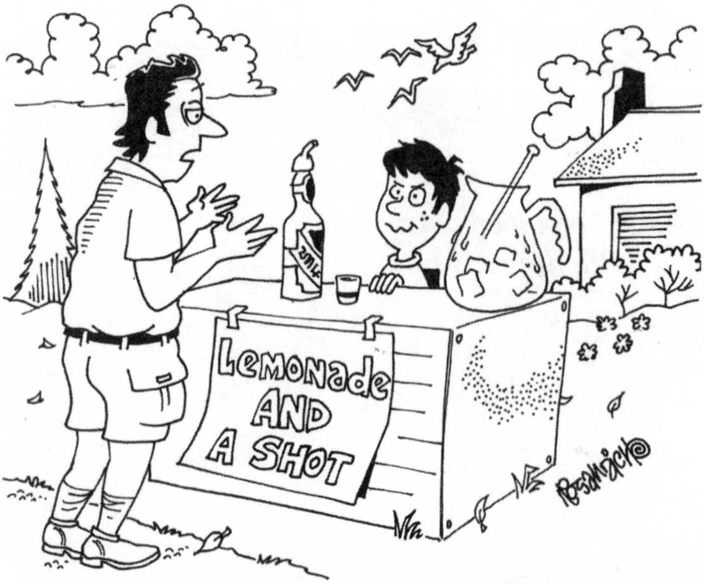
Lemonade
AND
A SHOT

"Son, we have to talk."

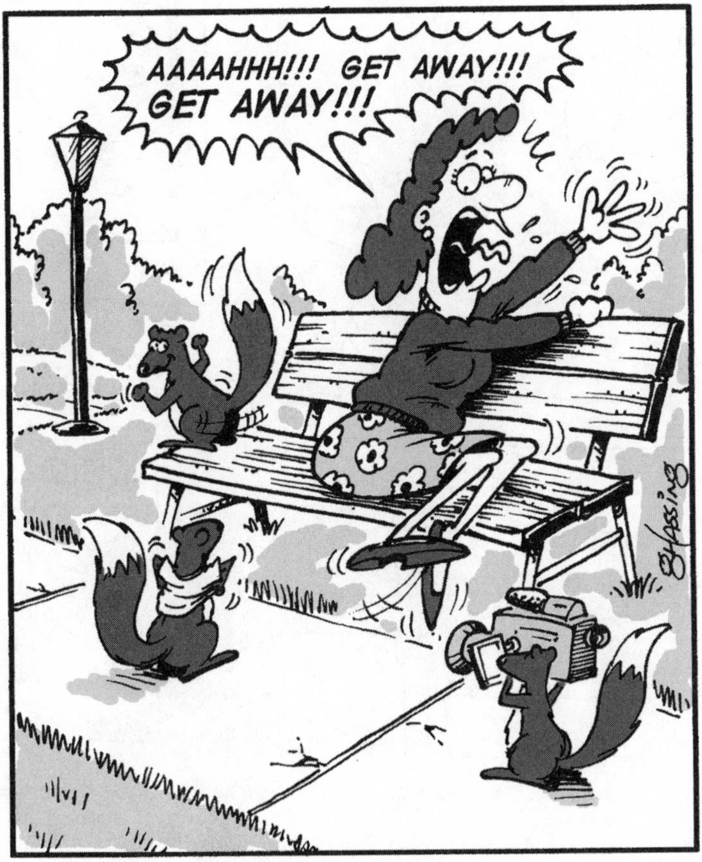
AAAAHHH!!! GET AWAY!!!
GET AWAY!!!

Squirrels Gone Wild

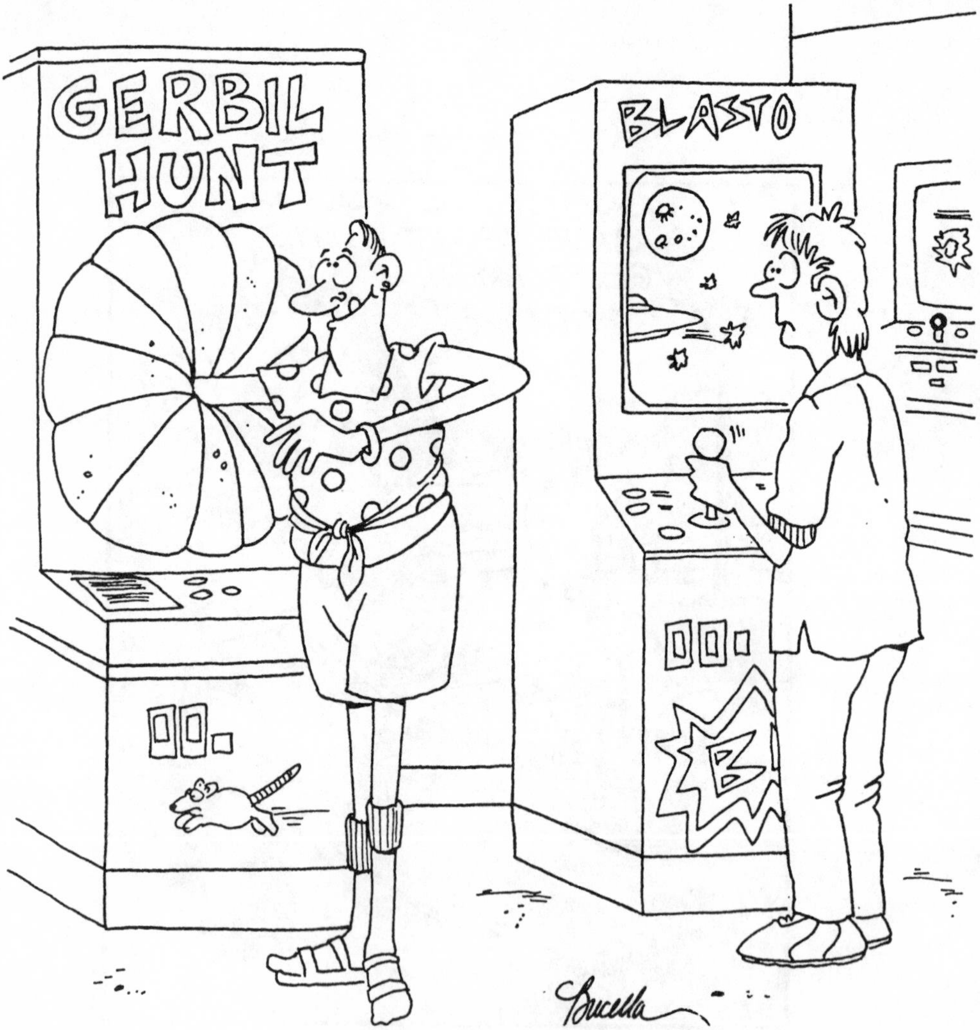
GERBIL HUNT
BLASTO
Bucella

LET AUTOMOBILE MANUFACTURING PLANT NO. 7
IF YOU WORKED HERE, YOU'D BE HOME LAYED-OFF BY NOW.
ROY DELGADO

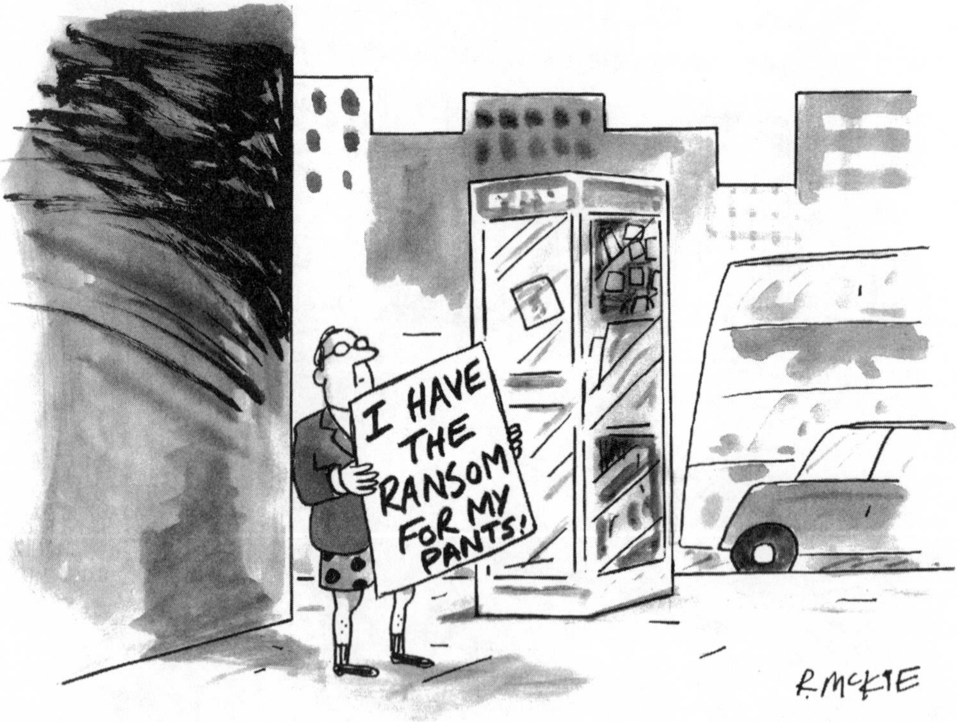
I HAVE THE RANSOM FOR MY PANTS!
R. McKIE

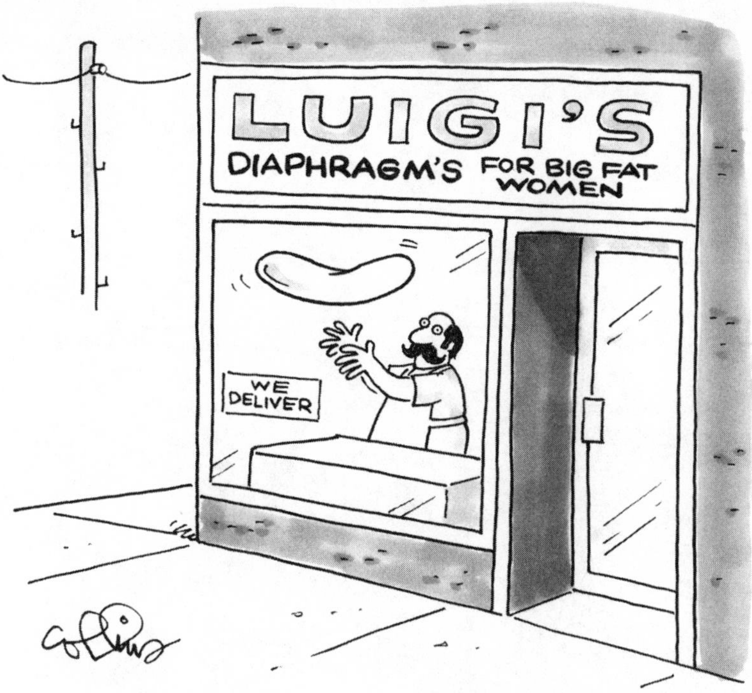
LUIGI'S
DIAPHRAGM'S FOR BIG FAT WOMEN
WE DELIVER

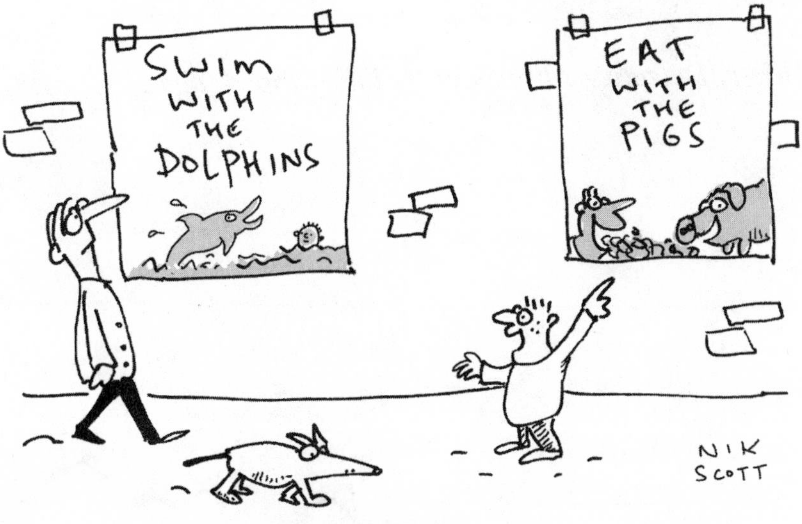
SWIM WITH THE DOLPHINS
EAT WITH THE PIGS
NIK SCOTT

POLICE LINE DO NOT
NOT CROSS
LINE DO N

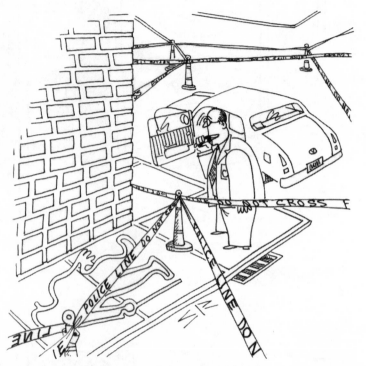

"This is Detective Abramowitz. I'm trapped, again."

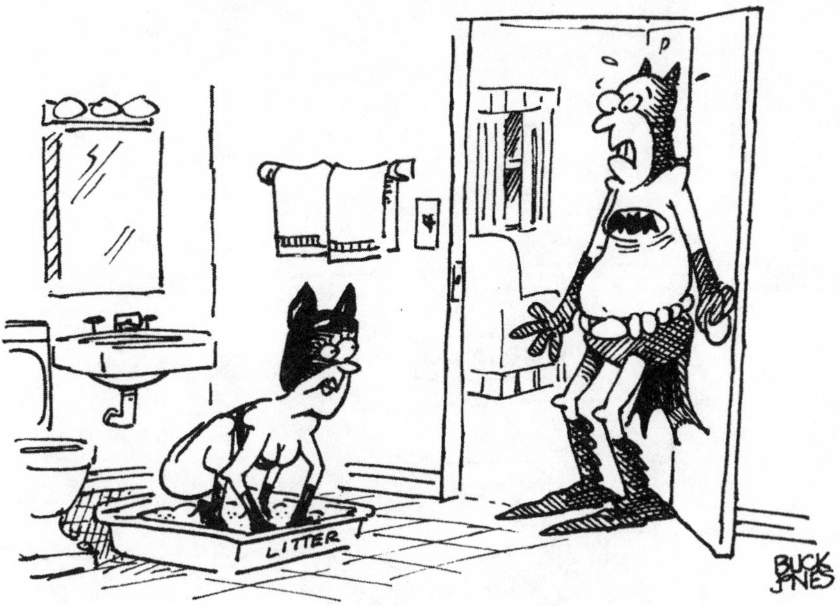
LITTER

Batman walks in on Catwoman

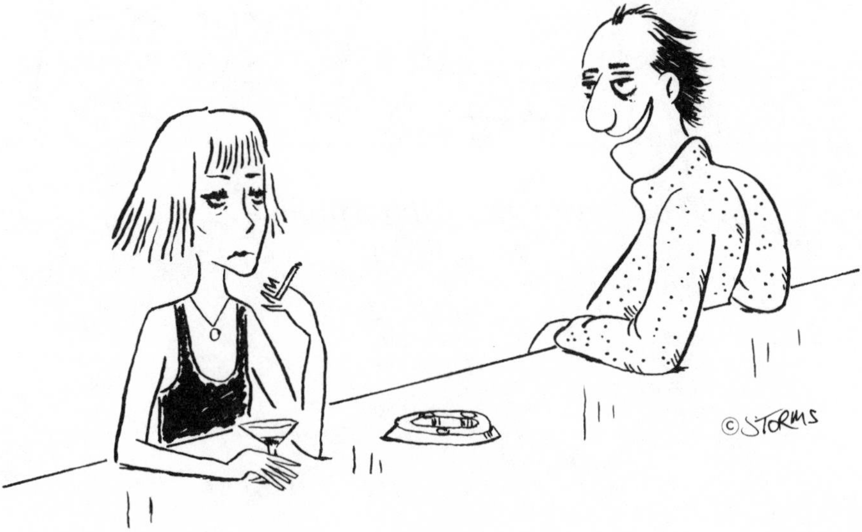

"I've got piercings on that jingle jangle jingle."

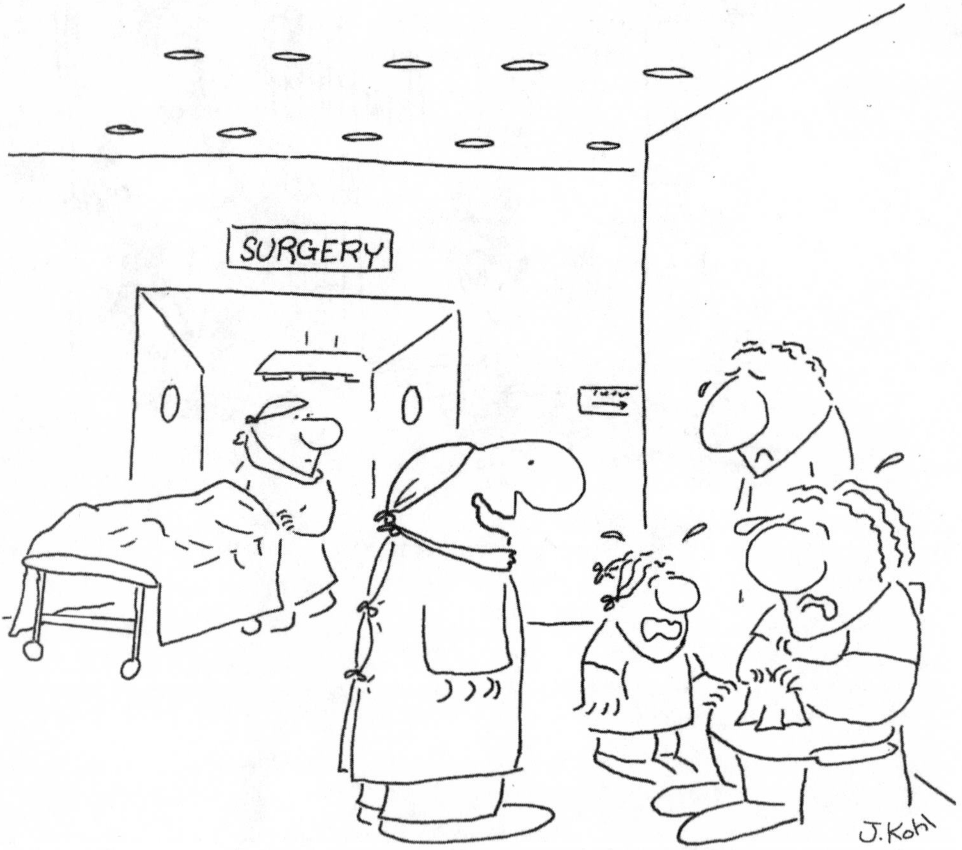
SURGERY
J. Kohl

"Can I have some of those funny 'get well' cards he got?"

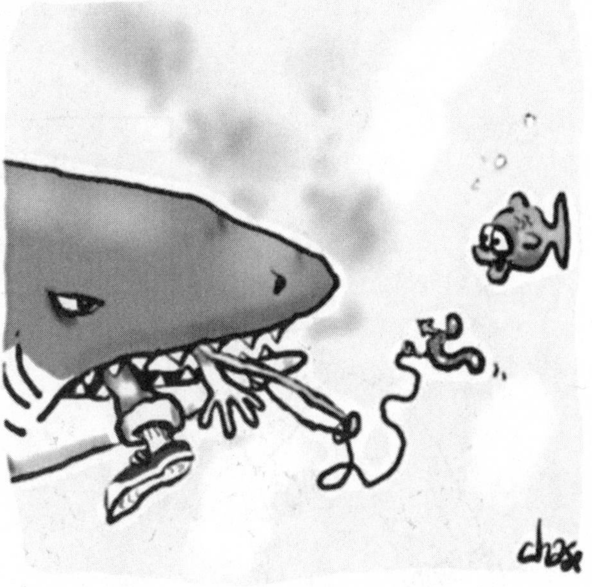
chase

"Are you gonna eat the worm?"

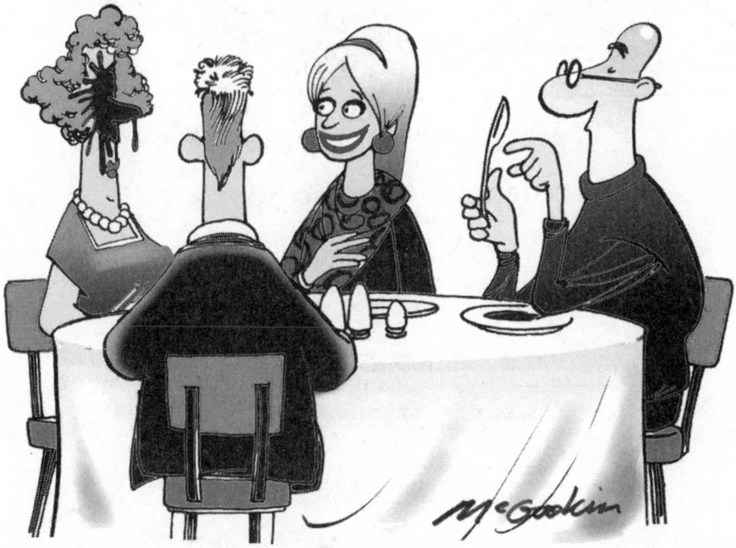
McGookin

Not everybody gets Roger...

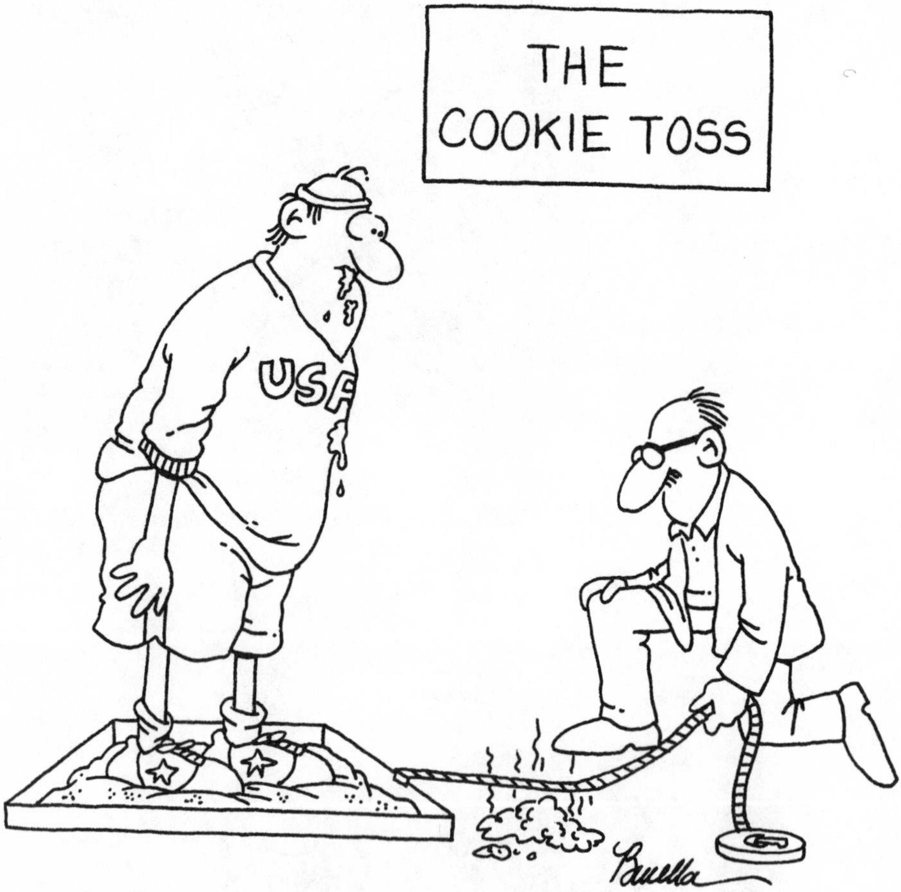
THE COOKIE TOSS
USA
Bauella

Unrecognized Olympic Sports

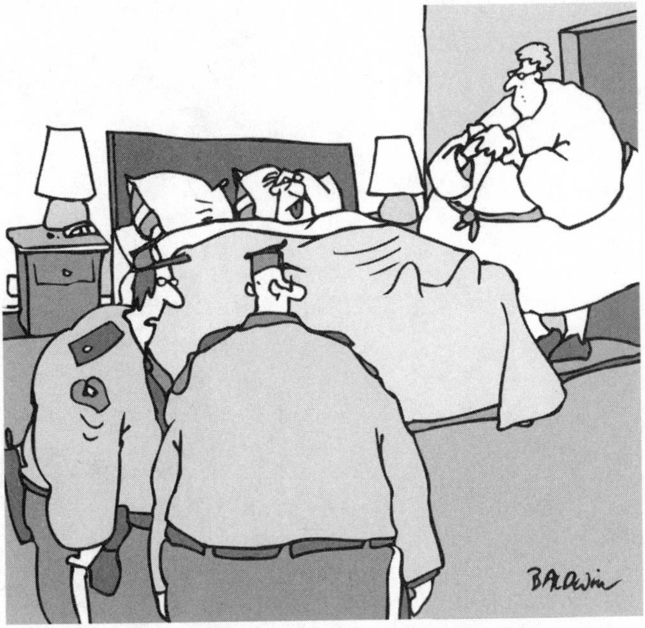

"Poor guy was crushed like a bug. Looks like someone woke up on the wrong side of the bed this morning."

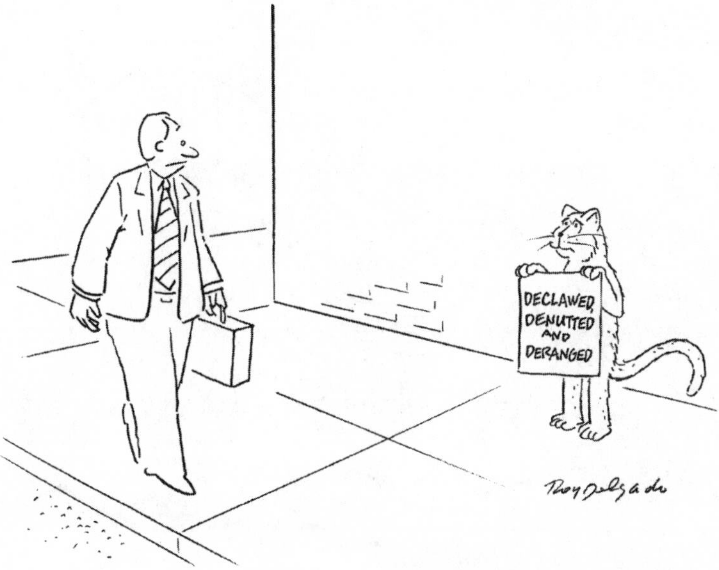
DECLAWED, DENUTTED AND DERANGED

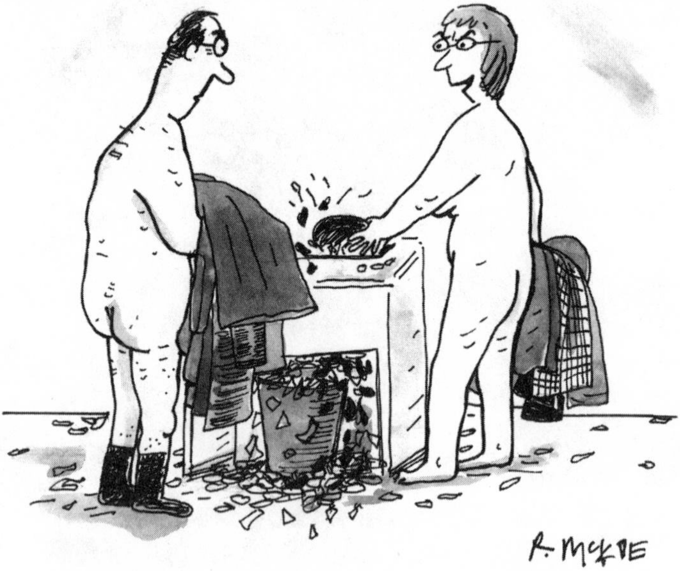
R. McKEE

"Okay, here's your silly little golf hat, and here's what I'm doing to it."

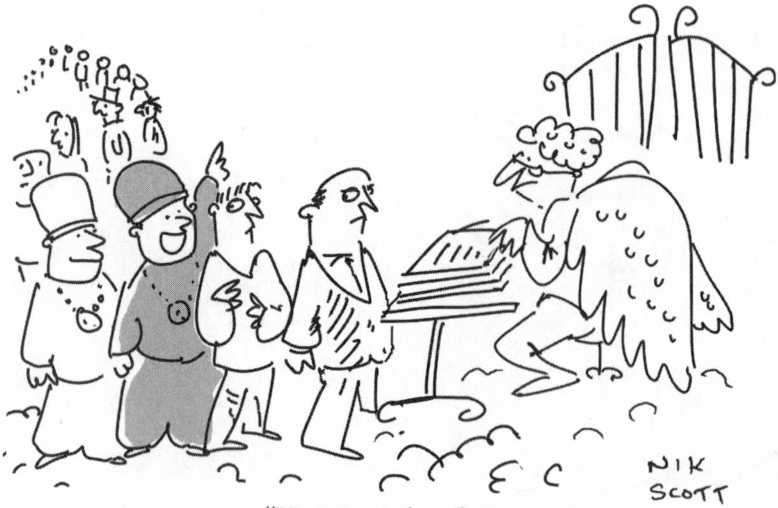
NIK
SCOTT

"Yo! Doorbitch!"

Stick with me kid, and you'll be a hit with the ladies. Hey, you got any money?
JERK IN A BOX
Royston

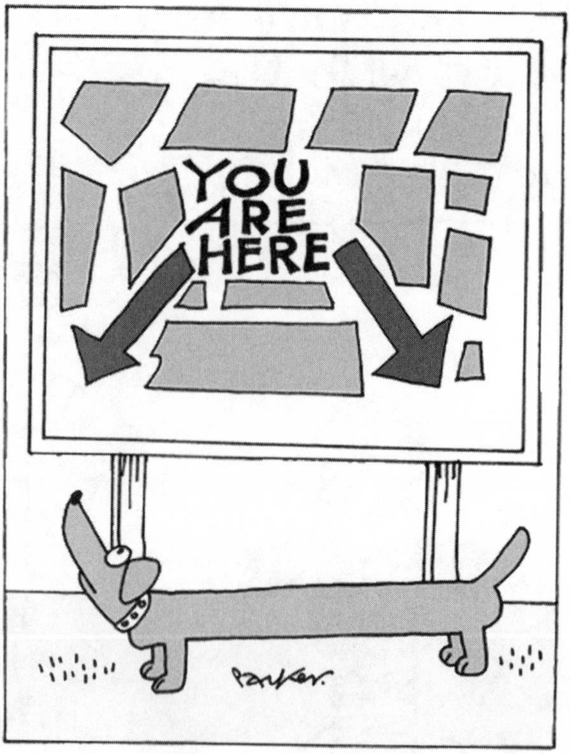
YOU
ARE
HERE
Parker.

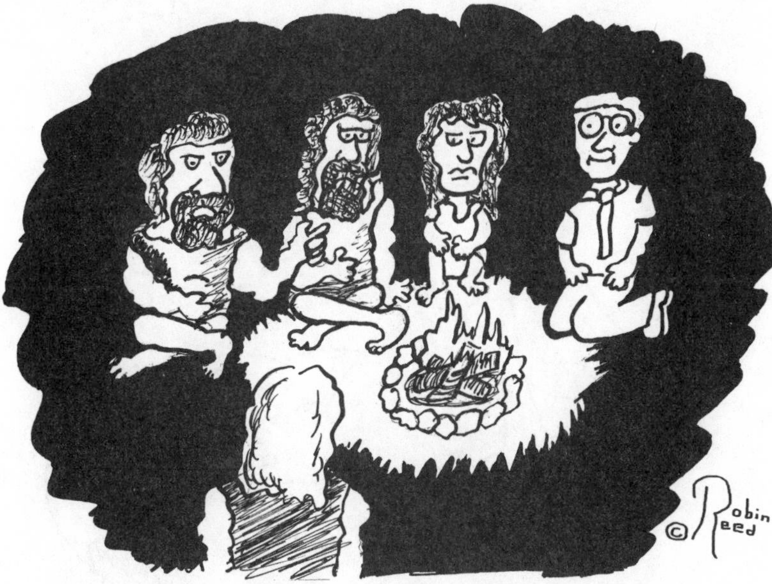
© Robin Reed

"Me Og. Him Ug. Her Ek. Him Arnie Brennerman."

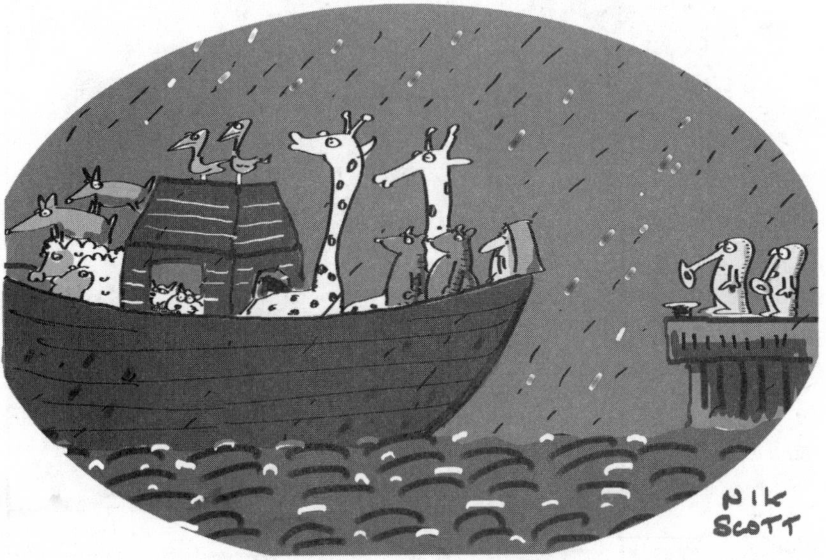
NIK SCOTT

"Is it because we're gay?"

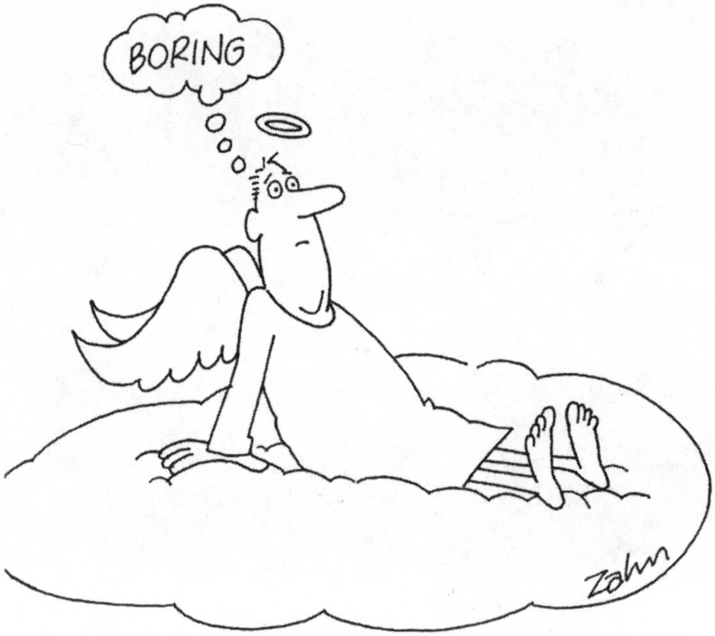
BORING
Zahn

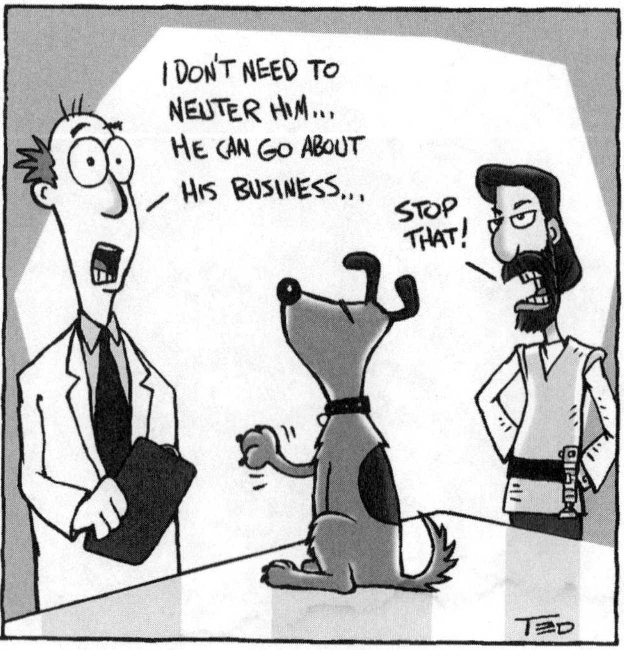
I DON'T NEED TO NEUTER HIM... HE CAN GO ABOUT HIS BUSINESS...
STOP THAT!
TED

Obi-wan Kenobi's dog.

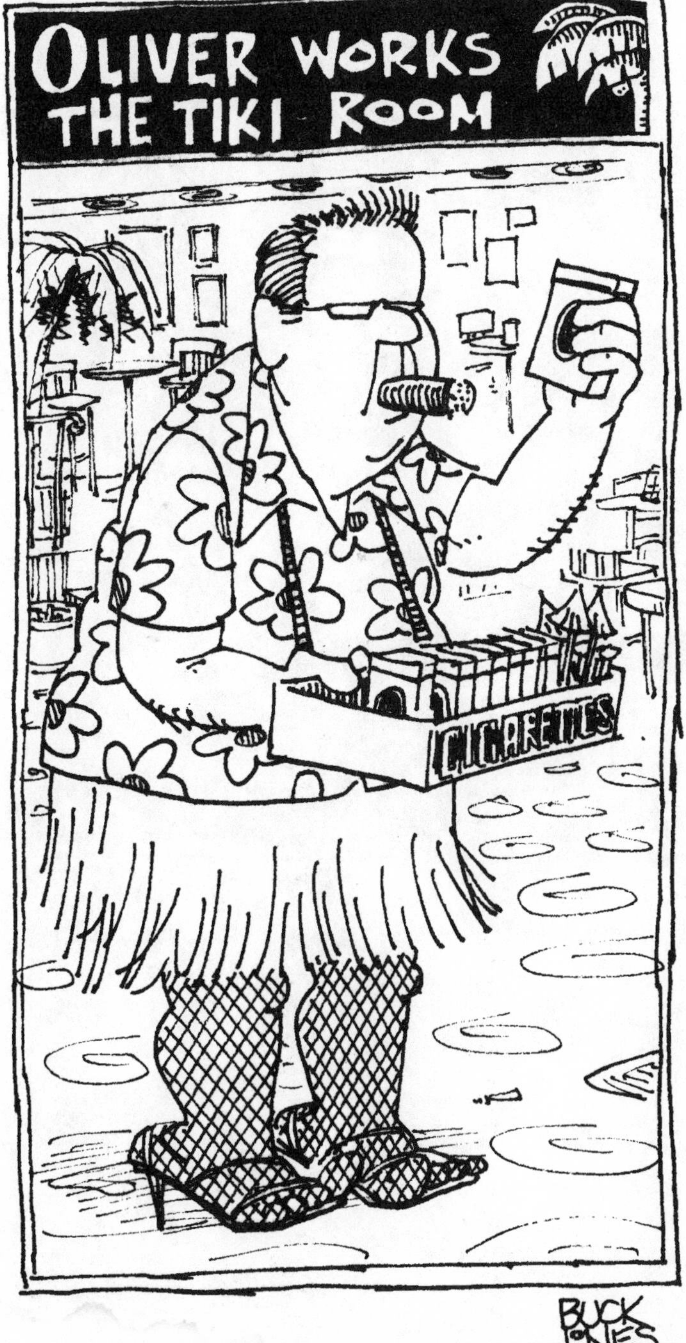
OLIVER WORKS THE TIKI ROOM
CIGARETTES
BUCK JONES

"She's very interested in the opposite sex..."

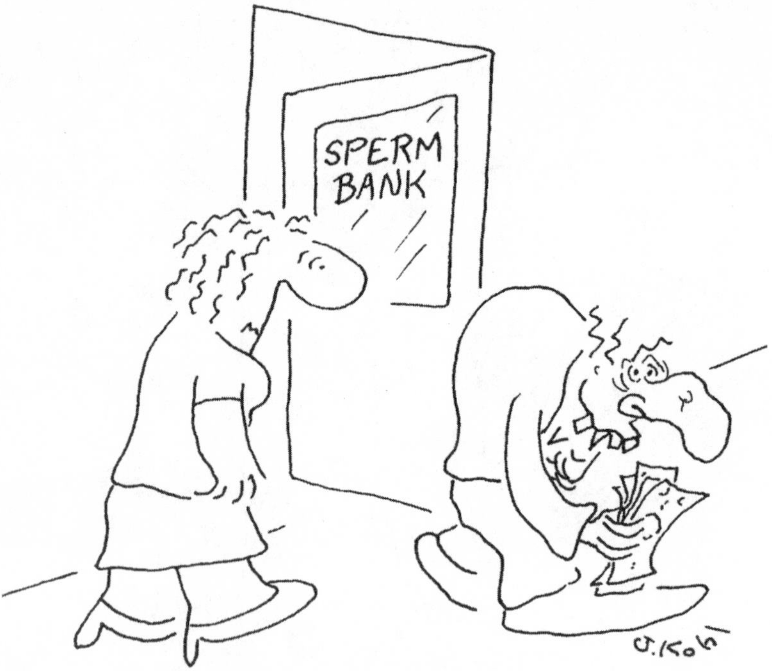
SPERM BANK
J.Kohl

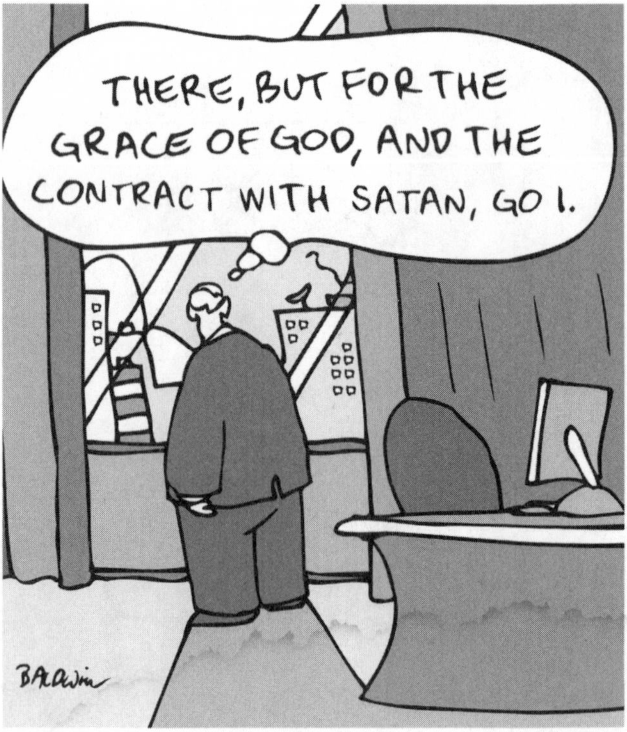
THERE, BUT FOR THE GRACE OF GOD, AND THE CONTRACT WITH SATAN, GO I.
BALDWIN

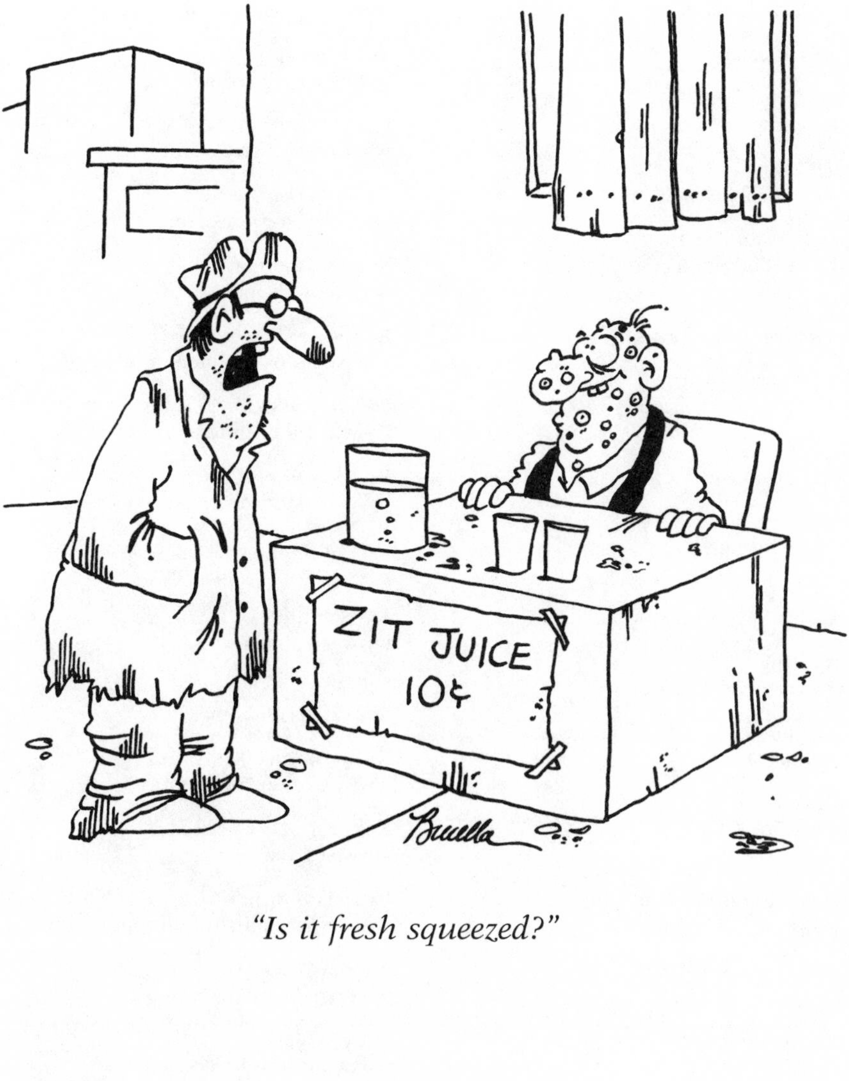
ZIT JUICE
10¢

"Is it fresh squeezed?"

National Lampoon's Favorite Cartoons of the 21st Century features the talents of

Mike Baldwin
www.cornered.com

Ian Baker
www.cartoonstock.com

Srini Bhukya
www.toonbag.com

Marty Bucella

John Chase
www.chasetoons.com

Dan Collins
www.dancollinscartoons.com

Roy Delgado
roy.delgado@gmail.com

Stan Eales
www.cartoonstock.com

Craig Eyles
www.cartoonstock.com

Clive Goddard
www.cartoonstock.com

Geoff Hassing
www.geofftoons.com

Buck Jones
www.buckjonesillustrator.com

Jerry King
www.cartoonstock.com

Joe Kohl
www.joekohl.com

Kit Lively
www.kitlively.com

Jason Love
www.cartoonstock.com

Mark Lynch
www.cartoonstock.com

Mazur
www.sickthings.org

Malcom McGookin
www.malcolmmcgookin.com

Andy McKay ("Naf")
www.cartoonstock.com

Rod McKie
www.onlinecartoonist.com

Ed McLachlan
www.cartoonstock.com

Joel Mishon
www.cartoonstock.com

Kim Naughton
www.jknaughton.com

Ted Nunes
www.tedtoons.com

Fran Orford
www.cartoonstock.com

David Parker
www.cartoonstock.com

Steamy Raimon
www.nowcartoons.com

Robin Reed
www.barstowproductions.com

Dan Reynolds
www.reynoldsunwrapped.com

Royston Robertson
www.roystonrobertson.co.uk

Dan Rosandich
www.danscartoons.com

Joe Schmidt
www.joestoons.com

Nik Scott
www.nikscott.com

Kevin Smith ("Kes")
www.cartoonstock.com

Stik
www.stik.biz

Patricia Storms
www.stormsillustration.com

Andrea Wayne-von Konigslow
www.snafustudios.com

Andy White
www.cartoonservices.com

Bob Zahn
www.zahntoons.com

Jay Naughton
www.jknaughton.com
Submission inquiries:
jnaughton@nationallampoon.com

WWW.NATIONALLAMPOON.COM

One Day In The Editor's Office

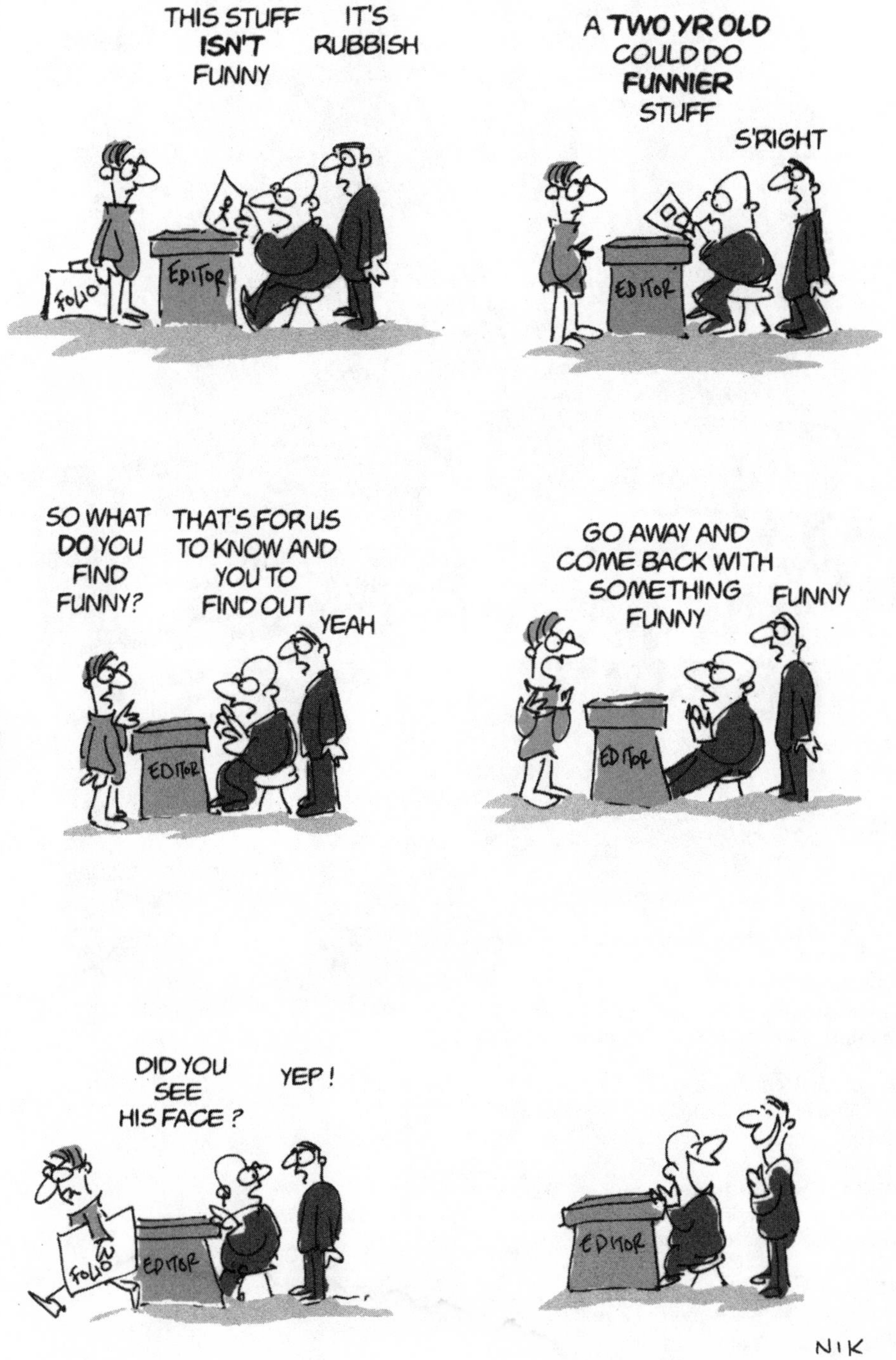
THIS STUFF ISN'T FUNNY
IT'S RUBBISH
FOLIO
EDITOR
A TWO YR OLD COULD DO FUNNIER STUFF
S'RIGHT
EDITOR
SO WHAT DO YOU FIND FUNNY?
THAT'S FOR US TO KNOW AND YOU TO FIND OUT
YEAH
EDITOR
GO AWAY AND COME BACK WITH SOMETHING FUNNY
FUNNY
EDITOR
DID YOU SEE HIS FACE ?
YEP !
FOLIO
EDITOR
EDITOR
NIK SCOTT

Also from NATIONAL LAMPOON® PRESS

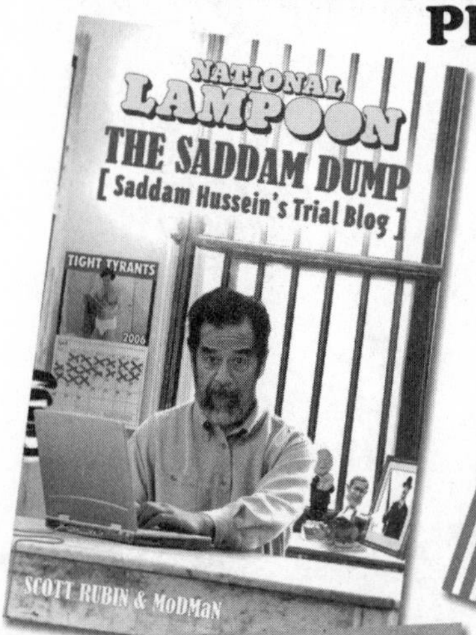

NATIONAL LAMPOON
THE SADDAM DUMP
[Saddam Hussein's Trial Blog]
TIGHT TYRANTS
2006
SCOTT RUBIN & MoDMaN

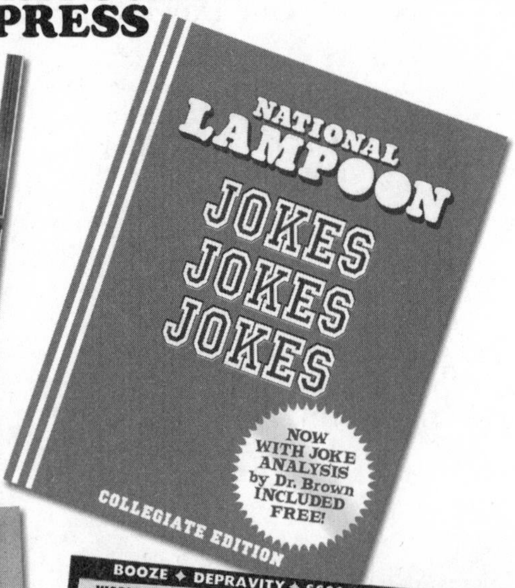

NATIONAL LAMPOON
JOKES
JOKES
JOKES
NOW WITH JOKE ANALYSIS by Dr. Brown INCLUDED FREE!
COLLEGIATE EDITION

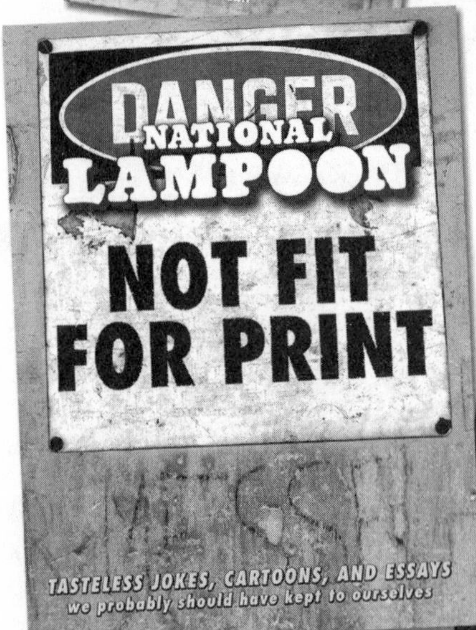

DANGER
NATIONAL LAMPOON
NOT FIT FOR PRINT
TASTELESS JOKES, CARTOONS, AND ESSAYS
we probably should have kept to ourselves

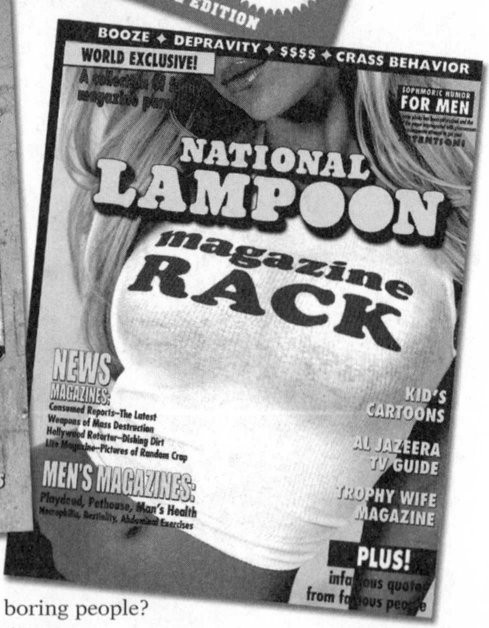

BOOZE ✦ DEPRAVITY ✦ $$$$ ✦ CRASS BEHAVIOR
WORLD EXCLUSIVE!
SOPHMORIC HUMOR
FOR MEN
NATIONAL LAMPOON
magazine RACK
NEWS MAGAZINES:
Consumed Reports–The Latest Weapons of Mass Destruction
Hollywood Retorter–Dishing Dirt
Life Magazine–Pictures of Random Crap
MEN'S MAGAZINES:
Playdead, Pethouse, Man's Health
KID'S CARTOONS
AL JAZEERA TV GUIDE
TROPHY WIFE MAGAZINE
PLUS!

The Saddam Dump
Why waste your time reading the blogs of boring people?
An imprisoned dictator has so much more to say.

Jokes Jokes Jokes
Finally! A collegiate edition of sophomoric jokes.
Didactic and scholarly analysis included FREE!

Magazine Rack
A hilarious collection of parodies of magazines in a magazine format!
What could be harder to explain?

Not Fit For Print
All the stuff that was too vile and too tasteless for us to publish anywhere else.
Guaranteed to offend.

NATIONAL LAMPOON® dotcom

NATIONAL LAMPOON TOGA! TogaTV.com